FAUST

PART ONE

JOHANN WOLFGANG GOETHE was born in 1749, the son of a well-to-do citizen of Frankfurt. As a young man he studied law and briefly practised as a lawyer, but creative writing was his chief concern. In the early 1770s he was the dominating figure of the German literary revival, his tragic novel *Werther* bringing him international fame.

In 1775 he settled permanently in the small duchy of Weimar where he became a minister of state and director of the court theatre; in 1782 he was ennobled as 'von Goethe'. His journey to Italy in 1786–8 influenced the development of his mature classical style; in the 1790s, he and his younger contemporary Schiller (1759–1805) were the joint architects of Weimar Classicism, the central phase of German literary culture.

Goethe wrote in all the literary *genres* but his interests extended far beyond literature and included a number of scientific subjects. *Faust*, written at various stages of his life and in a variety of styles, became a constantly enlarged repository of his personal wisdom. His creative energies never ceased to take new forms and he was still writing original poetry at the age of more than 80. In 1806 he married Christiane Vulpius (1765–1816), having lived with her for eighteen years; they had one surviving son, August (1789–1830). Goethe died in 1832.

DAVID LUKE is an Emeritus Student (Emeritus Fellow) of Christ Church, Oxford. He has published articles and essays on German literature and various prose and verse translations, including Goethe's *Selected Verse*, Stifter's *Limestone and Other Stories*, Kleist's *The Marquise of O and Other Stories*, *Selected Tales* by the brothers Grimm, Goethe's *Iphigenia in Tauris* and *Hermann and Dorothea*, a volume of Goethe's erotic poetry (*Roman Elegies* and *The Diary*), and Thomas Mann's *Death in Venice and Other Stories*. His translation of *Faust* Part One was awarded the European Poetry Translation Prize in 1989.

THE WORLD'S CLASSICS

JOHANN WOLFGANG VON
GOETHE

FAUST

PART ONE

Translated with an
Introduction by
DAVID LUKE

Oxford   New York
OXFORD UNIVERSITY PRESS

Oxford University Press, Walton Street, Oxford OX2 6DP

Oxford New York
Athens Auckland Bangkok Bombay
Calcutta Cape Town Dar es Salaam Delhi
Florence Hong Kong Istanbul Karachi
Kuala Lumpur Madras Madrid Melbourne
Mexico City Nairobi Paris Singapore
Taipei Tokyo Toronto

and associated companies in
Berlin Ibadan

Oxford is a trade mark of Oxford University Press

Translation and editorial material © David Luke 1987

First published 1987 by Oxford University Press as a
World's Classics paperback and simultaneously in a hardback edition

British Library Cataloguing in Publication Data
Data available

Library of Congress Cataloging in Publication Data
Goethe, Johann Wolfgang von, 1749-1832.
Faust, part one.
(The World's classics)
Translation of: Faust, 1. Theil.
I. Luke, David, 1921-   . II. Title. III. Title:
Faust, part 1. IV. Series.
PT2026.F2L85 1987 832'.6 87 1559
ISBN 0-19 281666-7 (pbk.)

9 10 8

Printed in Great Britain by
BPC Paperbacks Ltd
Aylesbury, Bucks

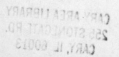

For Lawrence Brown

CONTENTS

Preface   viii

Introduction   ix

Synopsis of the composition of *Faust Part One*   lvi

Select Bibliography   lviii

Chronology   lxii

FAUST, PART ONE   1

Explanatory Notes   149

PREFACE

The present translation is from *Faust, der Tragödie erster Teil*, which Goethe published in 1808. I have used the edition by L. J. Scheithauer (Reclams Universal-Bibliothek, Stuttgart, revised 1986) which is itself based on the monumental 'Weimarer Ausgabe', the historical-critical edition of Goethe's writings by E. Schmidt and other authorities (Weimar 1887–1919; *Faust I* in vol. 14). I have also consulted this edition and the text and annotations in certain others, such as that by Erich Trunz (in the 'Hamburger Ausgabe' of Goethe's works, vol. 3, 1949) and that by Ernst Beutler in vol. 5 (1953) of the Zürich 'Gedenkausgabe'. Goethe's text has been transmitted by these and other standard modern editions virtually without variation or dispute. The prehistory or 'Entstehungsgeschichte', however, of this 1808 version of his Faust drama (that is, the process of its development from earlier fragmentary conceptions) is a more significant and complex matter, necessarily affecting any interpretation of the work and especially of this 'first part', which Goethe composed at intervals over a period of more than thirty years. This fundamental genetic problem is discussed in the Introduction, which is followed by a diagrammatic synopsis (pp. lvi f.). Additionally I have entered the abbreviations used in this synopsis ('UR', 'FRA', and 'F.I') alongside the text itself; these inform the reader to which of the widely separated 'phases of composition' any particular passage, or its unrevised equivalent, originally belonged.

Matters of detail and miscellaneous points requiring explanation or comment are dealt with in the Notes, on pp. 149–76, to which the asterisks in the text refer. The line-numbering of the English text corresponds to that of the German throughout. For convenience of reference I have also numbered the scenes (1–28), though this is not done by Goethe.

Special thanks are due to the Rockefeller Foundation for generously enabling me to spend a month in 1985 at its study-centre in Bellagio during work on this edition.

D.L.

INTRODUCTION

THE legend of Faust grew up in the sixteenth century, an age of renewal and rebirth in Germany and Europe, a time of transition between medieval and modern culture. Goethe's *Faust* was conceived in the 1770s, when his own creativity in its first flower was giving a new impetus to the German literary revival, and when as in the later eighteenth century generally Europe stood at a turning-point between the Enlightenment and Romanticism. *Faust* could thus hardly fail to become something like a myth of European man, as well as a myth of the young poet's own development. It is certainly his most famous single work, regarded both in and outside Germany as—along with his poetry —the most characteristic product of his genius. Both it and the poems did indeed have a certain centrality in his long creative career, which extended (if we disregard its first immature phase) from 1770 until his death in 1832. The poems are central in the fairly simple sense that, during these sixty years or so, he never really ceased writing them or developing as a poet, the result being a corpus of lyric and other shorter poems which is even now commonly underestimated in its range and complexity, far exceeding as it does the relatively small collection of texts that have been familiarized internationally by the great composers. *Faust* also, which is the work of a poet at least as much as of a dramatist, may be said to have accompanied Goethe through his life (Part One until he was in his fifties, Part Two mainly much later) though not, of course, in the sense that he was constantly preoccupied with it. He wrote it at intervals over the sixty years, in four clearly distinguishable and widely separated phases—short periods of creative work on a project which, as we might therefore expect and as Goethe himself conceded, turned out to be something rather less than unitary in its conception or homogeneous in its execution. We must here leave aside the complex question of whether the posthumously published 'Part Two' can properly be regarded, or was even strictly intended, as a completion of Part One or anything other than a rather tenuously connected sequel to it; to divide the whole work into two parts was in any case certainly not Goethe's original plan. As it is, we are here confronted with the extraordinary and unique phenomenon of 'Part One' itself, about which there are problems enough. It was begun when Goethe was in his early twenties, then set aside unpublished for about fifteen years, then revised and slightly extended (though also cut) for publication in this incomplete form (*Faust. A Fragment*, 1790) in the first edition of his collected works; then perhaps even abandoned as a project before being taken up again when he was nearly 50. In this third phase of composition, mainly from June 1797 to April 1801, it was enlarged very significantly; Goethe then lost interest in it again for a few years, but decided in 1805 to publish nearly all he had done so far, as a 'first part'. After further revisions and some delay due to external causes, this appeared in 1808 as *Faust. The First Part of the Tragedy*. A few scenes for Part Two had also been sketched at the turn of the century, but a long period of abandonment or latency now followed. Part Two, the in many ways very different continuation (and its differences rather than its links with Part One are what Goethe's own recorded comments emphasize), belongs essentially to the last years of his life (fourth phase of composition, 1825–31) and in accordance with his wish was first delivered to the bemused public in 1832 when he was safely in his grave.

The whole complex poetic drama or dramatic poem, which defies all normal categories in both form and content, thus combines a number of genetically disparate elements into an extraordinary and puzzling synthesis. Its poetic vitality is undeniable and probably only enhanced by its stylistic diversity and what Goethe himself called its 'fragmentariness' and 'incommensurability'. But ever since his own lifetime the history of *Faust* criticism has been that of a controversy between two methods. One is the historical or genetic approach which emphasizes the discrepancies, inconsistencies, or incongruities in the text and is content to explain them in terms of the long and complicated process of composition and Goethe's changes of plan or sheer forgetfulness in the course of it. The other is the 'unitarian' insistence that the work must be assumed to be an integrated dramatic whole, sprung from a single and unvarying conception, and that any apparent contradictions may be resolved by sufficiently ingenious argument, or shown to be unimportant matters of detail. The controversy has a certain similarity to the disputes that have arisen in the last century or two from the application of historical scholarship to the Bible. At its most extreme, geneticism tears *Faust* to pieces and leaves the reader wondering why this is accounted a masterpiece of world dramatic literature at all; at its worst, the unitarian special pleading becomes an exercise in perverse piety and blindness to textual and biographical fact. A balanced approach will wish to credit the poem with at least a profound human and personal unity and to see its creation as a kind of organic growth: at each stage of revision and expansion, we must assume, Goethe respected what he had already written and indeed for the most part already published, but sought to develop and enlarge his earlier conception and so far as possible to integrate the old with the new. The analogy of a work of architecture built progressively at different periods is only partly appropriate; in *Faust*, the architect is always Goethe.

Whatever eventual critical synthesis we may try to achieve, however, the fact that Part One took him some thirty years to write is inescapable and demands to be taken into account. If as readers we are content with mere impressions, we may ignore this genetic process; otherwise we are under an obligation to be aware of it, in outline at least. Most of its main details are in fact well enough known. We should above all note, and distinguish from the rest of the poem, those parts of it which are based on its original core: this was the long unpublished, mysteriously fragmentary version of the early 1770s (written probably between 1772 and 1775, though certain scenes may go further back) which in Goethe studies is now always referred to as the 'original *Faust*' or *Urfaust*. Goethe later destroyed this manuscript, but by a sensational chance an unknown contemporary copy of it was discovered sixty-five years after his death and almost exactly a century ago (1887). This 'Göchhausen transcript', so called after the lady of the Weimar court circle who made it at some time in the late 1770s, is thought to be a substantially accurate copy of Goethe's lost text, though we cannot of course know this for certain, and it is also possible that he had other *Faust* plans at that time of which the transcript contains no indication. Those parts of the final 1808 version which clearly correspond to this known pre-1775 nucleus, and most of which represent only slight revisions of the youthful material, comprise Faust's opening soliloquy and conjuration of the Earth Spirit (lines 354–517), two episodic scenes of anti-academic satire (518–605, 1868–2050), the episodic tavern scene (2073–336), and above all the sequence (beginning with 2605 and ending with 4614, between which the 1808 text contains some later insertions) of comic, touching, and tragic scenes telling the story of Faust's seduction and abandonment of Margareta (Gretchen) which so powerfully dominates the second half of Part One. Most of this *Urfaust* material has always more strongly appealed to both German and non-German readers than most of Goethe's complex and sophisticated later additions; indeed, the Gretchen story especially, which was entirely the young Goethe's invention and had no precedent in any earlier version of the Faust story, has exercised such imaginative fascination, and in particular so dominated theatrical productions and adaptations of the play throughout the nineteenth century, that the general public tends to associate Faust with the Gretchen affair almost to the exclusion of anything else.

The youthful *Urfaust* reflected the preoccupations not only of the youthful Goethe but of his generation. It has been said that if he had decided to publish it at the time, even in its fragmentary form, it might well have eclipsed the success and notoriety of his tragic first novel *The Sorrows of Young Werther* (1774) and possibly changed the whole course of German literary history. At the time of writing the *Urfaust* and *Werther* and his most famous early poems, the young Goethe, born in 1749 and still living in his native city of Frankfurt, was a restless, rebellious, highly individualistic genius, the son of a well-to-do middle-class family and therefore in practice free (unlike any other German writer of his day) to devote himself chiefly to literature. He had taken a degree in law and briefly practised it, but never bound himself to the legal profession, nor had he yet settled into any permanent position or become beholden to a patron. His emergence as a miraculously original and almost at once internationally famous writer coincided with that upsurge or breakthrough in German literature which by a quirk of historical terminology came to be known as the 'Storm and Stress' period, but which in a wider world perspective may be seen as a precursory and provocative German form of European Romanticism. The young Goethe, indeed, may be said to have virtually invented this avant-garde movement single-handed. True, there had been pioneer theorists and essayists, notably the highly influential cultural historian and philosopher Herder (1744–1803) whose encounter with Goethe in 1770 was one of the turning-points in the latter's development. There were about half-a-dozen minor writers, mostly dramatists, clustering round Goethe and treating him as a cult figure, but it was Goethe alone whose creative 'genius' (the word first became fashionable at this time) was not merely *soi-disant*—he alone who raised the values of eighteenth-century sentimentalism and early romanticism to a European level of literary expression. What is more, the Storm and Stress movement of the 1770s was Goethe's own 'Storm and Stress' phase, just as the 'Weimar Classicism' of the 1790s corresponded to a maturer and so to speak 'classical' period in his life. German literary history lends itself to personalization, and so centrally pre-eminent in it is Goethe that in his time its stages were not so much reflected in and by his personal evolution, as rather vice versa: they reflected him, he virtually constituted them. In Goethe, German literature underwent a peculiar evolution from Storm and Stress to a new classicism or romantic-classical synthesis; and nowhere is this more succinctly documented than in the development, as we may trace it in the genesis of Part One, of his modern, highly personal yet historically momentous conception of the old Faust story. In this sense, too, *Faust* is a 'central' work, and for the same reason the genetic or 'diachronic' examination of it (as distinct from merely reading through the final text synchronically in the normal way) gains added interest, at least as a supplementary or introductory exercise.

The sixteenth century was an age of forbidden exploration: old dogmas and certainties were being challenged, a new humanism was developing, the sciences were emancipating themselves from their magical antecedents, and all this could in the popular imagination easily be invested with an aura of dread and a savour of blasphemy. The legend of the daring magus who sells himself to the Devil for new knowledge and new powers was one that flourished in this atmosphere. A shadowy historical figure existed to give it a name: from a few scattered sources we hear of a certain Georg Faust who lived between about 1480 and 1540, a disreputable wandering academic charlatan who laid claim to out-of-the-way knowledge and healing gifts and was said to have come to a violent end. After his death legend credited him with academic titles, he became 'Dr Johannes Faustus' (the name in its Latinized form meaning favoured or fortunate), he had been a professor at Wittenberg, the Devil had kept him company in the shape of a black dog, he had conjured up characters from Homer in front of his students, played tricks on the Pope and Emperor and other princes, and on the expiry of his agreed term of twenty-four years had duly been torn to pieces by demons and carried off to hell. In the course of the century crude folk-narratives came into circulation in Germany, retailing the magician's sensational adventures and moralizing piously about his dreadful example. These Faust chapbooks, of which the first known example was printed in Frankfurt in 1587, continued to be published until the early eighteenth century in successive variants. From the outset translations quickly appeared in other countries, and an early English version inspired the first dramatic treatment of the theme: Christopher Marlowe's *Tragical History of Doctor Faustus*, written probably in 1592 and published posthumously in 1604. It was common in Elizabethan times for English actors to travel with their repertoires to foreign courts, and thus it was not long before debased versions of Marlowe's tragedy became well known in the German-speaking territories, entering also the repertoire of the popular puppet theatres (in which they still survive today). Goethe seems first to have encountered the legend in the form of a puppet play when he was a child, and also to have read at an early stage the 1725 version of the Faust chapbook. Rather surprisingly, he did not himself read Marlowe's play until 1818 (and even then in a German translation), though indirectly and in vulgarized form he would know something of its contents, especially from the puppet tradition. We do not know exactly when he first thought of using the legend for his own purposes. But Goethe's age, like Marlowe's, was one of change and ferment, of emergent humanism, of challenge to cultural establishments; and it is evident that either during or shortly after his student days in Leipzig in the late 1760s he perceived the expressive value of the Faust story, its relevance to his own generation and his own interests. For one thing it was folklore, a folk-tale, the kind of popular anonymous literature which the prevailing taste of the eighteenth century had despised. But the new enthusiasm, inspired by Rousseau, was for the natural, the primitive, the uneducated, and the unspoilt; and nowhere were these ideals embraced with more fervour than by the young Goethe and his Storm and Stress followers. From Herder in 1770 he had learnt the cult of old folk-songs and ballads, an interest reflected in the *Urfaust* and in his early poetry. This was in large part also a quest for the national past as such, at a time when Germany was not a nation and was seeking a sense of cultural identity. The Storm and Stress Goethe, looking for antecedents and roots, turned his attention to the great age of Reuchlin and Ulrich von Hutten, of Paracelsus and Luther and Hans Sachs. It was also in 1770 that he conceived his dramatic chronicle of the life of Gottfried von Berlichingen, the 'knight with the iron hand': his play (published in its final version as *Götz von Berlichingen* in 1773) idealized this sixteenth-century robber-baron (1480–1562) as a champion of simple natural German virtues against the sophistication of the Latinized court class (paralleled in Goethe's time by the French-speaking aristocracy against which the German and middle-class literary revival had to assert itself). It was also a work which provocatively cast aside, as the *Urfaust* was to do, all the neoclassical dramatic conventions still imposed on Germany by the influence of French taste, and it brought the young Goethe immediate fame in his own country. A clearly parallel project was the idealization and heroicization of Berlichingen's legendary contemporary 'Faust'. Prometheus, the rebellious demigod who had symbolized the protest of the human spirit in one of Goethe's most powerful early poems, could now be unbound.

Marlowe, indeed, who at the time of his early death in 1593 was under threat of prosecution for atheism, had perhaps already taken a step in this direction by investing his Faustus with some measure of heroic dignity, especially in the famous and moving final scene. But the time had now come for dispensing with his damnation as well. By the late eighteenth century it had long been less fashionable to burn heretics, witches, and wizards or even to believe in the Devil; this was common ground between the Storm and Stress and the Enlightenment, and Goethe was not the first important writer to consider Faust's eligibility for salvation. His immediate precursor, the critic and dramatist Lessing (1729–81), was essentially a sophisticated representative of mature Enlightened culture, but he also decisively influenced the thought and literary values of the incipient *Goethezeit*. Motivated both by his antagonism to dogmatic supernaturalistic Christianity and by his interest in possible characteristically national themes for German writers, Lessing had himself projected and partly written a salvationist treatment of the once notorious and now neglected legend. He published one scene of it as an 'anonymous' fragment in 1759, but his salvationist conception was not clear from this and did not become known until much later, some years after his death, although whatever else existed of his Faust manuscript had by then unaccountably disappeared. It is thus not clear to what extent the young Goethe was influenced by Lessing, nor do we in any case know whether or not he intended a salvationist version of the story at the *Urfaust* stage. What we do know, however, is that in 1768 a new factor had entered into his interest in the theme, when he immersed himself in the works of various occultistic and alchemistic writers of the sixteenth and seventeenth centuries, including Paracelsus (who became in some ways his model for Faust) and Giordano Bruno, as well as the eighteenth-century Swedish theosophist Swedenborg. This was after he had fallen ill in Leipzig and returned to Frankfurt to recover, breaking off his studies. In Book XI of his autobiography *Poetry and Truth*, written more than forty years later, he recalls how deeply dissatisfied he had been as a student with the aridly rationalistic and materialistic philosophy and cosmology which then, in the name of Enlightenment, dominated the academic world at Leipzig and elsewhere: the French *encyclopédistes*, he felt, had reduced Nature to a dead system. It must have seemed to Goethe that the bold theological and demonological adventurer 'Faust' could well be used as a symbolic mouthpiece for the anti-scientific, anti-rationalistic, pantheistic, and mystical world-view to which he himself felt drawn. The influence of this conception is quite evident in the opening pages of the *Urfaust*. The young Goethe's Faust exists not in a Christian but in a pantheistic frame of reference; he summons up not the traditional Devil but the Earth Spirit (cf. Note 14). There is every indication that in Goethe's original conception it was not Mephistopheles or God, but this Earth Spirit—representing as it seems the divine yet at the same time demonic creative and destructive forces of Nature and earthly activity—who was to preside over the destiny of his hero.

Goethe evidently found that for the time being at least he could not satisfactorily develop this original and fascinating idea. The Faustus legend had from the first been born out of Christian assumptions, and though the young Goethe personally, after (and no doubt as a result of) his Pietistic phase, was out of sympathy with Christianity, the artistic pull of its tradition was too strong. In the *Urfaust*, which is of course not dramatically complete or continuous, the hero's dialogue with the Earth Spirit breaks off inconclusively, and soon after this we encounter for the first time Mephistopheles, engaged in academic badinage with a naïve student, his presence and relationship to Faust left unexplained in a vast lacuna corresponding to the still unwritten lines 606 to 1867. Nor did Goethe ever explain, even when this gap came to be filled, why the *Urfaust* Mephistopheles appears from certain indications in the text (cf. Note 124) to be subordinate to the Earth Spirit and the latter to be responsible for Faust's bondage to Mephistopheles. Further questions then arise about the 'Gretchen tragedy', into which the *Urfaust* version presently resolves itself. Like the Earth Spirit passage, it is a personal invention by the young Goethe, a characteristic and quite new contribution to the Faustus theme, though its connection with the Faustus story as such remains puzzlingly tenuous, and it is even possible that he originally conceived it quite independently of his *Faust* project. Goethe's Gretchen story is not simply an episode in the career of a magician, a supernatural amorous encounter like the traditional chapbook episode made famous by Marlowe, in which Helen of Troy is procured as Faust's succubus; and it goes far beyond the passing mention, in the 1674 chapbook, of a 'very pretty but poor servant-girl' whom the doctor loves but because of his satanic contract cannot marry. Rather, it is a compelling romantic love-story in which the whole emphasis shifts to the innocent female partner and her tragic fate. It takes over and dominates the entire *Urfaust* conception, displacing the specifically Faustian themes. We must look outside the Faust tradition for explanations of why the young Goethe's Faust drama, and our attention, are suddenly sidetracked in this way.

They lie partly in the preoccupations of the later eighteenth century and especially of the Storm and Stress phase. The Gretchen story reflects, for one thing, the current sentimental enthusiasm about natural simplicity. Gretchen appeals so strongly to Faust because he is an intellectual and she is not, because of her naïvety, intuitiveness, integrity and fundamental innocence; Faust, like Werther, embodies a feeling that was the young Goethe's own experience. Secondly, there was the cult of folk-literature: the theme of the girl left pregnant by her lover and killing their child to avoid disgrace was known to Goethe as a folk-ballad motif current in and outside Germany. (The ballads with which he was familiar and which he would recite to his friends included some from Scotland which are still in our anthologies.) Goethe himself wrote a short poem in the ballad style about an abandoned unmarried mother (*Vor Gericht*, 'Before the Judge', ?1775). Gretchen, who sings a haunting ballad-like song at her first appearance and a song from a folk-tale at her last, is herself rather like a figure out of a ballad or a *Märchen*, as she herself almost seems to realize in the prison scene (lines 4448 f.). The laconic structure of the Gretchen drama —scenes that leap from high point to high point of the story, often over long periods of time and without connecting explanations—has itself been compared to that of the folk-ballad. A third factor was the powerful influence on Goethe and his generation of another sixteenth-century cult figure. Shakespeare was to them the supreme poet, the genius of geniuses, the inspired child of Nature, warbling his native wood-notes wild; Goethe had already invoked his authority for the structural and stylistic iconoclasm of *Götz von Berlichingen*. The Gretchen theme too must have seemed to lend itself naturally to 'Shakespearean' treatment: abandonment of the unities of time and place, mixture of tragic and comic scenes, and certain specific motifs which may well be conscious echoes. Fourthly, the strong emotional charge of the Gretchen drama may be partly explained by certain specific elements of Goethe's recent personal experience. It may be a mistake to attach as much importance as the earlier biographical critics did to his passing love-affair (probably not amounting to actual seduction) with Friederike Brion, the simple country girl in Alsace of whom he later wrote in idyllicizing terms in his autobiography but whom he abandoned with cruel suddenness after writing a few of his most famous poems about her. It is possible that he felt remorse about this which found indirect expression (little other evidence of it is extant) in his story of Faust and Gretchen. A probably more important stimulus from real life, however, was the execution for infanticide in January 1772 of Susanna Margaretha Brandt, a simple girl whose brother (like Gretchen's) was a soldier, who claimed to have been seduced on the promptings of the Devil, and with the help of a drug, by a young travelling goldsmith, and who had killed her child to avoid public disgrace. Her prison was only 200 yards from the Goethe family house in Frankfurt, where the poet was at that time practising as a lawyer. By a series of slightly uncanny coincidences, several members of his family and household were quite closely involved with aspects of this much-discussed case and even with details of the execution, which took place by beheading, with the usual macabre medieval ceremonial (cf. lines 4587–94 and Note 128). The question of whether the death penalty should be retained for infanticide was at that time a current legal controversy in the more enlightened German states (cf. Note 82). The Brandt case must have deeply affected the 22-year-old Goethe, and may well have been what chiefly moved him to introduce the Gretchen story into his Faust drama.

If this was a mistake, it was an inspired one, for in this part of the play the young Goethe, worthy of his model, achieves the highest levels of poetry and for once also a truly Shakespearean tragic pathos. We may, it is true, still wonder how we are meant to understand the integration of this powerful but essentially extraneous domestic tragedy into the specific story of a bargain between 'Faust' (whose real name and identity Gretchen never knows) and 'the Devil'. The traditional devil's-bargain (*Teufelspakt*) motif was evidently one that caused Goethe some difficulty, and this may well have been the chief reason for his long delay in completing Part One. In the *Urfaust* material there is no clarification whatever of the specific Faustian contract with Mephistopheles; Mephistopheles is simply there. But dramatically there is no difficulty about his role *as devil* (or, as the Devil) in the Gretchen affair. Whatever Goethe's personal scepticism as to the Christian doctrine of the Devil, there is no doubt that here at least he understood its aesthetic and theatrical possibilities, and to this extent the Gretchen story has indeed successfully attached itself to the Faust story. The Mephistopheles of the *Urfaust* is not simply the worldly companion of the hesitant seducer, cynically encouraging him to gratify his lust and then scoffing at the consequences. If he lacked the additional dimension of being (at least so far as Gretchen with her simple Catholic belief is concerned) the personal agent of transcendent evil, the drama would lose half its point: the ironies of the 'catechism' scene (Sc. 19, 3414–543), the sinister overtones of Sc. 26, and the dramatic climax of the closing scene (Sc. 28) in the prison, where Gretchen's instinctive shrinking from 'that man you have with you' becomes sudden clear recognition of what Mephistopheles really is and what this implies about her lover. Dramatically essential, too, is the young Goethe's identification of 'the Devil' with a kind of absolute cynicism. This enables him, by contrasting Mephistopheles with Faust and still more strikingly with Gretchen, to give the drama weight and balance—to make it embody a paradoxically realistic double view of human emotions and relationships which both fully expresses romantic sentimentalism and critically transcends it. This alone makes the Gretchen drama a profounder, more multidimensional work than the almost exactly contemporaneous *Sorrows of Werther*, in which Mephistopheles with his constant cynical commentary on the love-affair has no counterpart. Moreover, this brilliantly established motif of the Devil as cynic, and his dialectical relationship with Faust as romantic or idealist, remains constant on various levels throughout the later-written scenes of Part One as the maturing Goethe came to create it, and has strong claims to be considered the unifying and integrating theme of the work as a whole.

In 1775 came the main turning-point in Goethe's outward career, when at the invitation of the reigning Duke Karl August he went to Weimar, eventually settling in this tiny principality on a permanent basis. The young duke, one of the most enlightened of the numerous small-scale absolute monarchs in *ancien régime* Germany, greatly admired Goethe and soon appointed him to a number of public offices. The poet became involved in a host of practical affairs, partly as a result of which he began at this time also to develop a far-reaching interest in various scientific studies. For years he found he had too little time for creative literary work, but the constraints and responsibilities were also salutary. Before long he had lost sympathy with his 'Storm and Stress' friends and grown away from this whole tendency. He had brought the *Urfaust* manuscript with him from Frankfurt as an untidy jumble of papers, and is known to have given informal readings from it to members of the court circle; it was presumably after one such literary evening that Luise von Göchhausen, a lady-in-waiting to the dowager duchess, borrowed the precious autograph and copied it with or without the poet's knowledge. For Goethe there was for the time being no question of continuing work on this strange and fragmentary youthful masterpiece. But by 1786 he was increasingly chafing at the precarious accommodation he had reached with himself in these first Weimar years. In September he suddenly took temporary leave from his duties and travelled to Italy, where he remained, chiefly in Rome, until June 1788. He himself felt this flight to the south, more especially his stay in Rome and the contact with classical antiquity which this gave him, to be a new turning-point in at least his inner life, a deeply rejuvenating and transforming experience. It seems that some kind of sexual self-liberation was also involved, in that immediately upon his return to Weimar he set up house with the beautiful if scantly educated Christiane Vulpius, who continued to live with him (after 1806 officially as his wife) until her death in 1816. All this—the anagram, so to speak, of ROMA/AMOR—was celebrated around 1790 in the *Roman Elegies*, a cycle of erotic poems in elegiac distichs which now count among Goethe's greatest achievements. The Italian journey, however, had also coincided with preparations for the first complete edition of his writings so far, and this practical stimulus had led him not only to collect and revise his poems, finish unfinished works (including two major plays in the classical style, *Iphigenia in Tauris* and *Torquato Tasso*, both continued or completed in Italy and published respectively in 1787 and 1790) but also, in February 1788, to reconsider the problem of *Faust*.

   He evidently decided that he would not now attempt to finish it, but publish it as 'a fragment' with a few revisions and additions. The chief difficulty was still the 'great lacuna' (as he himself later called it) between what are now lines 605 and 1868. He had an effective beginning (354–605), and an ending so overwhelming that it must have been difficult to see what could ever be made to follow it. What was to be done about the missing middle? At the very least, Mephistopheles must not be allowed

simply to appear without explanation from nowhere, in a comic
scene, with no hint of his standing or of the nature of his business
with Faust. Even if Goethe could not yet work out his own
modernized version of the terms of their traditional bargain, the
reading public must at least be given some hint that an unspeci-
fied bargain has taken place. He therefore wrote a short new piece
of dialogue between Faust and Mephistopheles (which now
appears as lines 1770–850 of Sc. 7). To make it quite clear that a
still unfilled gap precedes this passage, he inserted a row of dashes
before the first line (as may still be seen in the 1790 edition) and
began in the middle of a sentence with the word 'and', as well
as in the middle of a rhymed quatrain (1768–71). In this new
dialogue, and in the soliloquy by Mephistopheles which follows
it (1851–67), Goethe set out what at that stage seemed to him
to be appropriate as the aims, or programmes, respectively of his
hero and of the Devil. Faust idealistically demands an expansion
of his life to include all human experience; and Mephistopheles,
left alone to reveal his true intentions in a soliloquy rather
resembling those of Shakespeare's Iago, rejoices in the prospect
of destroying Faust by a process of disillusionment, disgust, and
frustration. Goethe leaves it open what exactly is meant by
Mephistopheles' prediction (1867) that his victim will 'perish'
(zugrunde gehn; by suicide? in madness?), since the literalistic
Christian concept of damnation is evidently one that he wishes
to supersede. Nevertheless, this is still a comparatively straightforward Teufelspakt situation, though with the actual terms of
the bargain left out—indeed, Mephistopheles' concluding lines
(1866 f.) even read like a hint by Goethe to his readers that the
precise terms of the contract itself are unimportant.

   We do not know exactly at what point between February
1788 and the appearance of Faust. A Fragment in 1790 Goethe
wrote this new Faust–Mephistopheles material, the most significant of the second-phase scenes; merely that it comes first in the
sequence of the 1790 text. At least one of the new scenes was
written in Rome, in the gardens of the Villa Borghese; this is
thought to have been the one called A Witch's Kitchen (Sc. 9,
2337–604). Its main theme is Faust's rejuvenation and sexual
invigoration, and Goethe may have decided to add it because
(being now fifteen years older than when he had written the
Urfaust) he felt that the Urfaust's transition between Faust the

disillusioned professor of uncertain age and 'Heinrich', the passionate wooer of a young girl, was rather too sudden. We may
also detect, in this scene as in Faust's new speech to Mephistopheles about human totality, and in the third of these new
Fragment scenes (A Forest Cavern, 3217–373), a general tendency
of this second composition-phase to ennoble Faust, to emphasize
his intellectual and philosophical nature—rather as if the post-
Storm-and-Stress Goethe felt that there was here some kind of
imbalance in the *Urfaust* version which now, for publication,
needed redressing. The Faust of the *Witch's Kitchen* is not seen
to be at once pursuing a particular German girl of humble station,
not seen to be initiating a German domestic tragedy, but to be
longing for ideal Womanhood (2429–40). In Mephistopheles'
concluding comment (2603 f.) Goethe subtly contrives to suggest
to the reader an association of this lofty abstraction both with the
already-written story of Gretchen (whose first appearance now
follows, in 2605) and with the legendary Helen whose procure-
ment, or that of a phantasm in her shape, had always been an
essential motif in the Faustus tradition. Here Goethe seems to
suggest, *en passant*, his awareness that it would be desirable to
include a Helen episode in his own version if he were to complete
it. The 'classical' Goethe, moreover, now seems to have distanced
himself from the kind of north-European, Germanic folkloristic
element which had been so striking a feature of the youthful and
'romantic' *Urfaust*. In the closing scenes of the latter there had
been a savage devil-dog accompanying Faust (Sc. 26, lines <16–
19>; cf. Note 125), magic black horses on which Faust and
Mephistopheles ride and which must vanish at dawn (Sc 26, line
<65>, Sc. 27, Sc. 28 lines 4599 f.), and gallows-witches at whom
Faust gazes with fascinated horror (Sc. 27); and none of this had
been treated with the least trace of irony. Not only are all these
closing scenes omitted from the 1790 *Fragment*, but the Faust of
this version also finds witches ridiculous and contemptible
(2337 ff., etc.) and Goethe writes his new witch-scene in a comic
spirit, inserting dramatically irrelevant satirical material (2450 ff.,
2557–62, etc.) and in general treating witchcraft and magic as
motifs which are no longer imaginatively serious to him.
Mephistopheles himself sums the matter up in 2497 f., ironically
dismissing 'the northern fiend' as a thing of the past.

Equally, in Sc. 8 (*Auerbach's Tavern*), which for purposes of the 1790 version Goethe now improved by revising it completely into verse, Faust no longer does the traditional chapbook trick with the wine himself; this piece of magical slapstick is left to Mephistopheles, with Faust remaining a bored spectator. The tendency is to dignify him, and to 'classicize' the material at as many points as possible. Thus the next of the new scenes (Sc. 17, 3217-373, A Forest Cavern) begins with a lofty and rhetorical soliloquy by Faust, a kind of prayer to the Earth Spirit, and the only passage in the whole of Part One to have been written in iambic blank verse—the metre of Iphigenia and Tasso on which Goethe was working at this time. Faust here also gives thanks to the Earth Spirit for initiating him (when?) into the secrets of Nature, into contemplative knowledge of the ordered 'sequence' or 'series' of living creatures (3225 f.). Since this has no relevance to the dramatic context, that is to say the seduction of Gretchen, it seems probable that in inserting this speech in 1788 or 1789 Goethe was more concerned with a poetic celebration of his own scientific studies, which he was then actively pursuing in Italy, than with keeping close to the events or atmosphere of the Urfaust. Interestingly, he has retained the Earth Spirit, presumably for want of any more suitable idea for the time being, but the 'terrible vision' of Scene 4 (482) has become hard to recognize through the stately iambics. So, too, has Gretchen: her name in this classicizing speech has become stylistically unusable, so she is identified with the vision in the witch's magic mirror, 'that lovely woman's image' (3248).

The Forest Cavern scene is in fact a rather strange amalgam of new material written at this time, and old motifs retained from the Urfaust. One reason for the retentions is Goethe's already mentioned decision not to include the last three scenes of the Gretchen tragedy (Sc. 26, 27, 28) in the 1790 Fragment, but to end the latter with the Cathedral scene (Sc. 23)—a very unfortunate truncation dramatically, to be explained partly by the fact that the three scenes in question were in prose. Goethe evidently now regarded it as stylistically necessary to complete Faust as a verse drama if at all, yet for some reason he could not, at the Fragment stage, bring himself to rewrite these closing scenes in verse as he had done in the case of Auerbach's Tavern. On the other hand, he felt it to be important, for purposes of the Fragment, to retain and publish in some form the passage (Sc. 26, <37–41>) which

assigns responsibility to the Earth Spirit for Faust's dependence
on Mephistopheles (cf. Note 72). This was after all, in the whole
of his existing pre-1775 material, the only hint of Mephistopheles' status and provenance—a demonological question about
which Goethe by 1790 had evidently still not made up his mind.
Accordingly, the lines <37–41> are rewritten in iambic verse
and inserted at the end of Faust's soliloquy (3241–6); and in addition to the ascription of responsibility to the Earth Spirit ('you
added a companion', 3243) it is notable that the central motif of
Mephistopheles' *cynicism* ('cold mocking breath . . . turn your
gifts to nothing', 3245 f.) is retained and indeed made clearer than
in the corresponding *Urfaust* passage. There is one further highly
significant *Urfaust* retention in *A Forest Cavern*, namely the
passage which is now lines 3345–65. Originally it had been part of
that unfinished *Urfaust* sketch (also omitted from the *Fragment*)
which was to become, in the final 1808 version, the scene of
Gretchen's brother's death (Sc. 22). In this speech Faust, with
passionate and tormented eloquence, expresses his remorse at
having ruined Gretchen, and compares himself to a kind of
wandering Cain figure cursed by God, rushing like a mountain
torrent down his course of destruction: a brilliant Storm and
Stress outburst, anticipating as it did, in the early 1770s, a whole
nineteenth-century generation or more of English, French, and
Russian late-Romantic villain-heroes and Byronic *hommes
fatals*. Goethe, in 1788 or 1789, must have recognized that this
inspired *Urfaust* passage was too good not to use. Accordingly,
without significant textual alteration and preserving its irregular
verse form, he simply shifted its dramatic position forwards and
included it in *A Forest Cavern* (cf. Notes 71 and 75). Here it not
only provided this scene with a dramatic climax but also, as a
passage which showed Faust to be capable of remorse, further
dignified him and thus served one of Goethe's general purposes at
the *Fragment* stage.

   The new material added at this second phase of composition
(1788–90) has something of a transitional and provisional
character and makes a rather mixed and inconclusive impression.
Faust as a character becomes more elevated and dignified, the
stylistic changes tend in the same direction; magical and folkloristic themes, including that of the Devil (in 2495–513 for
instance), are treated more distantly. as occasions for miscel-

laneous satire and amusing ribaldry. But the main problem, that of how to treat Faust's bargain with Mephistopheles, has still not been solved, and it appears that Goethe, while seeking to integrate earlier material into a modified and expanded conception, still wishes to keep his options open. The new *Fragment* scenes, more particularly Mephistopheles' soliloquy, have elements of continuity with the *Urfaust*, and are at least as consistent with a tragic as with a non-tragic (salvationist) treatment of the story as a whole.

By 1797, when the third phase of work on *Faust* began, Goethe had been for about ten years the creator and central representative of what is now known as Weimar Classicism and generally regarded as the high noon of German literary history: a sophisticated literary culture emerging, in a manner not paralleled elsewhere in Europe, between the Storm and Stress (which it had transcended but by which it was at a deeper level still nourished) and the official German 'Romantic' movement in which, from the late 1790s onward, a generation of relatively minor talents attempted the thankless task of giving German creative writing a new direction in reaction against the still developing Goethe. By this time the latter's important published works included the *Roman Elegies* (which appeared after some delay in 1795), his second novel *Wilhelm Meister's Apprenticeship* (1794–6), and above all his masterly symbolic 'answer' to the French Revolution, *Hermann and Dorothea* (1797), a small-scale idyllic epic in Homeric verse celebrating stability, normality, the values of German middle-class life, and the indestructible natural cycle. Since 1794 Goethe had also been joined, as a close friend and literary ally, by Schiller (1759–1805) whose development through his own Storm and Stress phase had by a different route reached a position very similar to Goethe's, and who in the last few years of the decade produced his mature masterpieces, the classical historical tragedies *Wallenstein* and *Maria Stuart* (first performed respectively in 1799 and 1801). Had it not been for the stimulus of Schiller's active interest in the *Faust* project, it is doubtful if Goethe would ever have finished Part One or for that matter written Part Two. As it was, when he turned his attention to *Faust* again in the summer of 1797, just after completing *Hermann and Dorothea*, he did so with reluctance and mixed feelings. In his letters to Schiller at this time he refers to the unfinished project in deprecating terms: 'This misty and murky path' (*Dunst und Nebelweg*, 22 June 1797), 'this symbolic, ideal and nebulous world' (24 June), 'airy phantoms . . . a great proliferation of fungi . . . these tomfooleries' (1 July), 'the northern phantoms' (5 July), 'this tragelaphus' (i.e. mythical goat-stag hybrid; 6 December), 'this barbarian production' which 'by its northern nature should appeal to a vast northern public' (28 April 1798). By 'barbarian' and 'northern' he means 'unclassical'. He specifically concedes on 27 June 1797 that he does not think of *Faust* as a work governed by the highest principles of classical dramaturgy (such as he and Schiller in their correspondence of those years had been trying to formulate) but as a loosely constructed commodious dramatic poem: '. . . I shall see to it that its parts are pleasing and entertaining and give food for thought, . . . (whereas) the whole will always remain a fragment . . .' Yet it is significant and moving that at this very time (24 June), and using the very same phrase (*Dunst und Nebel*) as in his letter of the 22nd, the 48-year-old Goethe wrote the beautiful *ottava rima* stanzas called *Dedication* which were to preface the finished Part One: the ghosts of the *Urfaust* world here rise around him 'out of the mist and murk' (line 6) as with plangent nostalgia, over an interval of twenty-five years, he evokes his youth and its genius. The ambivalence of his present feelings becomes all the clearer when we read a poem called *Valediction*, written in the same metre as *Dedication* and probably at the same time, which he intended as a corresponding epilogue to the whole work, but did not in the end publish. Here he 'takes leave' of *Faust* in lines such as the following:

> . . . Who would portray the heart's confusions, when
> His path has led him into clarity?
> Enough! Farewell now to the limitations
> Of this barbarian world of incantations!

The great personal importance which *Faust* evidently had for him, and his own considerable aesthetic doubts about this 'not wholly worthless poetic monstrosity' (to Schiller, 16 September 1800), are both reflected in the continuation which he now nevertheless achieved, and we should lose sight of neither.

Our impression that Goethe was by this time treating the *Faust* project not more than half seriously is reinforced by the curious prefatory conversation-piece (also in all probability written in the summer of 1797) which he calls *Prelude on the Stage*. This discussion of general theatrical and literary problems between a director, a poet, and a comic actor contains nothing specifically relevant to *Faust* as such; it has even been suggested that it originally had no connection with *Faust* at all but was written in 1795 as a prelude (equally irrelevant in content) to Goethe's fragmentary sequel for the libretto of Mozart's *Magic Flute*. The *Dedication*, *Prelude*, and *Prologue in Heaven* nevertheless were all placed as 'prefaces' in front of *Faust*, and a common intention does arguably underlie all three of them. Each in its own way adds to the 'tragedy' itself a further, external, relativizing frame of reference. First, the solemn *Dedication* not only alludes to the play's fantastic and nebulous character, but also gives it the dimension of the poet's personal history, and indeed might almost be said to stand as the author's own invitation to us to interpret *Faust* by the genetic–biographical method. Secondly, the more lighthearted *Prelude* seems to offer the illusion-breaking ironic suggestion that the drama about to unfold is no more than a spectacular improvisation by a travelling theatrical company, intended merely to entertain German audiences. Thirdly, in the vast expanded perspective of the *Prologue in Heaven*, God and other eternal spectators contemplate the *theatrum mundi*, the human *commedia*; and Faust's (or man's) destiny, his tragedies and longings, his religious belief or unbelief, are all made subject in advance to a kind of cosmic irony, a relativizing overview. In these three prefaces Goethe seems to offer a symbolic threefold apologia, hinting (especially in the *Prelude*) that the reader or audience should not take the ensuing substantive drama with absolute seriousness. In this connection we should note yet another important letter, written only five days before his death (to Wilhelm von Humboldt, 17 March 1832), in which he fascinatingly refers to *Faust* as 'these very serious jests (*diese sehr ernsten Scherze*)'; a similar phrase ('these seriously intended jests') occurs in a letter to Boisserée of 4 November 1831. Goethe was in both cases specifically referring to the still unpublished Part Two, but he would probably have regarded the description as applicable to the whole poem.

The real opening of the final version of Part One, and the real key to Goethe's mature conception, is of course the *Prologue in*

Heaven (Sc. 3), which was almost certainly (like the *Dedication* and the *Prelude*) written in the summer of 1797 and in any case, on manuscript evidence, not later than April 1798. Here the earlier themes—particularly that of the Earth Spirit—are not so much abandoned as put in a new and more complex perspective. Probably (but not only) because he felt that a better-known, less private symbolism was now needed, Goethe adopted biblical material: the opening of the Book of Job, in which God gives 'the adversary', Satan, permission to attempt to drive the representative righteous man to despair. Goethe develops the laconic biblical narrative with great impressiveness into a grandiose and yet ironically urbane summit-conference on the value of the terrestrial natural order and of human life within it. The 'adversary', Mephistopheles, at once reveals himself as the cynic, but the cynic with a new dimension: the cosmic mocker and spoiler, the sardonic ironist, unimpressed by the splendid solemnity of the archangels' song in praise of the creation, contemptuous of mankind and of Faust as its exemplar. He is the destructive critic on a maximum scale, the nihilist who literally (to adapt Wilde's definition of cynicism) knows the value of Nothing; in a word, the 'spirit of (perpetual) negation', as God calls him (338) and as he later (1338) calls himself. This is an entirely logical continuation of his role in the *Urfaust*; indeed, it must be said that of the two major characters who are carried through from the earliest to the latest version of Part One, Faust and Mephistopheles, it is the latter who shows by far the greater consistency in his function and personality (Gretchen does not come into this comparison since she is in all essentials fully developed in the *Urfaust* version). The difference is merely that the Mephistopheles of the *Prologue*, confronting 'the Lord' and the other angelic powers who unlike him have remained 'authentic' (344), has had a high-level philosophic role added to his human persona as a cross (with some Satanic overtones) between Iago and Mercutio. His low and reductive view now applies not only to love but to all that exists, including apparently himself; for him the whole of creation, or certainly of earthly creation, might as well explode as the joke in poor taste which it ultimately is. He represents genuine objective despair, as distinct from the subjective despair of the basically idealistic Faust.

It is insufficiently appreciated that this is what the mature

Goethe's modernized, de-Christianized, psychologized version of 'the Devil' really amounts to. Weimar Classicism was, in sophisticated and non-trivial senses, idealistic and optimistic, as well as *humanistic* in the sense that it saw the world anthropocentrically rather than theologically, and in the sense that it took a positive, indeed Pelagian view of human nature and human potential. In Goethe's other great symbolic drama *Iphigenia*, with the publication of the final version of which in 1787 Weimar Classicism can more or less be said to have begun, the same view is clearly expressed: tragedy is reversed and repudiated, and man is 'saved' by 'pure human-ity' alone. The classical Goethe's Mephistopheles is even further than the young Goethe's from being the Satan of Christian tradition (indeed, it is even interestingly doubtful whether the visiting critic in Job has been rightly identified with that later development). He is neither Milton's nor Marlowe's Devil, he is de-theologized. Equally, 'the Lord' himself is not so much the Christian or even the Old Testament God as the impressive spokesman of the mature Goethe's positive and life-affirming view of things. It is notable that the *Prologue* both begins (243–70) and ends (344–9) with the characteristically Goethean celebration of cyclic Nature and the process of eternal Becoming. Notably also, in the Lord's interview with Mephis-topheles, all reference to sin and evil or hell and damnation is studiously avoided, and even death is only mentioned as this latter-day Devil's cue for declaring that he is not interested in whatever may happen to a man after he physically dies (318–21; the same naturalist-humanist emphasis is reiterated in the con-temporaneously written 'pact' scene (1660–70). Goethe has thus completely surmounted the literalistic modes of belief which are presupposed by the traditional Faustus story. He gives us, not so much the drama of a human soul's salvation or damnation, as a confrontation of opposite visions of the world. And by writing the *Prologue in Heaven* he also makes it quite clear that the 'divine' view will in the end be upheld and the Mephistophelean view confuted, the nobility of man vindicated (as in *Iphigenia*) and tragedy dissolved in the healing substance of hope—in other words, that 'Faust' will be 'saved'. This is now Goethe's decision on the point which the *Fragment* still left open.

It is also clear that with the introduction of 'the Lord' in 1797

Goethe was meeting his own need for a new spokesman, marking
his own shift away from a youthful, more unreserved identification with his hero—or rather with the polarity of his hero and
anti-hero, Faust and Mephistopheles, of whom it has always been
suggested that they represented opposite aspects of his own
nature. In the maturer final version of Part One we now hear a
third voice: that of the divine arbiter of the *Prologue*, who
perceives Faust's confusion and immaturity but confidently
predicts his future development (308–11), and who has 'never
hated' Mephistopheles but regards him as in effect yet another of
his servants, who is given permission to visit him when he
pleases (336–43). The addition of this third voice, this higher
perspective, means that Goethe's presentation of Faust and his
dealings with Mephistopheles now contains a certain element of
authorial distance, as if the poet were looking back tolerantly at
the 'confusion', the 'mist and murk' of his own youth. At certain
important points in the new 1797–1801 scenes this authorial
irony shows itself.

   The Earth Spirit is nowhere mentioned in the *Prologue*, and
it is often said that this new scene represents a change of plan
which left two incompatible conceptions side by side in the 1808
text. The Earth Spirit was inherent, as we have seen, in the
Urfaust and *Fragment* material which Goethe had published in
1790 and which he clearly had no wish to repudiate or rewrite.
He now seems simply to leave it to the reader to integrate, as
best he may, this earlier theme into the new and expanded frame
of reference. Arguably, however, there is no irreducible incon-
sistency, in that we need not assume authorial commitment
either to the theism of the *Prologue* or to the kind of Nature-
mysticism which the Earth Spirit seems to represent. The latter
may be seen as relativized, rather than contradicted, by the
cosmic perspective of the present (later) scheme. Faust himself
does not appear to believe in the God of the *Prologue* or to be
aware of this transcendent dimension. His quest for God, whether
he recognizes it as such or not, is through the earth, through
earthly Nature and earthly experience; the Earth Spirit, we may
assume, is the disguise under which 'the Lord' encourages Faust
to be aware of him. And when God, like the God of Job, now
permits Mephistopheles to try his experiment with Faust (323)
and indeed 'gives' him to Faust (342 f., literally 'I *give* him the

companion'), we may with hindsight see this as the higher objective correlative of Faust's belief that Mephistopheles has been
'given' (3241 ff., literally) or 'chained' to him (Sc. 26, <37> ff.)
by the Earth Spirit. In any case, the difference between the Earth
Spirit and the God of the *Prologue* is not radical. The latter is
at most biblical but not really Christian; and although in the
other scenes written in the 1797–1801 phase Christian symbolism
in the narrower sense is deliberately introduced by the use of
New Testament material (especially in 737–807 at the end of Sc.
4) the *specifically* Christian theme of salvific intervention by the
incarnate and therefore suffering Creator, is, as always in Goethe,
absent or at most peripheral: the new passage in Sc. 4 about
Christ's resurrection has an altogether different emphasis. A
Christology presupposing man's radical sinfulness and helpless-
ness which only a once-for-all divine act can remedy, seems to
have been quite alien to Goethe's mind. Although the idea of
salvific divine grace or at least guidance (309) does occur in the
Prologue, it seems that Faust is above all to be saved by the
organic development of his own rightmindedness (310 f.), com-
bined with an unfailing refusal to relapse into inactive com-
placency. On such a road, we might suppose, the Earth Spirit and
the God of Job would be equally suitable guides. But the essential
difference between them, and sufficient reason for replacing the
former by the latter, is perhaps the fact that the maturer Goethe
wished to expand the perspective, to provide a sovereign arbiter
more cosmic and 'celestial' than the Earth Spirit can be: a
remoter overlord who can represent the slightly ironic detachment with which he himself, in the late 1790s, had now come
to view his hero.

There are in fact two quite crucial and characteristic features
of the 'third phase' additions by which Part One was completed:
one is this new 'divine' perspective, and the other is the new
emphasis on 'activity' as the saving Faustian virtue. The three
most important of the 1797–1801 scenes are undoubtedly the
Prologue (Sc. 3), the scene of Faust's first encounter with
Mephistopheles (Sc. 6), and the newly written part (1530–769
in Sc. 7) of their second dialogue. In all three, the motif of
activity or striving (*Tätigkeit, Streben*) recurs with significant
frequency (317, 340 f., 1237, 1692–7, 1754–9). Here, too, it seems
that we may without too much difficulty integrate an earlier

conception with the final one, if we say that the Earth Spirit of the *Urfaust*, to which Faust seemed to commit himself, represented the principle of active energy (cf. Note 14), as contrasted with that of contemplation which was associated with the 'Macrocosm'. The Earth Spirit and Mephistopheles, whom Faust believed to be its servant (as indeed in the new perspective he perhaps still believes) can now both appear to the reader to be servants of 'the Lord'. In other words *activity*, to which in the earlier scenario the Earth Spirit lent a certain 'diabolic' colouring, has now become a more unambiguously positive value. In a note which Goethe made in 1797, moreover, the Earth Spirit itself is now referred to as 'world-spirit and spirit of activity (*Welt- und Tatengenius*)': the 'earthy' associations seem to have faded. This theme of the paramount value of activity, together with the suggestion of a new synthesis of the active and contemplative principles, is now central to Goethe's final conception as represented by the *Prologue in Heaven*. There has been a maturing, a modification, an integration of the earlier theme. Hand in hand with this goes the characteristic suggestion of the *Prologue* that it is the Devil's function, by means of ironic criticism and cynical comment, to stimulate and goad man into constantly renewed active endeavour (340 f.), and thus despite himself perform for him an educative, indeed salvific role. This is the basis of Goethe's famous paradoxical definition of Mephistopheles, who is made to describe himself (1335 f.) as a representative of

> that Power which would
> Do evil constantly, and constantly does good.

The optimistic, non-tragic character of this conception hardly needs underlining: it amounts in fact to a conciliatory integration of the traditional polarity of God and the Devil. The antithesis that now matters is that of action and inaction. It is activity as such that 'the Lord' values in man, it is Faust's motto 'in the beginning was the deed' (1237) that makes him God's 'servant' (300) and 'a good man' (328). Since, however, mere activity or 'striving' is not in itself either moral or immoral, this removes Goethe's scheme still further from a Christian basis as traditionally understood. The polarity of good and evil has itself been reduced, and this is entirely characteristic of Goethe's monistic and integrative way of thinking. It was already anticipated in an essay on Shakespeare written as early as 1771:

> What we call evil is only the other side of the good, a part of its existence, belonging to it and to the whole just as necessarily as the tropics must burn and Lapland must freeze if there is to be a temperate zone in between.

This constant tendency to balance out and reconcile opposites is something which Goethe's admirers find profound and his detractors infuriating. He himself, in a letter written in the last year of his life, described his nature as 'conciliatory' and with great perceptiveness gave this as the reason why he was 'not born to be a tragic poet' (to Zelter, October 1831). This has been held against him as a dramatist, and it might be held against *Faust*. Drama as such is about contrasts, conflicts, antitheses, dualities, polarities. What is, or was, the conflict in *Faust*? It resists simplistic understanding as a conflict between good and evil. Schiller, writing to Goethe on 23 June 1797 and still knowing only the *Fragment*, suggested another formulation: its main theme is 'the duality of human nature and the vain attempt to unite the divine and the physical in man'. Alternatively, we might say that from the outset the essential *opposita* in this dramatic dialectic were idealism and cynicism, the 'high' and the 'low' view of things. This is what the dramatic contrasts of the *Urfaust* were about: we miss its point unless we see that Mephistopheles is partly right in his assessment and prognosis of the Gretchen affair, the tragic outcome of which is his *quod erat demonstrandum*. Faust is torn by the conflict between an all-too-enlightened 'devil's' worldly realism and his own romantic vision. In another letter of 1797 (26 June) Schiller observes to Goethe that 'the Devil convinces our intelligence by his realism, and Faust convinces our hearts'. Faust's 'confusion' to which God in the *Prologue* refers (308) is a symptom of this continuing struggle —but it is a struggle that points towards conciliation. The hero's progress, the 'clarity' into which (like the poet of *Valediction*) he is to be 'led' (309), would involve the integration of these opposites, the development of higher syntheses beyond the *Urfaust's* tragically violent polarizations (idealism and cynicism, 'macrocosmic' contemplation and 'earthly' action). Whether or not this maturity is ever actually achieved by Faust in the poem, it is the direction in which Goethe himself, through his different stages of composing it, has seemed to be moving. It is perhaps in this sense that *Faust* may be read as the drama of an evolving human soul and of an evolving culture.

The longest sequence of new material added in the third phase runs from line 606 in Scene 4 to line 1769 in Scene 7, and with it Goethe at last closed the remaining 'great lacuna' between the end of Faust's first conversation with Wagner in the opening *Urfaust* scene and the beginning of the *Fragment* version of his first conversation with Mephistopheles. We now have the lengthy conclusion of Sc. 4 after Wagner's exit (606–807), the scene outside the town (Sc. 5, 808–1177), and most (1178–769) of the two ensuing scenes in Faust's study (Sc. 6, 7) in which Mephistopheles introduces himself. One of the interesting features of this important 'infill' sequence is that Faust has now developed a past of his own, a youth to which he refers, in two of the new scenes, with nostalgia or bitterness (720–9, 769–82, 1023–55). Another is that Faust undergoes several striking changes of mood between despondency and hope; and we should probably be wrong to try to explain these in terms of a clearly conceived intricate 'character' rather than of the poet's own wish to accommodate (as in the opening of Sc. 17 in the 1790 version) the expression of moods and thoughts of his own without over-much concern for the dramatic context. Were we to insist on seeking a clear dramatic line in the classical manner, we might for instance wonder how it is that a man about to 'sell himself to the Devil' is so often in a pious and life-affirming state of mind, or so easily moves back into one (762–84, 903–40, 1068–99, 1178–237, 1379–84). But the intervention, as Faust is about to commit suicide, of angelic choirs singing about the resurrection of Christ (Sc. 4, 737–807), is moving and effective for its own sake; there is also great poetic force in the ensuing praise of spring, which Goethe quite correctly couples with the Resurrection theme (Sc. 5, 903–28), and in Faust's translation of the Logos passage (Sc. 6, 1224–37). After the essentially comic exorcism of the poodle, we have the first confrontation between Faust and Mephistopheles, and it is notable that they are here at once polarized as spokesmen of life-affirmation and pure nihilism respectively (1363–84). It is also a matter of great interest and importance that Faust, both here and in the next scene (Sc. 7), treats the 'Devil' with scorn and contempt—an attitude very different from his helpless hanging on Mephistopheles' worldly advice in the 1790 *Fragment* passage (1776–1834). We are here brought back to the methodological controversy about how the interpretation of *Faust* should be approached.

Sc. 7 (*Faust's Study II*), which contains in its newly written part (1530–769) the actual negotiation of the 'pact' between Faust and Mephistopheles and is therefore often referred to as the 'Pact' scene, is the main stumbling-block for critics who insist on a logical exegesis of the finished 1808 text and refuse on principle to take its complex genesis into account. It is bound to be looked upon as a central scene, since it contains Goethe's long-delayed solution to what appears to have been his main problem in adapting the Faust legend, namely that of recasting the old motif of the devil's bargain in a modern and sophisticated form. A minor example of the methodological difficulty arises from the very fact that there is a hiatus, explicable historically but not otherwise, between the beginning of this scene (1530) and the end of the preceding Sc. 6 (cf. Note 25). As to Sc. 7 generally, it will best make sense if we bear in mind the following three points. (1) The whole Faust–Mephistopheles negotiation is a composite product, most of it belonging to the third (1797–1801) phase of composition, but an important part of it to the second (lines 1770–867, already published in the 1790 *Fragment*); indeed, if we also count the *Urfaust* dialogue between Mephistopheles and the student as part of the same scene, which it officially is, then we may say that Sc. 7 represents all three of the chronological levels of Part One. (2) The new pact-negotiation, written during the same years as the other new additions Sc. 3 (the *Prologue in Heaven*) and Sc. 6 (the Logos scene), is based on the same general conception as these and must be seen in the light of them. (3) In particular, the negotiation must be interpreted in the new ironic perspective of the *Prologue*; that is to say, Faust's attitude and utterances in this negotiation must be seen as subject in some degree to ironic authorial distance. This third consideration throws light, for example, on the otherwise obscure passage 1583–626. Faust here utters a grand rhetorical curse on human life and its vain deluding joys, and this is immediately followed (1607–26) by a 'chorus of spirits' lamenting his destruction of 'the beautiful world' and exhorting him

to build it again in his heart. There is here a quite clear parallel
with the contemporaneously written part of Sc. 4 in which the
suicidal Faust is brought to 'love the earth once more' (784;
literally, 'belong to the earth once more') by another chorus of
unseen singers with their message of affirmation. The invisible
chorus in the Pact scene is clearly not one of Mephistophelean
spirits, notwithstanding Mephistopheles' immediate claim that
they are and his cynical parody of their words (1627–34). The
spirit-chorus, if we are to judge by the content and tone of what
it actually says, can only be an answering, healing echo to Faust's
mood of subjective despair, an answer from deep within him—or
(which essentially comes to the same thing) from above him: a
concealed message from the divine Author to his 'confused
servant'. And what, except in such a perspective of tolerant
detachment, are we to make of the central passage 1635–707,
in which the deadly serious traditional *Teufelspakt* is paradoxically transformed into a mere wager? A bet or wager is a
kind of contract that is something more like a game, and this in
itself raises the question of how seriously we are to take it. The
conception seems to be relatively traditional as far as line 1674,
but at 1675 Goethe reverts emphatically to the new and paradoxical theme, characteristic of the third-phase material and quite
absent from the 1790 version, of Faust's *contempt* for the 'Devil'
to whom he is about to 'sell himself'. In Sc. 6 he mocked
Mephistopheles' vain life-destroying enterprise (1379–84); now
he mocks him as the purveyor of worthless because merely transi-
tory pleasures (1675–87). He then vows that none of these will
ever 'lull him into self-sufficiency' (1695) and challenges
Mephistopheles to prove him wrong.

This challenge constitutes the 'wager': Faust literally *bets his
life* that Mephistopheles can never make him complacent and
inactive (1692–8). Up to this point what he says is relatively
straightforward. But he now adds a further rhetorical development of his theme, passionately vowing (1699–706) to forfeit
his life at once if ever, deluded into mere enjoyment, he so far
forgets his embittered disillusionment as to bless a passing
moment, entreating it not to pass because it is so beautiful. The
poetic substance of these two celebrated lines (1699 f., 'Werd
ich zum Augenblicke sagen: Verweile doch, du bist so schön!')
is such, and so characteristic are they of the mature Goethe in

whose work the theme of the 'eternal moment' so often recurs, that it is impossible to read them as seriously expressing the formula for his problematic hero's 'damnation'. Faust longs, like Blake, to kiss the moment as it flies, and so live in Eternity's sunrise. This experience, and that of 'lying down in sloth and base inaction' (1692), sinking into the sty of contentment, are two very different things, though Faust's speech appears to identify them. The divine Observer, we may assume, sees this identification, like the earlier grand curse on 'the beautiful world', as yet another example of Faust's confusion. The idealist's divine discontent is not to be assimilated to a perverse restless rejection of the beauty of the world: the latter is merely a parody of it. The truly Goethean, truly human and divine Moment would be a paradoxical synthesis of contemplation and action, a union of complete satisfaction with continued longing, an intersection of the timeless with time. The Lord, in whom (as Goethe put it in a late poem) 'all striving and struggling is eternal rest', knows that Faust in his heart of hearts really desires such a Moment, and that his pretence that he does not is really a challenge to Mephistopheles to provide it for him; or again, that since it has of course only one Provider, Faust is here in a further irony confusing the Devil with God. In other words, Faust's defiant prediction that he will never experience the ultimately satisfying Moment, and Mephistopheles' ironic undertaking to see to it that he does, are only rhetorical: at a deeper level Faust is longing for something which Mephistopheles, if he could conceive it, would be determined he should never have. Once this is appreciated, then something more like the traditional Devil scenario re-establishes itself: the Devil as tormentor and frustrator, who will withhold from his client the very thing he appeared to offer him. We revert, in fact, to the scenario of Mephistopheles' concluding soliloquy (1851–67; see above, p. xxiv, and Note 37). In this soliloquy, the most crucial passage in that part of Sc. 7 (beginning at 1770) which was written and published at the *Fragment* stage, Mephistopheles looked forward to tantalizing and frustrating Faust, and there has been much discussion of the apparent discrepancy between this diabolic programme and the one now seemingly implied by the final Pact negotiation: namely, that if he is to win his bet with Faust he must try to satisfy him (1692–706). We might be content to leave the difference unresolved, merely pointing out that Goethe modified his plan after an interval of ten years or so, but was evidently unwilling to make consequential emendations in the text he had already published. In fact, however, we may say that in the later-written version too Mephistopheles' function is still, at a deeper level, that of frustrating Faust by denying him his profoundest wish. In any case, it also still remains the ultimate aim of Mephistopheles to destroy Faust, to destroy his idealism by exploiting his restless craving for experience: and we may now see him as pursuing this purpose pragmatically by whatever means come to hand, whether by frustrating his desires or by seeming to gratify them. The discrepancy thus disappears—if not altogether, then at least into a more marginal area of our attention. The composite genesis of the scene remains a historical fact which cannot be overlooked, but we may now at least credit Goethe with having in a subtle, perhaps over-subtle way, constructed a later and larger conception round an earlier and narrower one.

Another addition or interpolation made at the 1797–1801 stage was the curious *Walpurgis Night* sequence (Sc. 24, 25; cf. Notes 93, 111 and 121). After killing Gretchen's brother in Sc. 22, Faust has had to flee from the town where she lives, and some time has to pass while she bears their child, drowns it, and is arrested and condemned for infanticide. Dramatically it was reasonable enough that Goethe should feel it necessary to give Faust something to do during this interval, and his reference in the *Urfaust* prose scene to 'vulgar diversions' (Sc. 26, <10>) already hinted at this. It must be said, however, that Faust's sensual orgy (if that is what the Blocksberg scene is intended to be) is in practice more than a little tame. Here again a change of plan is involved. Goethe at first intended a thorough-going witches' sabbath, culminating in obscene and grotesque satanistic ceremonies at the top of the mountain, but regrettably he abandoned this idea, for which only a few manuscript jottings survive (cf. Note 121). Instead, as in the witch scene of the *Fragment* (Sc. 9), he seems to have decided that the whole satanistic scenario was not to be taken seriously but used for the insertion of miscellaneous satirical material, most of it intelligible only to an inner circle of his contemporaries. The result is that although Sc. 24 (the *Walpurgis Night* itself) contains some poetically remarkable passages, notably Faust's vision of the doomed Gretchen (4183–205) which should lead to a dramatic climax, it then simply breaks off into incongruous trivialities. To make matters worse, Goethe at this point permitted himself an extraordinary act of literary irresponsibility, by inserting the irrelevant collection of epigrams which he whimsically called A *Walpurgis Night's Dream* (Sc. 25, 4223–398; cf. Note 111). In any serious production of *Faust* as a play, this embarrassing piece of literary paraphernalia (which was certainly first intended for another purpose, as the *Prelude on the Stage* may have been) can only be quietly excised, along with about a quarter of the preceding Sc. 24.

A very much better feature of the final revision of Part One was of course the completion of the Gretchen tragedy by the restoration of the final *Urfaust* scenes which had been omitted from the *Fragment*. Valentine's *Urfaust* soliloquy in Sc. 22 had already been an effective and moving passage as it stood; Goethe now completed this scene in an entirely suitable style, adding Valentine's duel with Faust and his terrible dying speech in which he curses his sister as a whore. This is now followed (cf. Note 91) by the Cathedral scene and then, after the anticlimactic *Walpurgis* extravaganza, by the conclusion of the Gretchen tragedy with three more hitherto unpublished scenes of great dramatic power (cf. Note 122). It is sad to reflect that Schiller, but for whom Part One would probably never have been completed, not only did not live to see its publication but was apparently never even shown the text of these last *Urfaust* scenes (or for that matter the *Prologue in Heaven* or the new Faust–Mephistopheles dialogues). On 5 May 1798 Goethe wrote to him that he had been transcribing his old manuscript (the original *Urfaust* autograph) and had found that 'certain tragic scenes are written in prose, they have a naturalness and force which in comparison with the rest makes them quite unbearable'. In a revealing formulation of the classical, anti-naturalistic aésthetic which he and Schiller now shared, he continues: 'I am therefore now trying to put them into verse, so that the idea is seen as if through a veil, but the immediate impact of the dreadful subject-matter is softened.' One of the prose scenes to which he here refers was Sc. 26, that of Faust's violent recriminations with Mephistopheles over Gretchen's impending fate, the scene to which Goethe now gave the title A *Gloomy Day. Open Country.*

In this case, however, he decided on further consideration not only to drop the idea of versifying it but also to leave the wording of this characteristic Storm and Stress passage almost exactly as it was, despite the traces of abandoned conceptions which it contains (cf. Notes 124 and 125). It therefore now stands as the only prose scene in either part of *Faust*, a powerful and brilliant anomaly. The brief but haunting Sc. 27 which follows it could be considered to be in verse anyway and was therefore also left unchanged. The versification of the final Prison scene (Sc. 28) was, however, carried out, and whether or not we agree with Goethe's theory that it softens the impact of the poignant and harrowing material, this revision was probably an improvement, if any improvement was possible. One addition, not dictated by any requirements of metre, was made at the very end: in the *Urfaust* version Mephistopheles' exclamation *Sie ist gerichtet!* (literally 'judgement has been passed on her') were the last words spoken of Gretchen. In the final version (4597–612) Goethe has made 'a voice from above' echo them with the cry *Ist gerettet!* ('she is saved'). This represents no radical change, since the redemption of Gretchen was already clearly enough implied in the *Urfaust* version by her submission, then as now, to her earthly fate as God's judgement and by her renunciation of Faust. But Goethe evidently now wished to underline this point by adding the mitigating divine words, the effect of which is certainly dramatic. The tragedy of Gretchen's immediately following execution (described by anticipation in 4587–95) nevertheless remains as the implied conclusion of both versions.

'The First Part of the Tragedy', as published in 1808, ends at this point; and apart from a few notes, fragments, and sketches Goethe did not begin writing the 'Second Part' until nearly twenty years later, when he was in his late seventies. Of the many visitors who in the latter part of his life came from Germany and abroad to call on him, some would try to get him to satisfy their curiosity by divulging any plans he might have for the sequel which the designation 'Part One' seemed to hold in prospect. In particular, having evidently not read or not understood the *Prologue in Heaven*, they would ask about the hero's ultimate fate: 'Tell us, your Excellency, will the Devil carry off Faust?' On one occasion Goethe is reported to have replied impatiently: 'No, on the contrary, Faust will carry off the Devil.'

His readers were perhaps understandably confused by the presence in the title of the word 'tragedy'. This description was appropriate enough for what was predominantly the story of Gretchen, but it is a little difficult to account for its use, otherwise than as an ironic formality, in the title of what eventually appeared as *Faust. The Second Part of the Tragedy* in 1832. This extraordinary continuation in five long Acts, which it is here perhaps appropriate to summarize briefly, opens with Faust waking from a sleep of forgetfulness in the bosom of Nature, which has erased all memory of Gretchen from his mind. Much of the material that now follows is not so much drama as elaborate dramatic allegory which appears to be only loosely connected with the Faust theme. In largely comic scenes at the Imperial court, the spendthrift Emperor is first provided with 'magical' wealth by the printing of paper money, and then shown magical phantasms of Helen of Troy and her lover Paris. Faust is stricken with a passion for Helen, and Mephistopheles (on whom the new perspective of classical antiquity which predominates in Part Two now casts an ironic light) objects that he cannot assist in this matter since Helen is, so to speak, not his period. Faust is referred to subterranean mother-goddesses and an alchemical homunculus from whom we learn that he must seek Helen in ancient Greece. After he has encountered various other bizarre mentors in the course of an elaborate allegorical pageant (the *Classical Walpurgis Night* of Act III) Helen appears in ancient Sparta before the palace of her husband Menelaos, talking in the style of Euripidean drama to a chorus of women and to Mephistopheles, who is now disguised as a hideous old female servant and who persuades Helen to seek Faust's protection. In the central third Act Faust appears as a medieval crusading knight; his union with Helen seems intended as an allegory of the cultural union between ancient and modern, Greek and German, in the synthesis of Weimar Classicism. Their son Euphorion, expressly identified by Goethe as an allegory of Byron, falls to his death in an attempt to fly; the idyll ends with Helen's disappearance as she returns to the underworld, and with an impressive celebration of the eternally productive forces of Nature which outlast all cultures. In Act IV Faust floats back to Germany on a cloud and on the way observes the sea, the wasteful energies of which he desires to conquer and control. Mephistopheles wins a battle for the

Emperor by magical devices (an old chapbook motif) and in reward Faust is granted all the coastal lands that lie below the waterline. A grandiose reclamation programme begins, and is the theme of the final Act. In the last years of his life Goethe is reported to have expressed interest in future large-scale projects of this kind such as the building of canals through Panama and Suez. Faust's enterprise is of course charged with symbolic significance. On the one hand, having re-created (even if only temporarily) the perfect shape of Helen, he now seems to seek another medium in which to bring form out of chaos. More generally it is the confrontation between Man and Nature, the continuing struggle of civilization against the elemental forces which both the sea and Mephistopheles represent. Faust, now a hundred years old and with his activity still unflagging, dies in a vision of his project's accomplishment; and at this point Goethe feels it to be artistically necessary to revert (for the first time since line 1706 of Part One) to the unresolved and virtually forgotten motif of the Pact and Wager. By a *jeu de mots* (Faust enjoys his moment of supreme bliss in anticipation of a future achievement, and pronounces the 'fatal' words in this sense) Mephistopheles is put literally in the right, though essentially in the wrong. Faust falls dead, and with elaborate comedy Mephistopheles sets about the business of claiming his supposed victim's 'soul' (the medieval conceptions of which Goethe here takes occasion to satirize) and summons up diabolic underlings to assist him. But part of the celestial host now suddenly appears, scattering roses of love which burn the devils and put them to flight. Mephistopheles' own attention is distracted by a grotesque fit of homosexual lust inspired by the young angels: his skin erupts in boils and he recovers himself only to find that Faust's 'immortal part' (as the stage-direction puts it) has been carried off out of his reach. Cursing his discomfiture, he grudgingly acknowledges the power of Eros over even so hardbitten a cynic as himself. A concluding scene, set in a mysterious region between earth and heaven, shows the mute and inert Faust being carried upwards to where he can undergo further transformation and development. In this final passage, which has a mystical and syncretic character, Goethe uses largely Catholic symbolism and legend. Holy hermits and Church fathers pray and meditate, saints and choruses of penitent women mingle their voices with those of the angels, and as a climax the Mother of God appears in glory. Again all mention of Christ, and almost all suggestion of a personal judgement on the hero, is carefully avoided. Much of the material is reminiscent of Dante—though only of the *Paradiso*. Faust's long-forgotten beloved appears, as *'una poenitentium*, formerly called Gretchen', and intercedes for her 'returning' lover who is, as she puts it, 'no longer clouded (*getrübt*)'. The Mater Gloriosa invites her to 'rise to higher spheres' to which Faust, 'if he senses your presence', will follow her. The motif of a woman's redemptive goodness and love is paralleled elsewhere in Goethe (*Iphigenia*, *The Elective Affinities*) and of course in other writers before and since. Here, as a mystique of femininity, it is Goethe's touchingly personal version of the theme of divine grace, expressed in the often-quoted last two lines of the enigmatic *Chorus Mysticus* which closes this scene and the entire work:

> All that must disappear
> Is but a parable;
> What lay beyond us,* here
> All is made visible;*
> Here deeds have understood
> Words they were darkened by;
> Eternal Womanhood
> Draws us on high.

Such an ending may not be strictly Christian, but it expresses that deep-rooted trust in the maternal goodness and timeless meaningfulness of the world which was Goethe's form of all-sustaining love and faith.

The question of the overall dramatic unity of *Faust* in both its Parts, or even of Part One considered (if it is legitimate to do so) on its own, is vexed and controversial. If, for example, we reflect on the relationship between the Gretchen drama and the rest of Part One, a problem arises which can be explained, though not solved, in terms of the history of the play's genesis. The 'Wager' passage in Sc. 7, written about twenty-five years after the Gretchen material but preceding it in the final text, sets up, as we have seen, a scenario according to which Mephistopheles may claim Faust's life if Faust ever experiences a moment so beautiful that he wishes it to be prolonged. Theoretically, if Goethe had wanted Part One to be at all costs a dramaturgically consistent whole, he would before republishing the Gretchen scenes in 1808 have had to revise them in the light of this Wager, so that in the course of his passionate love-affair Faust would never be seen, or supposed, to experience a perfect moment of this kind. It would be the merest pedantry to insist that the fateful Moment does not count as such unless Faust actually also pronounces the fateful words. Tacitly and in effect, therefore, Faust must be presumed to have forfeited his life to Mephistopheles several times over when he was with Gretchen (perhaps in Sc. 16, perhaps on his first night with her and subsequently). To have revised the Gretchen drama in this way, however, would have been a radical and absurd operation, which Goethe quite rightly did not attempt. As we have seen in other contexts, the shaping of *Faust* into a logical whole was not his highest priority, and was certainly never allowed to override his respect for the compelling beauty of his already published youthful work. He therefore made no attempt to integrate the Gretchen tragedy with the Wager, but left it to all intents and purposes as he had originally written it, subject to certain revisions and additions which we have noted and which were made for quite different reasons. The effect is that since the whole Faust–Mephistopheles negotiation, culminating in the strongly emphasized Wager scene, precedes the whole Gretchen story in the finished 1808 version, any attentive and unprejudiced reader or spectator of the latter may well be puzzled, or even get the impression that Part One is a play falling into two halves (the second beginning with Sc. 10 or perhaps Sc. 8) which have little or nothing to do with each other. The difficulty is only partly met if we argue, hindsightedly and in unitarian fashion, that Faust's affair with Gretchen does not in a broader sense constitute loss of the Wager, if only because his passion for her appears to abate, and in any case because in the total perspective of Parts One and Two it may be seen as only one tragic episode among others in his career, and one that has not finally satisfied him. To assume (as indeed the ending of Part Two might suggest) that the Wager is not meant to be taken altogether seriously or literally, is perhaps our only recourse. But once again *Faust* here presents us, for historical reasons, with a structural problem which may or may not be a serious artistic flaw.

We have from Goethe himself a number of observations that may be regarded as relevant to this point and to the question of the 'unity' of *Faust* in general. Many of them date, as we have seen, from the summer of 1797 when he resumed work on Part One. A further such comment, probably also written at that time, was a nine-line verse epigram which he intended to place at the end of the play under the title *Curtain Speech* (*Abkündigung*), a counterpart to the *Prelude on the Stage* as the poet's *Valediction* would have been to *Dedication*. The actor was to call for applause, remarking:

> . . . Our play is rather like the life of Man :
> We make a start, we make an end—
> But make a whole of it? Well, do so if you can.

(*Des Menschen Leben ist ein ähnliches Gedicht: es hat wohl einen Anfang, hat ein Ende, allein ein Ganzes ist es nicht.*) Later, Goethe planned that this apologia should appear at the end of Part Two; in the event, like *Valediction*, it was left unpublished. But as we have already seen, Goethe conceded to Schiller at the time of finishing Part One that *Faust* could never claim to be an integral whole: 'the whole thing (*das Ganze*) will always remain a fragment' (27 June 1797); and it is noticeable how often he reverted to this point later on, especially in his last years when he was engaged on Part Two. The words 'fragment', 'fragmentary', and especially '*incommensurable*', turn up repeatedly, referring specifically to Part Two but probably applicable to Part One as well: '(I intended) the Second Part . . . to be less fragmentary than the first' (?1830/1, reported by Riemer); 'the more incommensurable and elusive to the understanding a work of literature is, the better it is' (conversation with Eckermann, 6 May 1827); '*Faust* is really a quite incommensurable quantity, and all attempts to make it rationally intelligible are vain' (Eckermann, 3 January 1830). To Eckermann, as to Schiller, he declares: 'In a work of this kind all that matters is that the individual component parts (*die einzelnen Massen*) should be meaningful and clear, although it will always be incommensurable as a whole—while nevertheless for that very reason remaining, like an unsolved problem, a constant stimulus to repeated study' (13 February 1831). The actor's valediction of 1800, by its choice of simile, made a further point: the poem, the drama, is like human life itself. It has been said of Goethe that fragmentariness was of the essence of his genius; also, that his poetry and his life were close to each other, as in a kind of symbiosis. The two points are related, as he himself seems to suggest by the much-quoted remark in his autobiography (*Poetry and Truth*, Book VII) that all his works are 'fragments of a great confession'. The description applies pre-eminently to *Faust*. It does not mean, of course, that all his works were themselves fragmentary. His shorter poems have their own kind of integrity and perfection, and some of his longer works as well (*Hermann and Dorothea*, *Iphigenia*, *Tasso*) have a classical unity or something closely approaching it. But if we look for dramaturgical and logical integration in *Faust* we shall be disappointed. Little purpose is served by crediting a work with qualities which its author himself disclaims. Most of the 'component parts' are of great interest in themselves or have great comic or tragic force; as a whole it is a fascinatingly flawed masterpiece. It seems to have had for Goethe the special status of a kind of creative side-show, to which (as he wrote to Schiller) the highest formal principles were not to be scrupulously applied. On the other hand, the fact that it remained, at each stage of its composition, close to his own life, documenting his current interests, an evolving and unfinished 'confession', a poetic extension of his organic growth so to speak, could not fail to give it a certain vitality, an endlessly stimulating variety and freshness. *Faust* is not so much a structure as a complex of structures, the drama not of one human problem but of a whole human development. Above all it is a generous and kaleidoscopic profusion of wit and poetry.

As a work for the theatre, even Part One was generally regarded during its author's lifetime as unperformable, though it was widely read. Goethe himself seemed to think it unsuitable for the stage, though his recorded pronouncements on this point are ambiguous. A production in Weimar was planned in 1810 but came to nothing. There were amateur or private performances of excerpts from the text, but the first full-length production of Part One in Germany by a professional company was in 1829, in Goethe's eightieth year and more than twenty years after its publication (strangely enough, a French première in Paris and even an English one in London, with accompanying fireworks, had been given a year or two earlier). The German première was at the Brunswick court theatre, produced by August Klingemann in an eight-act arrangement which was then quickly adopted in several other German cities. After this Part One continued to be performed, though always in adaptations which virtually reduced the text to the Gretchen tragedy. Gounod's opera of 1859 (often more correctly known in Germany not as *Faust* but as *Margarete*) reflects this conception and gave still wider currency to it. It was not until the last quarter of the century that German producers began to offer completer versions of Part One and to combine it with Part Two. The latter, published just after Goethe's death in 1832, had from the first been received with incomprehension, and only selected fractions of it had been performed; a few scenes were given in 1849 in honour of Goethe's centenary, and even in the so-called première of 1854, in Hamburg, the greater part of the text was cut. Not until 1876, in Weimar, did Otto Devrient put on the first production of both Parts, on two successive evenings. This was the year of the opening of the Bayreuth Festival, and indeed the influence of Wagner's unprecedently long operas, particularly the *Ring* tetralogy, is said to have encouraged producers to attempt full-scale multi-evening presentations of *Faust*. Dingelstedt of the Vienna Burgtheater planned to give one in Bayreuth itself, and in fact his successor Wilbrandt did so in Vienna in 1883; four-evening versions were given in 1877 in Hanover and in 1900 in Berlin. But theatrically speaking, neither Part One nor Part Two really came into its own until the twentieth century, in the hands of the great post-Naturalistic director Max Reinhardt. His 1909 production of Part One in Berlin was still a Faust–Gretchen version, but innovative by its use of the revolving stage; Part Two followed in 1911. In 1917 Reinhardt became, with Hofmannsthal and Strauss, a co-founder of the Salzburg Festival, and it was in his last years here, between 1933 and 1937, that he realized an extended and more integrated conception of Part One. His use of a vast, specially constructed 'simultaneous' stage in the *Felsenreitschule* was an achievement of genius, and his *Faust* productions became internationally famous. With the Second World War the Reinhardt era passed, and the Gustav Gründgens era began. Gründgens had first played the part of Mephistopheles (coveted by star actors even in Goethe's day) in 1932, and his first productions of Parts One and Two were in 1941 and 1942 respectively. A newly conceived version followed in Düsseldorf in 1949, and this developed into his revolutionary and now legendary Hamburg productions of 1957 (Part One) and 1958 (Part Two). Gründgens, taking a hint from the *Prelude on the Stage* which he had previously always cut but now reread, abandoned all the traditional illusion-making paraphernalia of realism and presented everything—the heavens, the Imperial court, Greece—as nothing but the stage itself, the play as a play, with boards and a few simple properties, just as a troupe of wandering players might have done it. His conception and his own acting won international acclaim, with guest performances in the United States and the Soviet Union. Gründgens had Part One made into a film in 1961, simply as a record of his stage version and without any exploitation of the film medium as such. Both parts also became available as sound recordings, Part One being particularly notable for the incomparable performance of Käthe Gold as Gretchen.

The notorious difficulty of translating *Faust* into any language is reflected in the history of attempts to put it into English. Of Part One alone, or of parts of it, there have been between fifty and a hundred English versions since it was first published in 1808, and the dust lies thick on most of them. The Bibliography gives details of some which have appeared on both sides of the Atlantic in the last forty years or so, and of one or two of the earlier ones. The existence of so many predecessors may well daunt the newcomer to this Sisyphean task, though paradoxically it is also encouraging: when the other versions are actually examined, the stimulus to try to do it differently is almost irresistible. Faust himself, we may hope, entertained no disrespect for his colleague and contemporary Martin Luther when he too felt this challenge and decided '*Ich muß es anders übersetzen*' (1227 f.). It is true that his career as a translator was shortlived: having considered three alternative renderings of his first five words he was interrupted by the Devil and promptly sold himself to him. In the beginning was the Word, and what have translators made of it? The intractability of the problem arises, I would suggest, from the constant conflict between three absolute requirements: (1) that a poem such as *Faust*, having been written almost entirely in rhymed verse, must be translated (even in the late twentieth century) into rhymed verse; (2) that it must nevertheless be translated into an English of the twentieth century and not of the nineteenth or earlier; and (3) that the essential elements of Goethe's meaning must be conveyed without significant distortion. In the present enterprise I have rightly or wrongly treated all three of these propositions as self-evident, though they are perhaps in need of some further clarification.

On the question of rhyme I emphatically agree in principle with those translators (now, it seems, increasingly unfashionable) who have reproduced it throughout, and fundamentally disagree with those who have abandoned it altogether or used it only intermittently. If one is trying to offer something like an autonomous English 'equivalent' of Goethe's text, and not merely the utilitarian reading-aid that may be appropriate to a bilingual edition, then one stands inescapably under formal demands similar—though they are less strict—to those imposed by Dante's *Divine Comedy* or Pushkin's *Eugene Onegin*. Dante has been put into English *terza rima* more than once with considerable virtuosity; as to Pushkin, Charles Johnston's prosodically meticulous and linguistically brilliant rendering of his relentlessly regular complex stanzas must surely stand as a model of what verse translation should and may rarely be. Goethe's schemes of rhyme and metre in most of *Faust* are more fluid and flexible, and some liberties may be taken with them, but they are still of the essence of the poem and must be imitated as closely as other considerations will allow. To use prose, or the kind of flat rhymeless verse which is tantamount to prose, is simply a counsel of despair, an evasion of the main technical challenge. Half the point of what Goethe says is lost if it lacks the musical closure and neatness of the way he said it. As Walter Arndt succinctly puts it in the introductory essay to his strictly rhymed version: '(the rhyme) is part of the "meaning" and the "meaning" is part of it ... Fidelity and prose are mutually exclusive goals.' Where one may differ is in some of the detailed applications of this fundamental principle. For example—given that English contains far fewer 'feminine' word-endings than German or Russian, to say nothing of Italian—it seems to me neither possible nor desirable to conform to Goethe's regular alternation of masculine and feminine rhymes, even in a prosodically strict passage such as the *ottava rima* stanzas of *Dedication* (1–32). (A similar point is made by Walter Kaufmann, who also uses predominantly masculine rhyming.) In addition, I have used far fewer end-stopped lines than Goethe, and have not often (except, again, in a piece such as *Dedication*) arranged the rhymes in exactly the same sequence as in the original or used exactly the same line-lengths. To eschew these licences—that of fairly frequent overrunning, for example —seems to me to increase the difficulty of rhyming to a point at which too much else has to be sacrificed for the sake of it; rhyme becomes, so to speak, too expensive.

This question of the *cost* of rhyme, of how expensive a luxury one is prepared to allow it to become, is one that constantly arises, and the answer must be a matter of personal judgement. The difficulty is created by the other two axiomatic constraints mentioned above, one of which is that of language and diction. Goethe's language was not archaic to his contemporaries, and it is absurd to translate it today into poetic archaisms. The insidious pervasiveness of archaic sub-Shakespearian diction in English verse is even now very hard to resist altogether, but we should continue to try harder—asking ourselves, for instance, as a constant routine test: how would this word, or this phrase, sound to a present-day audience in the mouth of a present-day actor? If we answer that to either of them it would probably sound even slightly laughable, then like Faust himself we must try another word (or another phrase, another arrangement). Our imaginary actor should not only not be asked to say 'methinks' as an equivalent of *mich dünkt*, or to use 'thou' and 'ye' for the *du* and *ihr* which modern German has been fortunate enough to preserve: we should also not expect him to talk constantly in dustily poetic inversions (the adjective following the noun, for instance, or the negative following the verb). At the other extreme, however, we should avoid up-to-the-minute, rapidly dating colloquial jocularities and obtrusive neologisms. The diction should be kept in a broad, quasi-timeless middle ground between the pallidly antiquated and the brashly modish. Worst of all is the incongruous mixture of the two. Better a discreet neutrality than the sudden jolt from one century to another, or from one register to another. The adage about art concealing art must mean, in this context, that it should ideally be made impossible for the reader of a rhyme-pair to guess which word was chosen to rhyme with which. If he can, then the chances are that the rhyme is too obtrusive, it has probably cost too much.

We come here to the problem of the third constraint, that of fidelity to the meaning—that is, to what I have advisedly called the *essential* meaning. Arndt, in this connection, is surely right in suggesting that in the technical process of creating rhymed verse, many words or phrases are not so much primary ends in themselves as 'acceptable fillers', co-opted into the poet's scheme for prosodic reasons. This seems to amount to a distinction between the *primary* semantic or expressive values in any given line or passage and its *secondary* or incidental details which have entered into combination with the main substance in one way or another. A translator's decision as to which elements are primary and which are secondary in any particular case will be a matter for his spontaneous aesthetic judgement. So will his decision on how much he can afford to pay for rhyme (and that is now to say, for suitable rhyming and suitable diction) in the currency of judicious paraphrase. His piety will incline him to treat every word of the German text as sacred, but he will find it necessary in practice to treat some as more sacred than others. He will also be compelled, in English, to use some degree of periphrasis or expansion, if only by the fact that his equivalent words are often several syllables shorter than their German originals (though the contrary can also be the case). How much can acceptably be modified, added, left out? Is not literalness, like rhymelessness, incompatible with fidelity in any sophisticated sense? What is the acceptable price for what effects and what fidelities? Translation is the art of the least intolerable sacrifice, of the instinctive choice between competing imperfections; it constantly exercises a kind of informed judgement which it is almost impossible to rationalize or to discuss with anyone else.

It follows, of course, that to compare other renderings with one's own is tedious as well as odious, but concrete examples are nevertheless the best way of making these general points clearer. For the main illustration I revert again to Walter Arndt, whose version starts from a sophisticated critical position and is particularly instructive as the most recent (1976) of a mere handful which seriously and thoroughgoingly attempt to reproduce Goethe's rhyming and metrical schemes in the unabridged whole of Parts One and Two. His translation of lines 315–35 is as follows:

THE LORD.   As long as on the earth he lives,
   So long it shall not be forbidden.
   Man ever errs the while he strives.

MEPHISTOPHELES. My thanks to you; I've never hidden
  An old distaste for dealing with the dead.
  Give me a full-cheeked, fresh-faced lad!   320
  A corpse with me is just no dice,
  In this way I am like a cat with mice.

THE LORD. So be it; I shall not forbid it!
  Estrange this spirit from its primal source,
  Have licence, if you can but win it,
  To lead it down your path by shrewd resource;
  And stand ashamed when you must own perforce:
  A worthy soul through the dark urge within it
  Is well aware of the appointed course.

MEPHISTOPHELES. May be—but it has never lasted yet;   330
  I am by no means worried for my bet.
  And if I do achieve my stated perpent,
  You grant me the full triumph that I covet.
  Dust shall he swallow, aye, and love it,
  Like my old cousin, the illustrious serpent.

What I find unsatisfactory here are the archaisms ('ever', 'the
while', 'aye', and the word-order in 315 and 334) and especially
their incongrous combination with racy contemporary col-
loquialisms ('no dice') or bizarre coinages ('perpent'). In addition,
'lad' and 'worthy soul' have the wrong connotations, and 'by no
means worried for' is lame as well as colloquial. Imperfect rhyme,
though almost wholly alien to Goethe, is difficult to avoid altogether, and to my ear 'lad' rhyming with 'dead' is at least
tolerable as prosody if not as diction, but 'he strives' rhyming
with 'he lives', in so famous and crucial a line, is not, and both
these rhymes can be improved quite easily. Arndt gives unneces-
sarily high priority to ending his lines on the same word as
Goethe, and to end-stopped lines generally; I should have preferred not only to avoid the imperfect rhymes but also to acknowledge, by simply shifting it from the rhyme-position, that there
is no acceptable rhyme for 'serpent'. Moreover, although unlike
Arndt I do not in general regard it as essential to preserve the
exact order of Goethe's rhymes, it is particularly important in
this passage to imitate the striking effect in 327–35 where he
uses only two rhymes in nine lines (in the German the sound
-ust recurs four times and -ange five; a similar rhyme-flow is

achieved in Mephistopheles' later soliloquy, where the sound
-eben is repeated six times in twelve lines, 1856–67). In my own
version of the *Prologue in Heaven* passage (315–35) I have
imitated this special effect and tried to steer round the other
pitfalls, while also aiming at natural word-sequences and a
broadly contemporary but suitable vocabulary. My rendering as
'ancestress' of Goethe's now archaic word *Muhme* which in fact
means cousin or aunt, is an instance of how an inessential detail
of literal meaning may be sacrificed for what seems to be a more
essential fidelity: in this case, to the nine-line flow of two rhymes.

One further short example is perhaps worth considering here.
The first stanza of *Dedication* (a particularly intractable piece
because of its prosodic strictness) ends with an instructive case
of what Arndt calls the 'filler' word. Goethe here (lines 7 f.)
writes:

> *Mein Busen fühlt sich jugendlich erschüttert*
> *Vom Zauberhauch, der euren Zug umwittert.*

Existing versions of this include the following:

> Deep stirs my heart, awakened, touched to song,
> As from a spell that flashes from your throng.   (Wayne)

> My breast is stirred and feels with youthful pain
> The magic breath that hovers round your train.   (Kaufmann)

> I feel youth's impulse grip my heart again
> At the enchantment wafting from your train.   (Passage)

> What wafts about your train with magic glamour
> Is quickening my breast to youthful tremor.   (Arndt)

My own rendering, I suppose, is based on (or can with hindsight
be analysed into) the following judgements: (1) *umwittert* is
probably the filler-word chosen to rhyme with *erschüttert*. Its
literal meaning suggests wind blowing about the 'procession' of
youthful memories which Goethe is apostrophizing, perhaps
carrying their scent; but this literal meaning is of secondary
importance, and 'waft' is in any case a weak equivalent for it.
(2) The literal meaning of *Zug* (procession, or less suitably 'train')
is also secondary; the memories are drifting back insistently towards him, an idea already twice suggested earlier in the stanza by
ihr naht euch (you draw near) and *ihr drängt euch zu* (you throng
upon me), and it should suffice to suggest this by some such

word as 'besiege'. (3) The essential or primary elements in the
sentence are *jugendlich erschüttert* (he feels rejuvenated and
moved by deep nostalgia) and *Zauberhauch* (the memories come
to him with magic force as if breathed into his heart by a gentle
wind—a suggestion which *umwittert* merely reinforces. Accordingly my proposed version is:

> (you . . .) who so
> Besiege me, and with magic breath restore,
> Stirring my soul, lost youth to me once more.

This loses certain details, but the gains include a natural word-
flow and a congruous diction.

To pursue such comparative analyses further would be weari-
some, but this much will serve to indicate the general guidelines
I have adopted in the present translation. On the whole, except
perhaps in certain important and much-quoted passages which
seemed to require a closer hugging of the text, I have proceeded
on the view that literalness is not the same thing as fidelity and
can indeed even amount to its opposite. It can also militate against
speakability, actability, and intelligibility. Goethe's lines have
all these qualities, though also much more. In the end we must
acknowledge again the inherent hopelessness of the whole
attempt to find an English equivalent for poetry of this order.
Faust belongs to the German language as such, and to read its
finest passages is to understand that no English will ever match
the texture and flavour, the weight and density, the wit and
magic of Goethe's native words. What can translate the despair-
ing romantic sensuousness of Faust's plea to Gretchen in the
final scene: *Komm! komm! schon weicht die tiefe Nacht!* (4506)
or the naïve and terrible monosyllabic finality of her last words
to him: *Heinrich! Mir graut's vor dir!* (4610)? A translation
must seek to stand by itself, but it must also point beyond itself,
back and on to the original. In such an undertaking one may
merely hope to avoid the worst faults, and be content if one can
add something to the anglophone world's understanding of the
status of *Faust* as poetry and its potential as actable drama.

SYNOPSIS OF THE COMPOSITION
OF FAUST PART ONE

This summary indicates to which composition-phase the various scenes and passages originally belong. The line-numerations in all three columns are those of the final version ('F.I'); when in square brackets they represent only approximately equivalent passages. Earlier material incorporated into later versions usually underwent at least slight revision, as mentioned here in the more significant cases.

FIRST PHASE	SECOND PHASE	THIRD PHASE
1772–5, Frankfurt: '*Urfaust*' (unpublished; discovered in Göchhausen transcript, 1887)	1788–90, Rome and Weimar: '*Faust, A Fragment*' (published 1790)	1797–1806 (chiefly 1797–1801), Weimar: '*Faust, Part One*' (published 1808)
= 'UR'	= 'FRA'	= 'F.I'
		1–353
		1 DEDICATION
		2 PRELUDE
		3 PROLOGUE IN HEAVEN
4a 354–597 +602–5 NIGHT (unfinished)	(4a) (as UR)	(4a) (as FRA, + 598–601)
		4b 606–807 remainder of NIGHT
	('great lacuna')	808–1529 5 OUTSIDE THE TOWN 6 FAUST'S STUDY I 7a FAUST'S STUDY II. 1530–769
	7b (*FAUST'S STUDY II*) 1770–867	(7b) (as FRA)
7c [1868–2050] (Meph. and the student)	(7c) (as UR, revised) 7d 2051–72 (*FAUST'S STUDY II*, concl.)	(7c) (as FRA) (7d) (as FRA)
8 [2073–336] AUERBACH'S TAVERN	(8) (as UR, revised)	(8) (as FRA)

	9 2337[-]604 *A WITCH'S KITCHEN*	(9)	(as FRA, +2366–77 & 2390–93)
	2605–3216	(10–16 as UR)	(10–16 as FRA, +3149–52)
10	*A STREET*		
11	*EVENING*		
12	*A PROMENADE*		
13	*THE NEIGHBOUR'S HOUSE*		
14	*A STREET*		
15	*A GARDEN*		
16	*A SUMMERHOUSE*		

(17a) (3217–373
(17b) as FRA,
(17c) repositioned)

	3374–586	(18–20 as UR)	(18 20 as FRA)
18	*GRETCHEN'S ROOM*		
19	*MARTHA'S GARDEN*		
20	*AT THE WELL*		

	17a	*A FOREST CAVERN* 3217—341
	(17b	3342–69 as UR, repositioned)
	17c	3370–3

21	3587–619 *BY A SHRINE*	(21)	(as UR)	(21)	(as FRA)
23	3776–834 *THE CATHEDRAL*	(23)	(as UR; FRA ends here)		

22a	3620–45 (Valentine's soliloquy)			(22a)	(3620–45) *NIGHT. THE STREET*
				22b	3646–9
22c	3650–9			(22c)	(3650–9)
17b	3342–69 (Faust's remorse)			**22d**	3660–775 (death of V.)
				(23)	(3776–834, *THE CATHEDRAL,* repositioned)
				24	*WALPURGIS NIGHT*
				25	*WALPURGIS NIGHT'S DREAM*

	Prose sc. and [4399–614]				Prose sc. and 4399–614
26	*A GLOOMY DAY*			(26)	(as UR)
27	*NIGHT*			(27)	(as UR)
28	*THE PRISON*			(28)	(as UR, revised)

SELECT BIBLIOGRAPHY

I. ENGLISH TRANSLATIONS OF FAUST

(The translations here chronologically listed are of Parts One and Two,
and wholly or largely in rhymed verse, unless otherwise indicated.)

Bayard Taylor (London and Boston, 1871; Part Two 1876). Revised
edn., Stuart Atkins (New York, 1962).

Theodore Martin (London, 1865; Part Two, New York 1886). Revised
edn., W. H. Bruford, Everyman's Library (London, 1954).

Philip Wayne, Penguin Books (London, 1949; Part Two 1959).

Louis MacNeice and E. L. Stahl (both parts abridged), Faber (London,
1951).

John Shawcross, Allan Wingate (London, 1959).

Walter Kaufmann, Part One with Act I, Sc. 1 and Act V of Part Two,
with facing German text (New York, 1961).

Charles E. Passage, with introd. and commentary (New York, 1965).

Barker Fairley, prose (Toronto, 1970).

John Prudhoe, Part One (Manchester University Press, 1974).

Walter Arndt, ed. Cyrus Hamlin with introd., documentation, and
commentary (New York, 1976).

Randall Jarrell, Part One, unrhymed verse (New York, 1976).

Stuart Atkins, unrhymed verse. Suhrkamp/Insel (Boston, 1984).

Robert David MacDonald (stage adaptation of both parts), Oberon
Books (Birmingham, 1988).

II. ENGLISH TRANSLATIONS OF OTHER WORKS
BY GOETHE

Poetry

Selected Verse, German text with prose tr. and introd., David Luke.
Penguin Books (London, 1964; ²1972, ³1981).

West-Eastern Divan, tr. J. Whaley. Oswald Wolff (London, 1974).

Roman Elegies and *The Diary*, German texts with elegiac and *ottava rima*
tr., David Luke, introd. H. R. Vaget. Libris (London, 1988).

Selected Poems, German text with verse tr., Michael Hamburger,
Christopher Middleton, David Luke and others. Suhrkamp/Insel
(Boston, 1982), Calder (London, 1983).

Hermann and Dorothea, hexameter verse tr., David Luke. Suhrkamp/
Insel (New York, 1987).

Plays

Ironhand, a free adaptation of *Götz von Berlichingen*, John Arden.
Methuen (London, 1965).

Egmont, tr. F. J. Lamport in *Five German Tragedies*, Penguin Books (London, 1969).

Torquato Tasso, verse tr. Alan Brownjohn, introd. T. J. Reed. Angel Books (London, 1985).

Iphigenia in Tauris, iambic verse tr. David Luke. Suhrkamp/Insel (New York, 1987).

Torquato Tasso, verse tr. Michael Hamburger. Suhrkamp/Insel (New York, 1987).

Novels

The Sorrows of Young Werther, tr. Victor Lange (New York, 1949).

Kindred by Choice (Die Wahlverwandtschaften), tr. H. M. Waidson. Calder (London, 1960).

Elective Affinities (Die Wahlverwandschaften), tr. Elizabeth Mayer and Louise Bogan (Chicago, 1963).

Elective Affinities, tr. R. J. Hollingdale. Penguin Books (London, 1971).

The Sorrows of Young Werther, tr. Elizabeth Mayer and Louise Bogan, foreword W. H. Auden (New York, 1971).

Wilhelm Meister (the *Years of Apprenticeship* and the *Years of Travel*), tr. H. M. Waidson, 6 vols. Calder (London, 1978–82).

Autobiography, etc.

Poetry and Truth (Dichtung und Wahrheit), tr. John Oxenford (as 'The Autobiography of Goethe', 1848), repr. Sidgwick and Jackson (London, 1971).

Conversations with Goethe in the Last Years of his Life, Eckermann, tr. John Oxenford (1850) repr. Everyman's Library (London, 1930).

Letters from Goethe, tr. Marianne Herzfeld and C. A. M. Sym, introd. W. H. Bruford (Edinburgh University Press, 1957).

Conversations and Encounters (with Goethe), ed. and tr. David Luke and Robert Pick. Oswald Wolff (London, 1966).

Italian Journey, tr. W. H. Auden and Elizabeth Mayer. Penguin Books (London, 1970).

III. WORKS IN ENGLISH ON FAUST AND THE FAUST LEGEND

E. M. Butler, *The Myth of the Magus* (Cambridge University Press, 1948); *The Fortunes of Faust* (Cambridge University Press, 1952).

Barker Fairley, *Goethe's Faust. Six Essays*. Clarendon Press (Oxford, 1953).

Eudo C. Mason, 'Some conjectures regarding Goethe's "Erdgeist" ' in *The Era of Goethe*, essays presented to J. Boyd. Blackwell (Oxford, 1959).

SELECT BIBLIOGRAPHY

Eudo C. Mason, 'The "Erdgeist" controversy reconsidered', *Mod. Lang. Review*, lv (1960).

Eudo C. Mason, 'The Paths and Powers of Mephistopheles' in *German Studies* presented to W. H. Bruford. Harrap (London, 1962).

The History of Doctor Johann Faustus (the 16th-century Faust chapbook), tr. and introd. H. G. Haile (Illinois University Press, 1965).

Eudo C. Mason, *Goethe's Faust. Its Genesis and Purport* (University of California Press, 1967), mainly on Part One.

John R. Williams, *Goethe's Faust*, Allen and Unwin (London, 1987).

IV. WORKS IN ENGLISH ON GOETHE

G. H. Lewes, *The Life and Works of Goethe* (London, 1855), repr. Everyman's Library (London, 1949).

W. H. Bruford, *Germany in the Eighteenth Century: The Social Background of the Literary Revival* (Cambridge University Press, 1935, repr. 1952).

Humphrey Trevelyan, *Goethe and the Greeks* (Cambridge University Press, 1941, repr. 1981 with foreword by H. Lloyd-Jones).

Barker Fairley, *A Study of Goethe*, Clarendon Press (Oxford, 1947).

W. H. Bruford, *Theatre, Drama and Audience in Goethe's Germany*, Routledge (London, 1950).

R. D. Gray, *Goethe the Alchemist* (Cambridge University Press, 1952).

Roy Pascal, *The German Sturm und Drang* (Manchester University Press, 1953).

Ronald Peacock, *Goethe's Major Plays* (Manchester University Press, 1959).

W. H. Bruford, *Culture and Society in Classical Weimar, 1775–1806* (Cambridge University Press, 1962).

E. M. Wilkinson, and L. A. Willoughby, *Goethe. Poet and Thinker* (essays), Edward Arnold (London, 1962).

Richard Friedenthal, *Goethe. His Life and Times*, Weidenfeld and Nicolson (London, 1965).

R. D. Gray, *Goethe: A Critical Introduction* (Cambridge University Press, 1967).

Georg Lukács, *Goethe and his Age* (essays), Merlin Press (London, 1968).

T. J. Reed, 'The Goethezeit and its Aftermath' in *Germany. A Companion to German Studies*, ed. J. M. S. Pasley, Methuen (London, 1972).

Ilse Graham, *Goethe: Portrait of the Artist*, de Gruyter (Berlin & New York, 1977).

T. J. Reed, *The Classical Centre. Goethe and Weimar 1775–1832*, Croom

Helm (London), Barnes & Noble (New York), 1980; Oxford
University Press (1986).

T. J. Reed, *Goethe*, Past Masters series (Oxford University Press,
1984).

E. M. Wilkinson, T. J. Reed, and others, *Goethe Revisited*, essays, ed.
E. M. Wilkinson, Calder (London), Riverrun Press (New York)
1984.

The *Publications of the English Goethe Society*, i–xii (1886–1912) and
new series i– (1924 to date) contain articles on numerous aspects of
Faust and Goethe; an index has also been provided by A. C. Weaver
(*Index to the P.E.G.S. 1886–1970* (Leeds, 1973)).

CHRONOLOGY

c.1480 Georg or Johann Faust born in ?Knittlingen (d.*c*.1540).

1506–36 Faust mentioned occasionally in contemporary documents.

1548–85 Various reports of Faust's legendary exploits.

1587 First known printed *Faustbuch* (Faust chapbook): *Historia of Doctor Johann Faust, the infamous magician and necromancer*, published in Frankfurt by Johann Spies; anonymous, and thought to be based on a lost earlier version.

?1592 Marlowe writes *The Tragical History of Doctor Faustus* (first attested performance 1594, first known edition 1604).

1599 Second *Faustbuch* published in Hamburg, in the version by Georg Rudolf Widmann.

1608 First attested performance of Marlowe's *Faustus* as a German popular play (in Graz).

1666 First attested Faust puppet-play (in Lüneburg).

1674 Third *Faustbuch* published in Nuremberg in the version by Nikolaus Pfitzer.

1725 Publication of the fourth *Faustbuch* 'by one of Christian intent' (*History of the universally notorious arch-necromancer and sorcerer Doctor Johann Faust, his alliance with the Devil . . .*); this was the version known to Goethe.

1749 Johann Wolfgang Goethe born in Frankfurt-am-Main (28 August).

1759 Lessing (1729–81) publishes in the seventeenth of his *Letters concerning Contemporary Literature* (but without claiming authorship) a scene from his projected and now lost dramatic version of the Faust story.

1765–8 Goethe studies at the University of Leipzig.

1768 The Faust play performed in Frankfurt by travelling players.

1768–70 Goethe in Frankfurt; Pietistic period, reading of cabbalistic literature.

1770 The Faust play performed in Strassburg by travelling players.

1770–1 Goethe at the University of Strassburg; meeting with Herder (1744–1803); collects folk-songs and writes poems to Friederike

Brion. First version of *Götz von Berlichingen* written in 1771 after Goethe's return to Frankfurt.

1772 Execution (14 January) of Susanna Brandt for the murder of her illegitimate child.

?1772 (possibly earlier): Goethe begins to write *Faust* ('*Urfaust*' phase of composition, till 1775).

1773 Publication of revised version of *Götz von Berlichingen*.

1774 Publication of *The Sorrows of Young Werther*.

1775 (November) Goethe arrives in Weimar at the invitation of the Duke Karl August (1757–1828).

c.1775–6 Copy made by Fräulein von Göchhausen of the unpublished *Faust* manuscript.

1775–86 Goethe's first Weimar years (ministerial duties, growing interest in the natural sciences, *amitié amoureuse* with Charlotte von Stein, end of 'Storm and Stress' phase, early versions of *Iphigenia in Tauris*, *Wilhelm Meister* and *Torquato Tasso*; 1782 Goethe ennobled by the Emperor Joseph II at Karl August's request).

1786 (September) Goethe's Italian journey (till June 1788).

1787 Publication of final (iambic) version of *Iphigenia in Tauris*.

1788 (February) Resumption of work on *Faust* (second phase of composition).

1788 Beginning of Goethe's liaison, on his return to Weimar, with Christiane Vulpius (1765–1816), whom he married in 1806.

1788–90 The *Roman Elegies* written.

1790 Publication of *Faust. A Fragment* and of *Torquato Tasso*.

1794 Beginning of the friendship between Goethe and Schiller (b.1759); over 1,000 letters exchanged between them in the next eleven years.

1795 Publication of the *Roman Elegies*; 1795–6 *Wilhelm Meister's Apprenticeship*; 1797 *Hermann and Dorothea*.

1797 (June) Resumption, with Schiller's encouragement, of work on *Faust* (third phase of composition; most of the new material written by 1801).

1805 Death of Schiller.

1808 Publication of *Faust. The First Part of the Tragedy*.

1809 Publication of *The Elective Affinities*.

1819 Publication of the *West-Eastern Divan*.

1823–32 Johann Peter Eckermann's conversations with Goethe (published after Goethe's death).

1825–31 Goethe completes *Faust. The Second Part of the Tragedy*. Publication in 1827 of Act III under the title *Helena. A Classical-Romantic Phantasmagoria. Interlude for Faust*; part of Act I published in 1828.

1829 First public performance of *Faust Part One*, in Brunswick.

1832 Death of Goethe (22 March). *Faust Part Two* published posthumously.

1854 Berlioz, *La Damnation de Faust*.

1857 Liszt, *A Faust Symphony*.

1858 Schumann, settings of scenes from both parts of *Faust*.

1859 Gounod's opera *Faust* (based on Part One).

1862 Friedrich Theodor Fischer's parody *Faust. The Third Part of the Tragedy*, published under the pseudonym Deutobold Symbolizetti Allegoriowitsch Mystifizinsky.

1868 Arrigo Boïto's opera *Mefistofele*.

1876 First production of *Faust Parts One and Two*, by Otto Devrient in Weimar.

1887 Erich Schmidt discovers the Göchhausen transcript of the '*Urfaust*' and publishes it as *Goethe's Faust in its original form*.

1910 Gustav Mahler's setting (in his 8th symphony) of the closing scene of *Faust* Part Two.

1925 Ferruccio Busoni's opera *Doctor Faust*.

1933–7 Max Reinhard's *Faust* productions at the Salzburg Festival.

1947 Thomas Mann's novel *Doctor Faustus*.

1957–8 Gustav Gründgens' *Faust* productions in Hamburg.

FAUST
PART ONE

Uncertain shapes, visitors from the past
At whom I darkly gazed so long ago,
My heart's mad fleeting visions—now at last
Shall I embrace you, must I let you go?
Again you haunt me: come then, hold me fast!
Out of the mist and murk you rise, who so
Besiege me, and with magic breath restore,
Stirring my soul, lost youth to me once more.

You bring back memories of happier days
And many a well-loved ghost again I greet;   10
As when some old half-faded legend plays
About our ears, lamenting strains repeat
My journey through life's labyrinthine maze,
Old griefs revive, old friends, old loves I meet,
Those dear companions, by their fate's unkind
Decree cut short, who left me here behind.

They cannot hear my present music, those
Few souls who listened to my early song;
They are far from me now who were so close,
And their first answering echo has so long   20
Been silent. Now my voice is heard, who knows
By whom? I shudder as the nameless throng
Applauds it. Are they living still, those friends
Whom once it moved, scattered to the world's ends?

And I am seized by long unwonted yearning
For that still, solemn spirit-realm which then
Was mine; these hovering lisping tones returning
Sigh as from some Aeolian harp, as when
I sang them first; I tremble, and my burning
Tears flow, my stern heart melts to love again.   30
All that I now possess seems far away
And vanished worlds are real to me today.

FAUST: PART ONE [F.I.

2 · PRELUDE ON THE STAGE*

[*The* DIRECTOR. *The* POET. *The* CLOWN]

DIRECTOR. Well, here we are on German soil,
My friends. Tell me, you two have stood
By me in bad times and in good:
How shall we prosper now? My toil,
Indeed my pleasure, is to please the mob;
And they're a tolerant public, I'll admit.
The posts and boards are up, and it's our job
To give them all a merry time of it.   40
They're in their seats, relaxed, eyes opened wide,
Waiting already to be mystified.
I know how to content popular taste;
But I've a problem here, it must be said:
Their customary fare's not of the best—
And yet they are appallingly well-read.
How shall we give them something fresh and new,
That's entertaining and instructive too?
I like to see them all throng through the gate
Into our wooden paradise, to watch   50
Them push and shove and labour up that straight
And narrow way, like babes about to hatch!
Our box-office, while it's still broad daylight,
Is under siege; before it's even four
They want their tickets. Tooth and nail they fight,
Like some half-famished crowd outside a baker's door.
Only the poet's magic so holds sway
Over them all: make it, my friend, today!

POET. Do not remind me of that motley throng,
Spare me the sight of them! Our spirits fail   60
And flounder in that stream, we are swept along,
Against the unruly flood what can prevail?
Give me the quietness where I belong,
The poet's place, the stillness never stale,
The love and friendship! Only there our art
Thrives on the blessed nurture of the heart.

Deep in the soul an impulse there can flow,
An early song still lisping and unclear;
Well-formed or ill, its momentary show
Too soon from Time's wild crest will disappear.   70
Often unseen and darkly it must grow,
Reaching its ripeness after many a year.
What glisters is the moment's, born to be
Soon lost; true gold lives for posterity.

CLOWN. Must we bring in posterity? Suppose
Posterity were all I thought about,
Who'd keep the present public's boredom out?
They must be entertained, it's what one owes
To them. And with a lad like me
Performing, they're enjoying what they see!   80
Communicate and please! You'll not retire
Then into semi-solitude,
Resentful of the public's fickle mood;
The wider circle's easier to inspire.
So do what's needed, be a model poet!
Let Fancy's choirs all sing, and interweave
Reason, sense, feeling, passion—but, by your leave,
Let a good vein of folly still run through it!

DIRECTOR. And let's have enough action, above all!
They come to look, they want a spectacle.   90
Let many things unfold before their eyes,
Let the crowd stare and be amazed, for then
You'll win their hearts, and that's to win the prize;
You'll join the ranks of famous men.
Mass alone charms the masses; each man finds
Something to suit him, something to take home.
Give much, and you'll have given to many minds;
They'll all leave here contented to have come.
And let your piece be all in pieces too!
You'll not go wrong if you compose a stew: 100
It's quick to make and easy to present.
Why offer them a whole? They'll just fragment
It anyway, the public always do.

POET. I note you don't despise such a *métier*,
And have no sense of how it ill beseems

True art. If I were to do things your way,
I'd join the bungling amateurs, it seems.
DIRECTOR. Such a reproach offends me not a whit.
My aim is our success: I must adopt
The proper method of achieving it.   110
What tool's best, when there's soft wood to be chopped?
Consider who you're writing for! They come,
Some of them, from sheer boredom; some
Arrive here fully sated after feeding;
Others again have just been reading
The newspapers, God help us all.
They come with absent thoughts, as if to a masked ball;
Mere curiosity brings them. As for the display
Of ladies and their finery, why, they
Eke out the show, and ask me for no pay!   120
Why do you dream your lofty dreams of art?
Why do full houses flatter you as well?
Take a look at our patrons: you can tell
Half of them have no taste, and half no heart.
One will be looking forward to a game
Of cards after the play, another to a night
In some girl's arms. Poor foolish poet, why invite
Your Muse to toil for this? Make it your aim
Merely to give them more—give them excess!
It's such a hard job to amuse them   130
That your best plan is to confuse them:
Do that, and you'll be certain of success—
Now what's the matter? Pain, or ecstasy?
POET. Leave me, and find some other willing slave!
Must the poet forgo what Nature gave
Him as his birthright, forfeit wantonly
For you that noble gift? How else does he
Move all men's hearts, what power but his invents
The conquest of the elements?
Song bursts forth from him, a harmonious whole   140
Engulfs the world and draws it back into his soul.
Nature spins out her thread, endlessly long,
At random on her careless spindle wound;
All individual lives in chaos throng
Together, mixed like harsh discordant sound.

Who divides up this dull monotonous drift
Into a living rhythm? Who can lift
Particular things into a general sense
Of some great music's sacred congruence?
When passions rage, who makes the tempest sing,   150
The sunset glow when solemn thought prevails?
Who scatters all the blossoms of the spring
On his beloved's path? Who makes a crown
Of mere green leaves the symbol of renown
For high distinction? What is this that fills
Olympus, joins the gods in unity?—
The power of Man, revealed in Poetry!

CLOWN. Use them then, these delightful powers,
And do your poet's work, rather as when
One falls in love to pass the amorous hours.   160
One meets by chance, one lingers, one is smitten,
And one's involvement gradually increases;
Happiness grows, but soon enough it ceases;
Joy ends in tears. And somehow then
It all becomes a novel, ready written.
Let's give them that, let's make that kind of show!
Use real life and its rich variety!
They're living it, but unreflectingly;
They'll notice this or that they didn't know.
Colourful changing scenes and little sense,   170
Much error, mixed with just a grain of truth—
That's the best drink for such an audience;
They'll be refreshed and edified. That way
It will attract the flower of our youth:
They'll hear your words, and think them revelation,
And every tender soul suck from your play
A sustenance of melancholy sensation.
Each will find something in it to excite him
For what he'll see's already there inside him.
They're young yet, ready still to laugh or cry;   180
Fancy still pleases, rhetoric lifts them high.
The old and hardened are a thankless brood,
But growing minds can still show gratitude.

POET. Ah, give me back those years when I

Myself was still developing,
When songs poured forth unceasingly
And thick and fast as from a spring!
Then still my world was misty-veiled,
Then promised wonders were in bud;
I picked the myriad flowers that filled   190
Those valleys in such plenitude.
My poverty was rich profusion;
I longed for truth and loved illusion.
Give unchecked passion back to me,
Those deep delights I suffered then,
Love's power, and hatred's energy—
Give back my youth to me again!

CLOWN. My friend, youth's what one needs, of course,
        when one
Is in the thick of battle with the foe,
Or when sweet girls are hanging on   200
One's neck and simply won't let go,
Or when the finish of a race
Beckons far off to victory,
Or when one's danced at furious pace
Then spends the night in revelry:
But boldly, gracefully to play
Upon the lyre, choose one's own goal
And reach it by some charming way
On random motions of the soul—
Such is the older poet's task; and we   210
Respect you none the less. The proverb's wrong, you see:
Age is no second childhood—age makes plain,
Children we were, true children we remain.

DIRECTOR. Come, that's enough of words! What I
        Want now is deeds. While you, my friends,
        Exchange these well-turned compliments,
        The time for useful work slips by.
        Why all this talk of the right mood?
        It won't just come by dithering.
        Command your Muses, and they'll sing   220
        To order, if you're any good!
        You know what we expect of you:

We're thirsty for a potent brew.
Prepare it now! What's not begun
Today will still be left undone
Tomorrow. Never miss a day,
But boldly and with resolution
Seize Chance's forelock and waylay
The possible before it slips away;
A started task compels completion.   230

On German stages, as you know no doubt,
Producers like to try things out;
So make sure now we have machines
And plenty of spectacular scenes!
Use the sunshine and moonshine lights,
Use starlight—we have stars galore,
Water and fire and rocky heights,
And birds and animals by the score!
Thus on these narrow boards you'll seem
To explore the entire creation's scheme—   240
And with swift steps, yet wise and slow
From heaven, through the world, right down to hell you'll
   go!

3 · PROLOGUE IN HEAVEN*   [F.I.

[*The* LORD. *The Heavenly Hosts, then*
MEPHISTOPHELES. *The three* ARCHANGELS
advance.]

RAPHAEL. The sun proclaims its old devotion
   In rival song with brother spheres,
   And still completes in thunderous motion
   The circuits of its destined years.
   Angelic powers, uncomprehending,
   Are strengthened as they gaze their fill;
   Thy works, unfathomed and unending,
   Retain the first day's splendour still.   250

GABRIEL. The glorious earth, with mind-appalling
   Swiftness, upon itself rotates,
   And with the deep night's dreadful falling

Its primal radiance alternates.
High cliffs stand deep in ocean weather,
Wide foaming waves flood out and in,
And cliffs and seas rush on together
Caught in the globe's unceasing spin.

MICHAEL. And turn by turn the tempests raging
   From sea to land, from land to sea,   260
Build up, in passion unassuaging,
   Their chain of furious energy.
The thunder strikes, its flash is faster,
   It spreads destruction on its way—
But we, thy messengers, O master,
   Revere thy gently circling day.

THE THREE IN CHORUS. And each of us,
    uncomprehending,
   Is strengthened as we gaze our fill;
For all thy works, sublime, unending,
   Retain their first day's splendour still.   270

MEPHISTOPHELES. Your Grace, since you have called on
    us again
To see how things are going, and since you
Have been quite pleased to meet me now and then,
I thought I'd come and join your retinue.
Forgive me, but grand words are not my trick;
I cut a sorry figure here, I know,
But you would laugh at my high rhetoric
If you'd not left off laughing long ago.
The solar system I must leave unsung,
And to mankind's woes lend my humbler tongue.   280
The little earth-god still persists in his old ways,
Ridiculous as ever, as in his first days.
He'd have improved if you'd not given
Him a mere glimmer of the light of heaven;
He calls it Reason, and it only has increased
His power to be beastlier than a beast.
He is—if I may say so, sir—
A little like the long-legged grasshopper,
Which hops and flies, and sings its silly songs
And flies, and drops straight back to grass where it belongs. 290

Indeed, if only he would stick to grass!
He pokes his nose in all the filth he finds, alas.

THE LORD. And that is all you have to say?
Must you complain each time you come my way?
Is nothing right on your terrestrial scene?

MEPHISTOPHELES. No, sir! The earth's as bad as it has
    always been.
I really feel quite sorry for mankind;
Tormenting them myself's no fun, I find.

THE LORD. Do you know Faust?

MEPHISTOPHELES.   The doctor? Do you mean—

THE LORD. My servant.

MEPHISTOPHELES.   Ah, he serves you well, indeed!   300
He scorns earth's fare and drinks celestial mead.
Poor fool, his ferment drives him far!
He half knows his own madness, I'll be bound.
He'd pillage neaven for its brightest star,
And earth for every last delight that's to be found;
Not all that's near nor all that's far
Can satisfy a heart so restless and profound.

THE LORD. He serves me, but still serves me in confusion;
I will soon lead him into clarity.
A gardener knows, one day this young green tree   310
Will blossom and bear fruit in rich profusion.

MEPHISTOPHELES. If I may be his guide, you'll lose him
    yet;
I'll subtly lead him my way, if you'll let
Me do so; shall we have a bet?

THE LORD. He lives on earth, and while he is alive
You have my leave for the attempt;
Man errs, till he has ceased to strive.

MEPHISTOPHELES. I thank your Grace; for dead men
    never tempt
Me greatly, I confess. In this connection
I like to see a full and fresh complexion;   320
A corpse is an unwelcome visitor.
The cat-and-mouse game is what I prefer.

THE LORD. Well, go and try what you can do!
  Entice that spirit from its primal source,
  And lead him, if he's not too hard for you
  To grasp, on your own downward course—
  And then, when you have failed, with shame confess:
  A good man, in his dark, bewildered stress,
  Well knows the path from which he should not stray.

MEPHISTOPHELES. No doubt; it's a short journey   330
  anyway.
  I'll win my wager without much delay.
  And when I do, then, if I may,
  I'll come back here and boast of my success.
  I'll make him greedy for the dust, the way
  The serpent was,* my famous ancestress!

THE LORD. Indeed, you may feel free to come and call.
  You are a type I never learnt to hate;
  Among the spirits who negate,
  The ironic scold* offends me least of all.
  Man is too apt to sink into mere satisfaction,   340
  A total standstill is his constant wish:
  Therefore your company, busily devilish,*
  Serves well to stimulate him into action.
  But you, the authentic sons of God, enfold
  With praise the abundant beauty of the world;
  Love, as you do, the eternal Process, which
  Is ever living and forever rich;
  Its vanishing phenomena will last,
  By your angelic thoughts made firm and fast.

    [*The heavens close, the* ARCHANGELS *disperse.*]

MEPHISTOPHELES. I like to see him sometimes, and take   350
  care
  Not to fall out with him. It's civil
  Of the old fellow, such a *grand seigneur,*
  To have these man-to-man talks with the Devil!

THE FIRST PART
OF THE TRAGEDY

4 · NIGHT*

[*A high-vaulted, narrow Gothic room.*]

FAUST [*sitting restlessly at his desk*].
    Well, that's Philosophy I've read,*
    And Law and Medicine, and I fear
    Theology too, from A to Z;
    Hard studies all, that have cost me dear.
    And so I sit, poor silly man,
    No wiser now than when I began.
    They call me Professor and Doctor, forsooth,   360
    For misleading many an innocent youth
    These last ten years now, I suppose,*
    Pulling them to and fro by the nose;
    And I see all our search for knowledge is vain,
    And this burns my heart with bitter pain.
    I've more sense, to be sure, than the learned fools,
    The masters and pastors, the scribes from the schools;
    No scruples to plague me, no irksome doubt,
    No hell-fire or devil to worry about—
    Yet I take no pleasure in anything now;   370
    For I know I know nothing, I wonder how
    I can still keep up the pretence of teaching
    Or bettering mankind with my empty preaching.
    Can I even boast any worldly success?
    What fame or riches do I possess?
    No dog would put up with such an existence!
    And so I am seeking magic's assistance,
    Calling on spirits and their might
    To show me many a secret sight,
    To relieve me of the wretched task   380
    Of telling things I ought rather to ask,
    To grant me a vision of Nature's forces
    That bind the world, all its seeds and sources
    And innermost life—all this I shall see,
    And stop peddling in words that mean nothing to me.

Oh sad full moon, my friend, why must
You see me suffer? Look your last!
Here at this desk so many a night
I've watched and waited for your light
To visit me again and shine   390
Over this paper world of mine.
Oh, take me to the hilltops, there
To wander in the sweet moonlit air,
By mountain caves, through fields to roam,
Hovering with spirits in your gloam,
Cleansed of book-learning's fog and stew
And healed by bathing in your dew!

God, how these walls still cramp my soul,
This cursèd, stifling prison-hole
Where even heaven's dear light must pass   400
Dimly through panes of painted glass!
Hemmed in by books to left and right.
Which worms have gnawed, which dust-layers choke,
And round them all, to ceiling-height,
This paper stained by candle-smoke,
These glasses, boxes, instruments,
All stuffed and cluttered anyhow,
Ancestral junk—look at it now,
Your world, this world your brain invents!

And can you still ask why your heart   410
Is pent and pining in your breast,
Why you obscurely ache and smart,
Robbed of all energy and zest?
For here you sit, surrounded not
By living Nature, not as when
God made us, but by reek and rot
And mouldering bones of beasts and men.

Come, flee into the open land!
And this great book of magic lore,
By Nostradamus'* very hand,   420
Shall be my guide, I'll need no more;
By it I'll see the stars in course,
And as great Nature rules my mind

Discover the inner psychic force,
The spirit speaking to its kind!
This arid speculation's vain,
The sacred diagrams are clear:
Spirits, you hover close—be plain
And answer me, if you can hear!

[*He throws open the book and sees the Sign of the Macrocosm.**]

Ha! as I look, what sudden ecstasy   430
Floods all my senses, how I feel it flowing
Through every vein, through every nerve in me,
Life's sacred joy and youth's renewal glowing!
Did not some god write these mysterious
Signs, by whose might my soul is filled
With peace again, my poor heart healed,
And by whose secret impetus
The powers of Nature all about me are revealed?
Am I a god? Light fills my mind;
In these pure lines and forms appear   440
All Nature's workings, to my inner sense made clear.
That sage's words at last I understand:
'The spirit-world is open wide,
Only your heart has closed and died;
Come, earth-disciple, boldly lave
Your bosom in the dawn's red wave!'

[*He gazes at the sign.*]

How it all lives and moves and weaves
Into a whole! Each part gives and receives,
Angelic powers ascend and redescend
And each to each their golden vessels lend;   450
Fragrant with blessing, as on wings
From heaven through the earth and through all things
Their movement thrusts, and all in harmony it sings!
How great a spectacle! But that, I fear,
Is all it is. Oh, endless Nature, where
Shall I embrace you? Where, you breasts that flow
With life's whole life? All earth and heaven hangs
On you, who slake the thirsty pangs
Of every heart—and must I languish vainly so?

[He turns impatiently to another page of the book and
   sees the Sign of the Earth Spirit.*]

How differently this sign affects me! You,   460
Spirit of Earth, are closer to me,
Fresh strength already pulses through me,
I glow already from wine so new!
Now, to go out into the world and bear
The earth's whole pain and joy, all this I dare;
To fight with tempests anywhere,
And in the grinding shipwreck stand and not despair!
Clouds gather over me—
The full moon hides its face—
My lamp burns low!   470
Mist rises—red fire flashes round
My head, and from the vaulted roof
A chill breathes down and strikes
A shudder into me!
Spirit I long to summon, now I feel
You hovering round me, oh reveal
Yourself! Ha, this pain tears my heart!
A new sensation
Stirs all my senses into perturbation!
I am committed: you shall come, you must   480
Appear to me, though you may strike me into dust!

   [He seizes the book and secretly pronounces the spirit's
   sign. A red flame flashes, the spirit appears in the flame.]

THE SPIRIT. Who is calling me?

FAUST *[turning away]*.   Ah, you are too terrible!

THE SPIRIT. You have drawn me to you with mighty
      power,
   Sucked at my sphere for many an hour,
   And now—

FAUST.   Alas, this sight's unbearable!

THE SPIRIT. You groan and sigh to have me appear,
   To hear my voice, to behold my face:
   Your soul's great plea compels me to this place
   And I have come! What pitiable fear
   Seizes you, Faust the superman! Where is the call   490

Of your creative heart, that carried all
The world and gave it birth, that shook with ecstasy,
Swelling, upsurging to the heights where we,
The spirits, live? Where are you, you whose song
I heard besieging me so loud and strong?
Can this be you? Now that my breath blows round you,
In the depths of terror I have found you,
Shrinking and writhing like a worm!

FAUST. Am I to quail before you, shape of flame?
It is I, Faust! you and I are the same!   500

THE SPIRIT. In life like a flood, in deeds like a storm
I surge to and fro,
Up and down I flow!
Birth and the grave
An eternal wave,
Turning, returning,
A life ever burning:
At Time's whirring loom I work and play
God's living garment I weave and display.

FAUST. Oh busy spirit! from end to end   510
Of the world you roam: how close you are to me!

THE SPIRIT. You match the spirit you can comprehend:
I am not he. [It vanishes.]

FAUST [collapsing]. Not you!
Who is he then?
I, made in God's image
And not even like you!
            [There is a knock at the door.]
Oh, devil take him, it's that dry-as-dust
Toady, my famulus!* Why must
He interrupt me and destroy   520
This supreme hour of visionary joy?

    [Enter WAGNER in a nightgown and nightcap, carrying
    a lamp. Faust turns to him impatiently.]

WAGNER. Excuse me, sir! I heard your declamation:
You were reading a Greek tragedy, no doubt?
That art is one of powerful persuasion
These days; I'd like to learn what it's about.

I've often heard it said an actor might
Give lessons to a parson.

FAUST.   You are right,
If the parson himself's an actor too;
As sometimes is the case.

WAGNER.   Oh dear, what can one do,
Sitting day after day among one's books!   530
The world's so distant, and one never looks
Even through a spyglass at it; so how can
One learn to bring about the betterment of man?

FAUST. Give up pursuing eloquence, unless
You can speak as you feel! One's very heart
Must pour it out, with primal power address
One's hearers and compel them with an art
Deeper than words. Clip and compile, and brew
From the leavings of others your ragoût
Of rhetoric, pump from your embers   540
A few poor sparks that nobody remembers!
Children will gape and fools admire,
If that's the audience to which you aspire.
But what can blend all hearts into a whole?
Only the language of the soul.

WAGNER. But one must know how to deliver a tirade.
I fear my training still is uncompleted.

FAUST. Why don't you learn to ply an honest trade?
Why be a fool with tinkling bells?
Stick to right thinking and sound sense, it tells   550
Its own tale, little artifice is needed;
If you have something serious to say,
Drop the pursuit of words! This play
Of dazzling oratory, this paper decoration
You fiddle with and offer to the world—
Why, the dry leaves in autumn, whirled
About by foggy winds, carry more inspiration!

WAGNER. Alas, our life is short,
And art is long, they say!
My scholarly pursuits, how sore they weigh   560
Upon my heart and mind! One ought
To learn the means of mounting to the sources,

Useless mechanical contrivances, retained
Because my father used them, old smoke-stained
Parchments that have lain here, untouched by toil,
Since my dull lamp first burnt its midnight oil!
I should have squandered all my poor inheritance,   680
Not sat here sweating while it weighed me down.
What we are born with, we must make our own
Or it remains a mere appurtenance
And is not ours: a load of unused things,
Not the live moment's need, raised on the moment's wings.

But what is this? My eyes, magnetically drawn,
Are fixed on that one spot, where I can see
That little flask: why does sweet light break over me,
As when in a dark wood the gentle moonbeams dawn?

Unique alembic! Reverently I lift   690
You down and greet you. Now, most subtle gift
Compounded of the wit and art of man,
Distilment of all drowsy syrups, kind
Quintessence of all deadly and refined
Elixirs, come, and serve your master as you can!
I see you, and am healed as with a balm,
I seize you, and my striving soul grows calm;
And borne upon my spirit's ebbing tide,
Little by little drifting out to sea,
I tread on its bright mirror—far and wide   700
As new dawn breaks, new shores are beckoning me!

A fiery chariot on light wings descends
And hovers by me! I will set forth here
On a new journey to the heaven's ends,
To pure activity in a new sphere!
O sublime life, o godlike joy! And how
Do I, the ertswhile worm, deserve it now?
I will be resolute, and turn away
For ever from the earth's sweet day.
Dread doors, though all men sneak and shuffle past   710
You, I'll confront you, tear you open wide!
Here it is time for me to prove at last
That by his noble deeds a man is deified;

Yet even this task almost passes my resources;
For we poor devils, by the time we've got
Less than halfway, we die, as like as not.

FAUST. A manuscript—is that the sacred spring
That stills one's thirst for evermore?
Refreshment! it's your own soul that must pour
It through you, if it's to be anything.

WAGNER. Excuse me, but it's very pleasant   570
Studying epochs other than the present,
Entering their spirit, reading what they say,
And seeing how much wiser we have grown today.

FAUST. Oh yes indeed, a wisdom most sublime!—
My friend, the spirit of an earlier time,
To us it is a seven-sealed mystery;
And what you learned gentleman would call
Its spirit, is its image, that is all,
Reflected in your own mind's history.
And what a sight it often is! Enough   580
To run a mile from at first glance. A vast
Old rubbish-dump, an attic of the past,
At best a royal tragedy—bombastic stuff
Full of old saws, most edifying for us,
The strutting speeches of a puppet-chorus!

WAGNER. But the great world! the heart and mind of man!
We all seek what enlightenment we can.

FAUST. Ah yes, we say 'enlightenment', forsooth!
Which of us dares to call things by their names?
Those few who had some knowledge of the truth,   590
Whose full heart's rashness drove them to disclose
Their passion and their vision to the mob, all those
Died nailed to crosses or consigned to flames.
You must excuse me, friend, the night's half through.
We shall speak further on the next occasion.

WAGNER. I'd stay awake all night, and gladly too,
Enjoying such a learned conversation.
Tomorrow morning, being Easter Day,   [F.I.
I'll ask you some more questions, if I may.
I've studied now for years with zeal and zest;   600
Already I know much, I must know all the rest. [Exit.]

FAUST. Why does he not despair? A mind so void   [UR
   And blinkered, so benighted and earthbound!
   Greedy for gold, he scratches in the ground,
   And when he finds some worms he's overjoyed.

   Why, when those spirit-voices filled the air*   [F.I.
   About me, must the speech of such a man
   Intrude? And yet for once I can
   Thank you, poor mortal wretch: for when despair
   Was close to me and madness had assailed   610
   My mind, when like a dwarf I seemed to shrink
   Before that giant vision, and I quailed,
   Dwindling to nothingness—you snatched me from the
     brink.

   I, God's own image! Ah, how close it shone,
   The mirror of eternal verity!
   I fed upon its light and clarity
   Within myself, all mortal limits gone,
   And with presumption too extreme
   Of free, superangelic strength, divine
   Creative life, thought even now to stream   620
   Through Nature's veins—what sudden shame was mine!
   A voice of thunder dashed me from that dream.

   Not close to you, not like you; this I dare
   No longer claim to be. I had the power
   To summon you, but could not hold you there.
   I felt in that ecstatic hour
   So small, and yet so great: and then
   You hurled me back so cruelly
   Into the changeful common state of men.
   What must I do now? who shall counsel me?   630
   What urge claims my obedience?
   Alas, not only pain, even activity
   Itself can stop our life's advance.

   The spirit's noblest moments, rare and high,
   Are choked by matter's alien obtrusion,
   And rich with this world's goods, we cry
   Scorn on those better things as mere illusion.

   Life-giving intuitions of great worth
   Are stifled in the muddle of the earth.

   Imagination, once a flight sublime   640
   That soared in hope beyond the swirl of time,
   Now, as each joy is drowned beyond redress,
   Sinks down inside us into pettiness:
   Care make its nest in the heart's deepest hole
   And secretly torments the soul;
   Its restless rocking motion mars our mind's content.
   Its masks are ever-changing, it appears
   As house and home, as wife and child, it will invent
   Wounds, poisons, fires and floods—from all
   These blows we flinch before they ever fall,   650
   And for imagined losses shed continual tears.

   I am not like a god! Too deeply now I feel
   This truth. I am a worm stuck in the dust,
   Burrowing and feeding, where at last I must
   Be crushed and buried by some rambler's heel.

   Is this not dust, filling a hundred shelves
   On these high walls that hem me in?
   These thousand useless toys that thrust themselves
   At me in this moth-mumbled rubbish-bin?
   How shall I find fulfilment in this gaol,   660
   Reading the thousand-times-reprinted tale
   Of man's perpetual strife and stress
   And rare occasional happiness?—
   You hollow skull, what does your grinning say?
   That brain, in the confusion of its youth,
   Like mine, once sought the ethereal dawn of truth
   But in the heavy dusk went piteously astray.
   And you old instruments, how you too mock,
   What scorn your wheels, cogs, pulleys pour on me!
   I reached the gate, you were to be the key: 670
   Your bit's a well-curled beard, but it won't fit the lock.
   We snatch in vain at Nature's veil,
   She is mysterious in broad daylight,
   No screws or levers can compel her to reveal
   The secrets she has hidden from our sight.

Time not to shrink from the dark cavern where
Our fancy damns itself to its own tortured fate;
Time to approach the narrow gate
Ringed by the eternal flames of hell's despair;
Time to step gladly over this great brink,
And if it is the void, into the void to sink!

Old goblet of pure crystal, come, now let   720
Me take you from your shelf and sheath. Long years
Have passed since last I thought of you; and yet
At bygone feasts you were the cup that cheers
The solemn guests, the gleaming beaker
Raised to the toast by many a speaker!
Your rich engraved pictorial decorations,
The drinker's task, his rhyming explanations
Before in one long draught he drained you down—
These I recall, from revels long ago;
I passed you round, I praised your art to show   730
My wit. Now I shall not do so.
I have a potion here whose work's soon done;
Its dizzying liquid fills you, dark and brown.
I made and mixed it well, as I know how.
And so, with all my heart, I raise it now:
With this last festive drink I greet the rising sun!

[He sets the cup to his lips. There is a peal of bells and a
sound of choral singing.]

CHORUS OF ANGELS. Christ is ris'n from the dead!*
                Hail to all mortal men,
                From sin's insidious bane,
                From their inherited   740
                Bondage set free again!

FAUST. What lilting tones are these, what notes profound
    Cry to me: Do not drink! Have they such power?
    And do these bells with their dull booming sound
    Announce the Easter festival's first hour?
    Is this already the angelic song
    Of solace, heard above the grave that night so long
    Ago, when the new covenant was sealed and bound?

CHORUS OF WOMEN. Spices we brought and myrrh,
      We who befriended him,   750
      Faithfully laid him here,
      Lovingly tended him;
      Clean linen, swaddling-bands,
      We wound with our own hands.
      Who can have come today
      Taking our Lord away?

CHORUS OF ANGELS. Christ is raised, Christ is blest!
      He bore mankind's ordeal,
      Loving their joys to feel,
      Suffering the stripes that heal: 760
      He passed the test!

FAUST. You gentle, puissant choirs of heaven, why
 Do you come seeking me? The dust is stronger!
 Go, chant elsewhere to tenderer souls! For I
 Can hear the message, but believe no longer.
 Wonders are dear to faith, by it they live and die.
 I cannot venture to those far-off spheres,
 Their sweet evangel is not for my ears.
 And yet—these strains, so long familiar, still
 They call me back to life. There was a time* 770
 Of quiet, solemn sabbaths when heaven's kiss would fill
 Me with its love's descent, when a bell's chime
 Was deep mysterious music, and to pray
 Was fervent ecstasy. I could not understand
 The sweet desire that drove me far away
 Out through the woods, over the meadowland:
 There I would weep a thousand tears and feel
 A whole world come to birth, my own yet real.
 Those hymns would herald youthful games we played
 To celebrate the spring. As I recall 780
 That childhood, I am moved, my hand is stayed,
 I cannot take this last and gravest step of all.
 Oh sing, dear heaven-voices, as before!
 Now my tears flow, I love the earth once more!

CHORUS OF DISCIPLES. Now from his burial
      Christ has gone up on high,
      Living, no more to die,

        Glorious, imperial;
        He in creative zest
        Into the heavens has grown.   790
        On the earth-mother's breast
        We still must weep alone;
        Yet though we here endure
        Exile and anguish,
        Master, it is in your
        Joy that we languish!

CHORUS OF ANGELS. Christ is raised from the tomb,
        Snatched from corruption's womb!
        Rise and be joyful, all
        You whom earth's bonds enthral!   800
        Brothers, o blessed few,
        Sharers of love's food, who
        Praise him in deeds you do,
        Pilgrims whose words renew
        Man's hope of glory: you
        Know that your Lord is near,
        See, he is here!

5 · OUTSIDE THE TOWN WALL   [F.I.

[A variety of people setting out on country walks.]

SOME APPRENTICES. Why are you going that way, you
    lot?

OTHERS. We're off to the hunting-lodge, why not?

FIRST GROUP. Well, we're going this way, out to the mill. 810

AN APPRENTICE. That inn by the river's worth a visit.

ANOTHER. Not much of a road for getting there, is it?

SECOND GROUP. What about you?

THIRD APPRENTICE.   I'll go with them.

A FOURTH.   Come up the hill
    To Burgdorf! I promise you you'll get
    The best girls there, the best beer yet,
    And plenty of good quarrels to pick.

A FIFTH. Well, you're a fine fellow, I must say!
  Keen for another dose of stick?
  I don't care for that place, I keep away.

A SERVANT GIRL. No, that I shan't, I'm going back home! 820

ANOTHER. But he's sure to be by those poplars—come,
  Over there!

THE FIRST. Oh, very nice for me too,
  I dare say! He'll be walking with you,
  He'll be your partner on the dancing-floor.
  Your fun isn't my fun any more.

THE OTHER. I'm sure he won't be alone; he did say
  The curly-haired boy would be with him today.

A STUDENT. Look at them, my friend! Come along—hell's
    bells,
  We must take a walk with those strapping girls!
  A good strong beer, a puff of weed   830
  And a fine smart lass are what I need.

A YOUNG LADY. Look at those nice boys! I do declare
  It's positively scandalous:
  They could keep company with us,
  And yet they chase those hussies there.

SECOND STUDENT [to the first]. Not so fast! There's
    another two behind,
  Just look, they're dressed up pretty neat!
  One of them lives near me; she's sweet!
  Now that's a girl I wouldn't mind.
  Both nice and quiet, ambling to and fro;   840
  They'll end by taking us in tow.

FIRST STUDENT. No, no, being polite's no fun, my friend!
  Quick, let's not lose our proper prey!
  A hand that holds a broom on Saturday
  Makes better love the rest of the weekend!

A CITIZEN. No, I don't fancy the new burgomaster,
  Insolent fellow! Why, he's a disaster.
  What's he done for the town? Since they
  Appointed him, things get worse day by day:
  More and more regulations to obey,   850
  Higher and higher rates to pay.

Yet even this task almost passes my resources;
For we poor devils, by the time we've got
Less than halfway, we die, as like as not.

FAUST. A manuscript—is that the sacred spring
That stills one's thirst for evermore?
Refreshment! it's your own soul that must pour
It through you, if it's to be anything.

WAGNER. Excuse me, but it's very pleasant   570
Studying epochs other than the present,
Entering their spirit, reading what they say,
And seeing how much wiser we have grown today.

FAUST. Oh yes indeed, a wisdom most sublime!—
My friend, the spirit of an earlier time,
To us it is a seven-sealed mystery;
And what you learned gentleman would call
Its spirit, is its image, that is all,
Reflected in your own mind's history.
And what a sight it often is! Enough   580
To run a mile from at first glance. A vast
Old rubbish-dump, an attic of the past,
At best a royal tragedy—bombastic stuff
Full of old saws, most edifying for us,
The strutting speeches of a puppet-chorus!

WAGNER. But the great world! the heart and mind of man!
We all seek what enlightenment we can.

FAUST. Ah yes, we say 'enlightenment', forsooth!
Which of us dares to call things by their names?
Those few who had some knowledge of the truth,   590
Whose full heart's rashness drove them to disclose
Their passion and their vision to the mob, all those
Died nailed to crosses or consigned to flames.
You must excuse me, friend, the night's half through.
We shall speak further on the next occasion.

WAGNER. I'd stay awake all night, and gladly too,
Enjoying such a learned conversation.
Tomorrow morning, being Easter Day,   [F.I.
I'll ask you some more questions, if I may.
I've studied now for years with zeal and zest;   600
Already I know much, I must know all the rest. [Exit.]

FAUST. Why does he not despair? A mind so void   [UR
  And blinkered, so benighted and earthbound!
  Greedy for gold, he scratches in the ground,
  And when he finds some worms he's overjoyed.

  Why, when those spirit-voices filled the air*   [F.I.
  About me, must the speech of such a man
  Intrude? And yet for once I can
  Thank you, poor mortal wretch: for when despair
  Was close to me and madness had assailed   610
  My mind, when like a dwarf I seemed to shrink
  Before that giant vision, and I quailed,
  Dwindling to nothingness—you snatched me from the
      brink.

  I, God's own image! Ah, how close it shone,
  The mirror of eternal verity!
  I fed upon its light and clarity
  Within myself, all mortal limits gone,
  And with presumption too extreme
  Of free, superangelic strength, divine
  Creative life, thought even now to stream   620
  Through Nature's veins—what sudden shame was mine!
  A voice of thunder dashed me from that dream.

  Not close to you, not like you; this I dare
  No longer claim to be. I had the power
  To summon you, but could not hold you there.
  I felt in that ecstatic hour
  So small, and yet so great: and then
  You hurled me back so cruelly
  Into the changeful common state of men.
  What must I do now? who shall counsel me?   630
  What urge claims my obedience?
  Alas, not only pain, even activity
  Itself can stop our life's advance.

  The spirit's noblest moments, rare and high,
  Are choked by matter's alien obtrusion,
  And rich with this world's goods, we cry
  Scorn on those better things as mere illusion.

Life-giving intuitions of great worth
Are stifled in the muddle of the earth.

Imagination, once a flight sublime   640
That soared in hope beyond the swirl of time,
Now, as each joy is drowned beyond redress,
Sinks down inside us into pettiness:
Care make its nest in the heart's deepest hole
And secretly torments the soul;
Its restless rocking motion mars our mind's content.
Its masks are ever-changing, it appears
As house and home, as wife and child, it will invent
Wounds, poisons, fires and floods—from all
These blows we flinch before they ever fall,   650
And for imagined losses shed continual tears.

I am not like a god! Too deeply now I feel
This truth. I am a worm stuck in the dust,
Burrowing and feeding, where at last I must
Be crushed and buried by some rambler's heel.

Is this not dust, filling a hundred shelves
On these high walls that hem me in?
These thousand useless toys that thrust themselves
At me in this moth-mumbled rubbish-bin?
How shall I find fulfilment in this gaol,   660
Reading the thousand-times-reprinted tale
Of man's perpetual strife and stress
And rare occasional happiness?—
You hollow skull, what does your grinning say?
That brain, in the confusion of its youth,
Like mine, once sought the ethereal dawn of truth
But in the heavy dusk went piteously astray.
And you old instruments, how you too mock,
What scorn your wheels, cogs, pulleys pour on me!
I reached the gate, you were to be the key: 670
Your bit's a well-curled beard, but it won't fit the lock.
We snatch in vain at Nature's veil,
She is mysterious in broad daylight,
No screws or levers can compel her to reveal
The secrets she has hidden from our sight.

Useless mechanical contrivances, retained
Because my father used them, old smoke-stained
Parchments that have lain here, untouched by toil,
Since my dull lamp first burnt its midnight oil!
I should have squandered all my poor inheritance,   680
Not sat here sweating while it weighed me down.
What we are born with, we must make our own
Or it remains a mere appurtenance
And is not ours: a load of unused things,
Not the live moment's need, raised on the moment's wings.

But what is this? My eyes, magnetically drawn,
Are fixed on that one spot, where I can see
That little flask: why does sweet light break over me,
As when in a dark wood the gentle moonbeams dawn?

Unique alembic! Reverently I lift   690
You down and greet you. Now, most subtle gift
Compounded of the wit and art of man,
Distilment of all drowsy syrups, kind
Quintessence of all deadly and refined
Elixirs, come, and serve your master as you can!
I see you, and am healed as with a balm,
I seize you, and my striving soul grows calm;
And borne upon my spirit's ebbing tide,
Little by little drifting out to sea,
I tread on its bright mirror—far and wide   700
As new dawn breaks, new shores are beckoning me!

A fiery chariot on light wings descends
And hovers by me! I will set forth here
On a new journey to the heaven's ends,
To pure activity in a new sphere!
O sublime life, o godlike joy! And how
Do I, the ertswhile worm, deserve it now?
I will be resolute, and turn away
For ever from the earth's sweet day.
Dread doors, though all men sneak and shuffle past   710
You, I'll confront you, tear you open wide!
Here it is time for me to prove at last
That by his noble deeds a man is deified;

Time not to shrink from the dark cavern where
Our fancy damns itself to its own tortured fate;
Time to approach the narrow gate
Ringed by the eternal flames of hell's despair;
Time to step gladly over this great brink,
And if it is the void, into the void to sink!

Old goblet of pure crystal, come, now let   720
Me take you from your shelf and sheath. Long years
Have passed since last I thought of you; and yet
At bygone feasts you were the cup that cheers
The solemn guests, the gleaming beaker
Raised to the toast by many a speaker!
Your rich engraved pictorial decorations,
The drinker's task, his rhyming explanations
Before in one long draught he drained you down—
These I recall, from revels long ago;
I passed you round, I praised your art to show   730
My wit. Now I shall not do so.
I have a potion here whose work's soon done;
Its dizzying liquid fills you, dark and brown.
I made and mixed it well, as I know how.
And so, with all my heart, I raise it now:
With this last festive drink I greet the rising sun!

> [*He sets the cup to his lips. There is a peal of bells and a
> sound of choral singing.*]

CHORUS OF ANGELS. Christ is ris'n from the dead!*
                Hail to all mortal men,
                From sin's insidious bane,
                From their inherited   740
                Bondage set free again!

FAUST. What lilting tones are these, what notes profound
    Cry to me: Do not drink! Have they such power?
    And do these bells with their dull booming sound
    Announce the Easter festival's first hour?
    Is this already the angelic song
    Of solace, heard above the grave that night so long
    Ago, when the new covenant was sealed and bound?

CHORUS OF WOMEN. Spices we brought and myrrh,
                    We who befriended him,   750
                    Faithfully laid him here,
                    Lovingly tended him;
                    Clean linen, swaddling-bands,
                    We wound with our own hands.
                    Who can have come today
                    Taking our Lord away?

CHORUS OF ANGELS. Christ is raised, Christ is blest!
                    He bore mankind's ordeal,
                    Loving their joys to feel,
                    Suffering the stripes that heal: 760
                    He passed the test!

FAUST. You gentle, puissant choirs of heaven, why
    Do you come seeking me? The dust is stronger!
    Go, chant elsewhere to tenderer souls! For I
    Can hear the message, but believe no longer.
    Wonders are dear to faith, by it they live and die.
    I cannot venture to those far-off spheres,
    Their sweet evangel is not for my ears.
    And yet—these strains, so long familiar, still
    They call me back to life. There was a time*   770
    Of quiet, solemn sabbaths when heaven's kiss would fill
    Me with its love's descent, when a bell's chime
    Was deep mysterious music, and to pray
    Was fervent ecstasy. I could not understand
    The sweet desire that drove me far away
    Out through the woods, over the meadowland:
    There I would weep a thousand tears and feel
    A whole world come to birth, my own yet real.
    Those hymns would herald youthful games we played
    To celebrate the spring. As I recall   780
    That childhood, I am moved, my hand is stayed,
    I cannot take this last and gravest step of all.
    Oh sing, dear heaven-voices, as before!
    Now my tears flow, I love the earth once more!

CHORUS OF DISCIPLES. Now from his burial
                    Christ has gone up on high,
                    Living, no more to die,

Glorious, imperial;
He in creative zest
Into the heavens has grown.   790
On the earth-mother's breast
We still must weep alone;
Yet though we here endure
Exile and anguish,
Master, it is in your
Joy that we languish!

CHORUS OF ANGELS. Christ is raised from the tomb,
Snatched from corruption's womb!
Rise and be joyful, all
You whom earth's bonds enthral!   800
Brothers, o blessed few,
Sharers of love's food, who
Praise him in deeds you do,
Pilgrims whose words renew
Man's hope of glory: you
Know that your Lord is near,
See, he is here!

5 · OUTSIDE THE TOWN WALL   [F.I.

[A variety of people setting out on country walks.]

SOME APPRENTICES. Why are you going that way, you
    lot?

OTHERS. We're off to the hunting-lodge, why not?

FIRST GROUP. Well, we're going this way, out to the mill.   810

AN APPRENTICE. That inn by the river's worth a visit.

ANOTHER. Not much of a road for getting there, is it?

SECOND GROUP. What about you?

THIRD APPRENTICE.   I'll go with them.

A FOURTH.   Come up the hill
    To Burgdorf! I promise you you'll get
    The best girls there, the best beer yet,
    And plenty of good quarrels to pick.

A FIFTH. Well, you're a fine fellow, I must say!
　　Keen for another dose of stick?
　　I don't care for that place, I keep away.

A SERVANT GIRL. No, that I shan't, I'm going back home! 820

ANOTHER. But he's sure to be by those poplars—come,
　　Over there!

THE FIRST. Oh, very nice for me too,
　　I dare say! He'll be walking with you,
　　He'll be your partner on the dancing-floor.
　　Your fun isn't my fun any more.

THE OTHER. I'm sure he won't be alone; he did say
　　The curly-haired boy would be with him today.

A STUDENT. Look at them, my friend! Come along—hell's
　　bells,
　　We must take a walk with those strapping girls!
　　A good strong beer, a puff of weed   830
　　And a fine smart lass are what I need.

A YOUNG LADY. Look at those nice boys! I do declare
　　It's positively scandalous:
　　They could keep company with us,
　　And yet they chase those hussies there.

SECOND STUDENT [to the first]. Not so fast! There's
　　another two behind,
　　Just look, they're dressed up pretty neat!
　　One of them lives near me; she's sweet!
　　Now that's a girl I wouldn't mind.
　　Both nice and quiet, ambling to and fro;   840
　　They'll end by taking us in tow.

FIRST STUDENT. No, no, being polite's no fun, my friend!
　　Quick, let's not lose our proper prey!
　　A hand that holds a broom on Saturday
　　Makes better love the rest of the weekend!

A CITIZEN. No, I don't fancy the new burgomaster,
　　Insolent fellow! Why, he's a disaster.
　　What's he done for the town? Since they
　　Appointed him, things get worse day by day:
　　More and more regulations to obey,   850
　　Higher and higher rates to pay.

A BEGGAR [*singing*]. Kind sirs, fair ladies plump and red,
    All dressed up in your finery!
    Pray look at me, who have no bread,
    And spare some coins, for charity!
    Come, hear my hurdy-gurdy plead!
    Happy who gives to one in need.
    On such a day, when all rejoice,
    Let me earn something by my voice!

ANOTHER CITIZEN. There's nothing better, on a holiday, 860
 Than talk and noise of war to while the time away.
 Some far-off war, in Turkey, let's suppose,
 Some place where armies come to blows.
 One watches from the window, sips one's glass,
 While down the river all those fine ships pass.
 And back home in the evening, we congratulate
 Each other on our peaceful happy state.

A THIRD CITIZEN. Yes, neighbour, I agree, quite so, quite
  so!
 Let them all split each other's skulls out there,
 Let the world go to pot for all I care, 870
 But here at home, let's keep the *status quo*!

AN OLD WOMAN [*to the young ladies*]. Why, how now,
  my proud beauties! What young sir
 Could see you and not fall in love?—
 Well, no offence, my dears! I've said enough.
 But I could find you what you're looking for.

FIRST YOUNG LADY. Agatha, come! In public I steer clear
 Of her; she's an old witch with second sight.
 It's true that on St. Andrew's night
 She caused my future sweetheart to appear.

SECOND YOUNG LADY. She showed me mine in a glass 880
  ball:
 A soldier-boy, with soldier friends to match.
 Now I look everywhere, and I can't catch
 Even a glimpse of him at all.

SOLDIERS. Show us a fortress
    Proudly defended,
    Give me a mistress

Haughty and splendid!
We are the valiant,
We are the gallant,
War-spoil and love-spoil   890
Are ours to be won!

Trumpets, sing out and
Sound our advances,
Stir us to action,
To joy and destruction!
This is the life for us,
This is the strife for us!
Castles or girls, we'll
Breach their defences!
War-spoil and love-spoil   900
Are ours to be won.
Soldiers, march on!

[*Enter* FAUST *and* WAGNER.]

FAUST. Ice thaws on the river, ice melts on the streams,
They are freed again as the spring sun gleams.
The valley is green with new life, new hopes;
Old winter is beaten—see how it withdrew
To skulk up there on rough mountain-slopes!
And now in its weakness all it can do
Is to scatter hail in impotent showers
Over the meadows as they turn green.   910
But the sun will allow no white to be seen:
It calls for colours as the earth revives,
As everything grows and stirs and strives;
And the countryside is still short of flowers,
So the people instead, dressed up so fine,
Are lured out into the sweet sunshine.
Look back at the town from where we stand,
Look down at its hollow, gloomy gate,
Where the glad throng pours out over the land!
They have something today to celebrate,   920
For the Lord's resurrection is theirs as well:
Today they have risen and been set free
From the mean damp houses where they dwell,
From their trades and crafts and drudgery,

From the gabled roofs' oppressive gloom,
From the choking streets where they fight for room,
From the churches' solemn devotional night—
They all have risen into the light!
Oh, look how so many are nimbly dispersing
Over the gardens, across the fields,   930
And the boats on the river happily coursing;
How the wide stream flows, how the water yields!
And that last one setting off, almost foundering
Under its load; and even up there
On the far-off hills there are people wandering,
We can see them by the bright colours they wear.
We're nearing the village, I hear the noise.
These are the simple folk's real joys.
They shout with delight, the whole motley crowd:
Here I am human, here it's allowed!   940

WAGNER. It is an honour to walk out with you,*
Doctor, and one I profit by;
But to come here alone would never do,
It's too vulgar and coarse for such as I.
Their fiddling, skittling, shrieking—I'm appalled
By it, such noises I detest.
They rave as if they were possessed,
And fun and singing's what it's called!

CHORUS OF VILLAGERS [dancing and singing under
    the linden-tree].
              A shepherd boy went out one night
              Dressed up to dance in colours bright,   950
              All in his fine array, oh!
              And all the village, full of glee,
              Was dancing round the linden-tree.
                  Hey-ho, hey-ho,
                  Hey-hoppie-hoppie-ho,
              The fiddlers they did play, oh!

              And as he joined the merry whirl
              His elbow jogged a buxom girl:
              Why was she in his way, oh?
              The saucy lass she turned about   960
              And said: 'Why, what a clumsy lout!'

> Hey-ho, hey-ho,
> Hey-hoppie-hoppie-ho,
> 'Sir, mind your manners, pray, oh!'
>
> But on they danced, and spurned the ground,
> And left and right and round and round,
> And skirts did swirl and sway, oh!
> They danced till they were flushed and warm
> And out of breath and arm in arm,
>   Hey-ho, hey-ho,   970
>   Hey-hoppie-hoppie-ho,
> And hips to elbows lay, oh!
>
> 'Now don't you get so fresh with me!
> That's how men cheat their brides-to-be
> When they have had their way, oh!'
> But she went with him by and by,
> And from the linden all did cry:
>   Hey-ho, hey-ho,
>   Hey-hoppie-hoppie-ho,
> They all did shout and play, oh!   980

AN OLD PEASANT. Why, Doctor, now that's very kind
   To join us for your Easter walk,
   Being such a learned gentleman,
   And not look down on us poor folk!
   Now, here's a jug of finest ale;
   You are the man we've filled it for,
   And in your honour this we wish,
   That it may quench your thirst, and more:
   There's many a drop in this cup I raise—
   May their number be added to your days!   990

FAUST. I thank you all; this drink refreshes,
   And I return your kind good wishes.

                [*The people gather round.*]

THE OLD PEASANT. Yes, sir, indeed! we all are glad
   To see you on this day of cheer,
   For long ago, when times were bad,
   You wished us well for many a year.
   There's many of us might now be dead*
   Who've lived on to a healthy age

Because your father stopped the spread
Of plague, and cooled the fever's rage.   1000
You were young then, you went about
Visiting every hospital:
So many corpses they brought out,
But you came out alive and well;
Though many a hard time you had too.
You helped us, and the Lord helped you.

ALL. Long life to our good doctor! May
He help us yet for many a day.

FAUST. Give thanks to Him who gave these skills
And helps mankind in all its ills.   1010

[*He walks on with* WAGNER.]

WAGNER. Ah, what a sense of your own greatness must
You have as all these people honour you!
Happy the man whose gifts bring him such true
Advantage, as is only just!
They all ask questions, fathers point you out
To sons, they all rush up to see
You pass, the fiddling stops, they stand about
To stare instead of dancing, and the sky
Is full of cheers and caps thrown high;
They very nearly drop on bended knee   1020
As if the Sacred Host were being carried by!

FAUST. A few steps further, to that rock up there;
Now let us rest here from our walk. This place is one
Where I would often sit and meditate alone,
Keeping strict fast, in anguished prayer.
Here, full of hope, firm in belief,
I sought to alter heaven's will;
I groaned, I wrung my hands in grief—
The pestilence continued still.
Now I feel mocked by this mob's adulation.   1030
If only you could read my mind and know
How little we did, so long ago,
I and my father, to deserve such commendation!
My father was a man respected, yet obscure,
Who laboured honestly with never a pause,

Though by his own eccentric methods to be sure,
Studying Nature's sacred cyclic laws.
With the initiated few
He practised in the Black Laboratory,
Mixing, by this or that strange recipe,   1040
Elements in an ill-assorted brew.
Thus in tepid immersion he would wed
The Lily to the Lion bold and red;
Then with intenser heat he forced this bridal pair
From one glass chamber to the other—by and by
The Young Queen was engendered there,
The rainbow-hued precipitate: this, then,
Was our specific. Still the sick would die,
But no one asked why none got well again.
So in these valleys and these villages,   1050
With those hell-sirups as our remedies,
We, worse than any plague, raged far and wide.
I myself poisoned thousands, I saw how
They all wasted away and perished—now
Men praise that cynical mass-homicide.

WAGNER. Sir, do not let that trouble you!
To practise a transmitted skill
With a good conscience and good will
Is all an honest man need do.
If one respects one's father in one's youth,   1060
One will have learnt from him with pleasure;
If as a man one then adds to our store of truth,
One's own son will do this in even greater measure.

FAUST. Happy are they who still hope this is so,
While ignorance surrounds us like an ocean!
The very thing one needs one does not know,
And what one knows is needless information.
But let us put these gloomy thoughts away
And let the precious present hour confound them!
Look how they gleam in the last light of day,   1070
Those little huts with green all round them!
Evening has come, our sun is westering now—
But it speeds on to bring new life elsewhere.
Oh if some wings would raise me, if somehow

I could follow its circuit through the air!
For then as I strove onwards I should see
A silent sunset world for ever under me,
The hills aglow, the valleys lost in dreams,
The silver brooks poured into golden streams;
No mountain-range would stop me, not with all   1080
Its rugged chasms; at divine speed I fly,
The sea already greets my wondering eye
With its warm gulfs where now the sun's rays fall.
Now the god seems at last to sink and set,
But a new impulse drives me yet:
I hasten on to drink his endless light,
The day ahead, behind my back the night,
The sky above me and the waves below . . .
A pleasing dream; but the sun vanishes
And it is over. Wings, alas, may grow   1090
Upon our soul, but still our body is
Earthbound. And yet, by inborn instinct given
To each of us, our hearts rise up and soar
For ever onwards, when we hear the lark outpour
Its warbling song, lost in the blue of heaven,
Or when we see the wing-spread eagle hover
Above wild cliffs which pine-trees cover,
Or across marsh and lakeland watch the crane
Fly homeward to its native haunts again.

WAGNER. I too have known fanciful states of mind,   1100
But to such moods as yours I never was inclined.
One soon grows tired of forests and of fields;
I never envied any bird its wings.
But the pursuit of intellectual things
From book to book, from page to page—what joys that
   yields!
How fine and snug the winter nights become,
What sweet life courses through one's veins!
Is an old parchment not a whole compendium
Of paradise itself, rewarding all our pains?

FAUST. Only one of our needs is known to you;*   1110
You must not learn the other, oh beware!
In me there are two souls, alas, and their

Division tears my life in two.
One loves the world, it clutches her, it binds
Itself to her, clinging with furious lust;
The other longs to soar beyond the dust
Into the realm of high ancestral minds.
Are there no spirits moving in the air,
Ruling the region between earth and sky?
Come down then to me from your golden mists on high,   1120
And to new, many-coloured life, oh take me there!
Give me a magic cloak to carry me
Away to some far place, some land untold,
And I'd not part with it for silk or gold
Or a king's crown, so precious it would be!

WAGNER. Oh do not call the dreaded host that swarms*
And streams abroad throughout the atmosphere!
They bring men danger in a thousand forms,
From the earth's ends they come to plague us here.
Out of the north the sharp-toothed demons fly,   1130
Attacking us with arrow-pointed tongues;
On the east wind they ride to drain us dry
And slake their hunger on our lungs;
The southern desert sends them to beat down
Upon our heads with fiery beams;
The west will bring refreshment, as it seems,
Till in their flooding rains we and the fields must drown.
Their spiteful ears are open to obey
Our summons, for they love to harm and cheat;
They pose as heaven's angels, and though all they say   1140
Is false, their lisping voice is sweet.
But come, the air grows chill, the world is grey
With dusk and mist already; come away!
When evening falls, indoors is best.—
Why do you stand and stare with such surprise?
What twilight thing has seized your interest?

FAUST. There—in the corn and stubble, do you see
That black dog?*

WAGNER.   Why, of course; of what account is he?

FAUST. What do you take him for? Come, use your eyes!

WAGNER. A poodle, acting as a dog will do   1150
  When it has lost its master, I suppose.

FAUST. He's getting closer; round and round he goes
  In a narrowing spiral; no, there's no mistake!
  And as he comes—look, can't you see it too?—
  A streak of fire follows in his wake!

WAGNER. An ordinary black poodle is all I
  Can see; no doubt some trick of light deceives your eye.

FAUST. It is some magic he is weaving, so
  Subtly about our feet, some future knot!

WAGNER. He's nervous, jumping round us, since we're not   1160
  His master, but two men he doesn't know.

FAUST. The circle shrinks; now he is on our ground.

WAGNER. You see! he's not a phantom, just a hound.
  He's doubtful still, he growls, he lies down flat,
  He wags his tail. All dogs do that.

FAUST. Come to us! Come to heel! Come here!

WAGNER. He's just a foolish poodle-beast, I fear.
  Stand still, and he will dance attendance on you;
  Speak to him, and he'll put his forepaws on you;
  Drop something, and he'll find it, that's his trick—   1170
  He'll jump into the water for your stick.

FAUST. No doubt you're right; no spirit after all,
  But merely a conditioned animal.

WAGNER. A well-trained dog is one who can
  Find favour even with a learned man.
  Our students taught him to behave this way;*
  He far excels his teachers, I must say.

  [*They pass through the gate into the town.*]

6 · FAUSTS'S STUDY (I)*   [F.I.

FAUST [*entering with the poodle*].
    Now I have left the fields and hills
    Where now the night's dark veil is spread;
    Night wakes our better part, and fills   1180

Our prescient soul with holy dread.
The active turmoil leaves my mind,
All wilder passions sleep and cease;
Now I am moved to love mankind,
To love God too, and am at peace.*

Stop running about, you poodle-clown!
Why are you snuffling there by the door?
Go behind the stove! Keep still, lie down!
You have my best cushion, I can't do more.
On that path down the hill you jumped and ran   1190
For our delectation, and that was fun;
I will entertain you now if I can,
As a welcome guest, but a silent one.

    Back in our little narrow cell
    We sit, the lamp glows soft and bright,
    And in our heart and mind as well
    Self-knowledge sheds its kindly light.
    Reason once more begins to speak,
    And hope once more is blossoming;
    We long to find life's source, to seek   1200
    Life's fountainhead, to taste life's spring.

Poodle, stop growling! It does not agree
With my high tone, and my soul's sacred joys
Are interrupted by your animal noise.
We know what scorn and mockery
Uncomprehending man will pour
On anything he has not heard before—
The good, the beautiful, the true;
Must dogs start muttering at it too?

But now, that deep contentment in my breast,   1210
Alas, wells up no more, in spite of all my best
Endeavours. Oh, how soon the stream runs dry,
And in what parching thirst again we lie!
How often this has happened to me!
And yet, there is a remedy:
We learn to seek a higher inspiration,
A supernatural revelation—
And where does this shine in its fullest glory,

If not in that old Gospel story?
Here is the Greek text; I am moved to read   1220
Its sacred words, I feel the need
Now to translate them true and clear
Into the German tongue I hold so dear.

[*He opens a volume and prepares to write.*]

'In the beginning was the Word': why, now
I'm stuck already! I must change that; how?
Is then 'the word' so great and high a thing?
There is some other rendering,
Which with the spirit's guidance I must find.
We read: 'In the beginning was the Mind.'
Before you write this first phrase, think again;   1230
Good sense eludes the overhasty pen.
Does 'mind' set worlds on their creative course?
It means: 'In the beginning was the Force'.
So it should be—but as I write this too,
Some instinct warns me that it will not do.
The spirit speaks! I see how it must read,
And boldly write: 'In the beginning was the Deed!'*

If we are to share this room in peace,
Poodle, this noise has got to cease,
This howling and barking has got to end!   1240
My invitation did not extend
To so cacophonous a friend.
In my study I won't put up with it.
One of us two will have to quit.
I am sorry that we must part so;
The door stands open, you may go.
But what is this I see?
Can it be happening naturally?
Is it real? Is it a dream or not?
How long and broad my poodle has got!   1250
He heaves himself upright:
This is no dog, if I trust my sight!
What hobgoblin have I brought home somehow?
He looks like a hippopotamus now,
With fearsome jaws and fiery eyes.
Aha! you'll get a surprise!

With this hybrid half-brood of hell
King Solomon's Key works very well.*

SPIRITS [outside in the passage].
        He's caught! There s one caught in there!
        Don't follow him, don't go in!   1260
        Like a fox in a gin
        An old hell-lynx is trapped; beware!
        But now wait and see!
        Hover round, hover
        Up and down, he'll recover,
        He'll set himself free;
        We'll lend a hand to him,
        We'll not abandon him;
        He's been polite to us,
        Always done right by us!   1270

FAUST. First, to defeat this beast,
  I need the Spell of the Four, at least.*
        Salamander, burn!
        Water-nymph, twist and turn!
        Sylph of the air, dissolve!
        Goblin, dig and delve!
When the elements are known,
Each in its own
Qualities and powers,
The mastery is ours   1280
Over all and each,
By this knowledge and speech.
        Salamander, in flame
        Vanish as you came!
        Murmur and mingle,
        Nymph of the sea-dingle!
        Blaze like a meteor,
        Sylph-creature!
        Serve in the house for us,
        Incubus, incubus!   1290
        Come out of him, show yourself thus or thus!
None of those four
Has passed through my door.
The beast just lies there grinning at me.

I've not yet hurt him, evidently.
Wait! I can sing
A more powerful spell!
   Are you from hell,
   You fugitive thing?
   Then behold this Sign   1300
   Which they fear and know,
   The black hosts below!
Now he swells up with bristling spine.
   Vile reprobate!
   Do you read this name?
   He who is nameless,
   Uncreated, timeless,
   In all worlds the same,
   Pierced in impious hate?
Behind the stove he shrinks from my spells; 1310
Like an elephant he swells.
The whole room is filled by this devil-dog.
He wants to dissolve into a fog.
Do not rise to the ceiling, I forbid you!
Lie down at your master's feet, I bid you!
You will see that I utter no idle warning;
With sacred fire I shall set you burning!
Do not dare the might
Of the Thrice-Effulgent Light!
Do not dare the might   1320
Of my strongest magic of all!

MEPHISTOPHELES [*stepping out from behind the stove as
  the mist disperses, dressed as a medieval wandering
  student*].   Why all this fuss? How can I serve you, sir?

FAUST. So that was the quintessence of the cur!
A student-tramp! How very comical.

MEPHISTOPHELES. Sir, I salute your learning and your
  wit!
You made me sweat, I must admit.

FAUST. What is your name?

MEPHISTOPHELES.   The question is absurd,
  Surely, in one who seeks to know

The inmost essence, not the outward show,
And has such deep contempt for the mere word.   1330

FAUST. Ah, with such gentlemen as you
The name often conveys the essence too,
Clearly enough; we say Lord of the Flies,*
Destroyer, Liar—each most fittingly applies.
Well then, who are you?

MEPHISTOPHELES.   Part of that Power which would
Do evil constantly, and constantly does good.

FAUST. This riddle has, no doubt, some explanation.

MEPHISTOPHELES. I am the spirit of perpetual negation;
And rightly so, for all things that exist
Deserve to perish, and would not be missed—   1340
Much better it would be if nothing were
Brought into being. Thus, what you men call
Destruction, sin, evil in short, is all
My sphere, the element I most prefer.

FAUST. You seem complete and whole, yet say you are a
    part?

MEPHISTOPHELES. I speak the modest truth, I use no art.
Let foolish little human souls
Delude themselves that they are wholes.
I am part of that part which once, when all began,
Was all there was; part of the Darkness before man   1350
Whence light was born, proud light, which now makes
    futile war
To wrest from Night, its mother, what before
Was hers, her ancient place and space. For light depends
On the corporeal worlds—matter that sends
Visible light out, stops light in its stride
And by reflected light is beautified.
So, light will not last long, I fear;
Matter shall be destroyed, and light shall disappear.

FAUST. Well! now I know your high vocation:
Failing that grand annihilation   1360
You try it on a smaller scale.

MEPHISTOPHELES. And frankly, I must own, here too I
    fail.

The Something, this coarse world, this mess,
Stands in the way of Nothingness,
And despite all I've undertaken,
This solid lump cannot be shaken—
Storms, earthquakes, fire and flood assail the land
And sea, yet firmly as before they stand!
And as for that damned stuff, the brood of beasts and men,
That too is indestructible, I've found;   1370
I've buried millions—they're no sooner underground
Than new fresh blood will circulate again.
So it goes on; it drives me mad. The earth,
The air, the water, all give birth:
It germinates a thousandfold,
In dry or wet, in hot or cold!
Fire is still mine, that element alone—
Without it, I could call no place my own.

FAUST. And so the ever-stirring, wholesome energy
  Of life is your arch-enemy;   1380
  So in cold rage you raise in vain
  Your clenched satanic fist. Why, you
  Strange son of chaos! think again,
  And look for something else to do!

MEPHISTOPHELES. On such a point there's much to say;
  We'll talk again another day.
  This time I'll take my leave—if, by your leave, I may.

FAUST. Why not? We are acquainted now,
  And you are welcome to come back
  And visit me some time, somehow.   1390
  Here is the window, there's the door;
  I even have a chimney-stack.

MEPHISTOPHELES. I must confess that on the floor,
  Across your threshold, you have put
  A certain obstacle—a witch's foot—*

FAUST. You mean, that pentagram I drew
  Hinders a gentleman from hell?
  Then how did you get in? Well, well!
  How did I fool a sprite like you?

MEPHISTOPHELES. It's not well drawn; look closely, sir! 1400
   One of the outside angles—there,
   You see? the lines do not quite meet.

FAUST. How curious! how very neat!
   And so you are my prisoner.
   A lucky chance, I do declare!

MEPHISTOPHELES. The poodle skipped in without
      noticing,
   But now it's quite another thing:
   The Devil can't skip out again.

FAUST. Why don't you use the window, then?

MEPHISTOPHELES. Devils and spirits have a law, as you 1410
      may know:
   They must use the same route to come and go.
   We enter as we please; leaving, we have no choice.

FAUST. So even hell has laws? Good; in that case
   One might conclude a pact with you
   Gentlemen, and a guaranteed one too?

MEPHISTOPHELES. Whatever is promised, you shall have
      your due,
   There'll be no quibbling, no tergiversation.
   But that all needs mature consideration;
   We shall discuss it by and by.
   Meanwhile I must most earnestly   1420
   Repeat my plea to be released.

FAUST. Come, stay a little while at least,
   To edify me with your conversation.

MEPHISTOPHELES. Excuse me now: I soon will reappear
   And tell you anything you wish to hear.

FAUST. I did not pursue you, you know;
   You put your own head in the noose.
   Don't catch the Devil and let go,
   They say—it's harder when he's on the loose.

MEPHISTOPHELES. Very well, if you wish, I will remain 1430
   And help you while the time away;
   But I insist you let me entertain
   You with my arts in a befitting way.

FAUST. Certainly, you are welcome to do so;
    But you must make it an amusing show.

MEPHISTOPHELES. My friend, you shall in this one night,
    In this one hour, know greater sensuous delight
    Than in a whole monotonous year!
    Delicate spirits now will bring
    You visions, and will charm your ear   1440
    With song; theirs is no empty conjuring.
    Your palate also shall be sated,
    Your nostrils sweetly stimulated,
    Your sense of touch exhilarated.
    We are all ready, all are in
    Our places—come, at once, begin!

SPIRITS.   Vanish, you darkling
                Vaults there above us!
                Now let the sweeter
                Blue of the ether   1450
                Gaze in and love us!
                Are not the darkling
                Clouds disappearing?
                Starlight is sparkling,
                Suns of a gentler
                Brightness appearing.
                Children of light dance
                Past in their radiance,
                Swaying, inclining,
                Hovering, shining: 1460
                Passionate yearning
                Follows them burning.
                And their long vesture
                Streams out and flutters,
                Streams out and covers
                Arbour and pasture,
                Where lovers ponder
                As they surrender
                Each to each other.
                Arbour and bower,   1470
                Full fruit and flower!
                Vines shed their burden

Into the winepress
Rich with their ripeness;
Wines foam unending
In streams descending,
Through precious gleaming
Stones they are streaming,
Leaving behind them
Heights that confined them,   1480
Pleasantly winding
Round the surrounding
Hills and their verdure,
To lakes expanding.
Birds drink their pleasure,
Soaring to sunlight,
Flying to far bright
Islands that shimmer,
Trembling, enticing,
Where the waves glimmer,   1490
Where echo answers
Songs of rejoicing
Shouted in chorus,
Where we see dancers
Leaping before us
Out over green fields;
Over the green hills
Some of them climbing,
Some of them over
Lake-waters swimming,   1500
Some of them hover;
All seeking life, each
Seeking a distant star
Where love and beauty are
Far beyond speech.

MEPHISTOPHELES. He sleeps! Well done, my airy
    cherubim!
How soon your lullaby enchanted him!
This concert puts me in your debt.
Faust, you are not the man to hold the Devil yet!
Go on deluding him with sweet dream-shapes,   1510

Plunge him into a sea where he escapes
Reality. As for this threshold, I know how
To split the spell: I need a rat's tooth now.
No need to conjure in this place for long!
I hear them scuttling, soon they'll hear my song.

The master of all rats and mice,
All flies and frogs and bugs and lice,
Commands you to poke forth your snout
And gnaw this floor to let me out!
I'll smear it for you with some drops　　　　1520
Of oil. Aha! see, out he hops!
Now set to work. The point where I was stuck
Is at the front here. What a piece of luck!
One little bite more and it's done. ——
Now, Faust, until we meet again, dream on!

FAUST [*waking*]. Have I been twice deluded in one day?
The spirit-orgy vanishes: it seems
I merely saw the Devil in my dreams,
And had a dog that ran away!

7 · FAUST'S STUDY (II)*　　　[F.I./FRA/UR

FAUST. A knock? Come in!—Who is this bothering me　　1530
Again?

MEPHISTOPHELES. I'm back!

FAUST.　　　　　　　　Come in!

MEPHISTOPHELES.　　　　　　You must say it three
Times over.

FAUST.　　Well, come in!

MEPHISTOPHELES [*entering*]. Well done!
I think we're going to get on
Together, you and I. To cheer
You up, I've come dressed as a cavalier:
In scarlet, with gold trimmings, cloak
Of good stiff silk, and in my hat
The usual cock's feather; take
A fine long pointed rapier,
And one's complete. So, my dear sir,　　　　1540

Be ruled by me and do just that:
Wear clothes like mine, strike out, be free,
And learn what the good life can be.

FAUST. The earth's a prison—one can't get away
From it, whatever clothes one wears.
I'm still too young to lack desires,
Not young enough now for mere play.
What satisfaction can life hold?
Do without, do without! That old
Command pursues us down the years   1550
Endlessly echoing in our ears—
The same old hoarse repeated song
Heard hour by hour our whole life long!
With each new dawn I wake aghast,
My eyes with bitter tears are filled
To think that when this day has passed
I'll not have had one single wish fulfilled,
That even my presentiments of joy
Will die of nagging scruples, and life's mess
Of trivial impediments destroy   1560
My active soul's creativeness.
When the night falls, I seek my bed
With anxious fears, with many a sigh,
But find no peace: with sights of dread
Wild dreams torment me as I lie.
And though a god lives in my heart,
Though all my powers waken at his word,
Though he can move my every inmost part—
Yet nothing in the outer world is stirred.
Thus by existence tortured and oppressed   1570
I crave for death, I long for rest.

MEPHISTOPHELES. And yet death never is a wholly
     welcome guest.

FAUST. Happy the man whom glorious death has crowned
With bloodstained victor's laurels, happy he
Whose sudden sweet surcease is found
In some girl's arms, after wild revelry!
And I, who saw that mighty Spirit's power,
Why did I not expire with joy in that same hour!

MEPHISTOPHELES. And yet, in that same night, someone
   who mixed a brown
  Elixir did not drink it down.   1580

FAUST. You seem to like eavesdropping.

MEPHISTOPHELES.   I am not
  Omniscient, but I know a lot.

FAUST. In that great turmoil and distress
  Sweet well-known echoing notes deceived
  My ear, old childhood joys relieved
  My homesick heart—this I confess.
  But now I curse all flattering spells
  That tempt our souls with consolation,
  All that beguilingly compels
  Us to endure earth's tribulation!   1590
  A curse first on the high pretences
  Of our own intellectual pride!
  A curse on our deluded senses
  That keep life's surface beautified!
  A curse upon our dreams of fame,
  Of honour and a lasting name!
  A curse upon vain property,
  On wife and child and husbandry!
  A curse on mammon, when his gold
  Lures us to rash heroic deeds,   1600
  Or when his easeful arms enfold
  Us softly, pampering all our needs!
  I curse the nectar of the grape,
  I curse love's sweet transcendent call,
  My curse on faith! My curse on hope!
  My curse on patience above all!

CHORUS OF INVISIBLE SPIRITS. Alas, alas,
        You have destroyed
        The beautiful world!
        At a blow of your clenched fist   1610
        It falls, struck down
        By a demigod, it disappears.
        Into the void
        We carry its fragments, with our tears
        We mourn

> The beauty that is lost.
> Mightiest
> Of the sons of earth,
> Let it be built anew
> More splendidly, let it come to birth   1620
> Again, within you:
> Begin new
> Ways of living,
> With your mind clear,
> New light receiving,
> New music to hear.

MEPHISTOPHELES. My little sprites
> Are performing their rites:
> Full of wise exhortations
> And invitations   1630
> To worlds unknown
> Of living and doing.
> Why sit here alone,
> They say, stifling and stewing?

Stop playing with your misery,
That gnaws your vitals like some carrion-bird!
Even the worst human society
Where you feel human, is to be preferred!
I don't of course propose that we
Should merely mingle with the common herd;   1640
I'm not exactly a grandee,
But if you'd fancy getting through
Your life in partnership with me,
I shall with pleasure, without more ado,
Wholly devote myself to you.
You shall have my company,
And if you are satisfied,
I shall be your servant, always at your side!

FAUST. And what is your reward for this to be?

MEPHISTOPHELES. Long years will pass till we need   1650
    think of that.

FAUST. No, no! The Devil has his tit-for-tat;
    He is an egoist, he'll not work for free,
    Merely to benefit humanity.

State your conditions, make them plain and clear!
Servants like you can cost one dear.

MEPHISTOPHELES. In this world I will bind myself to cater
For all your whims, to serve and wait on you;
When we meet in the next world, some time later,
Wages in the same kind will then fall due.*

FAUST. The next world? Well, that's no great matter;   1660
Here is a world for you to shatter—
Smash this one first, then let the next be born!
Out of this earth all my contentment springs,
This sun shines on my sufferings;
First wean me from all earthly things—
What happens then's not my concern.
That's something I've no wish to hear:
Whether there's hatred still or love
In that remote supernal sphere,
And who's below and who's above.   1670

MEPHISTOPHELES. Why, in that case, be bold and dare!
Bind yourself to me, begin life anew:
You soon will see what I can do.
No man has ever known a spectacle so rare.

FAUST. Poor devil! What can you offer to me?
A mind like yours, how can it comprehend
A human spirit's high activity?
But have you food that leaves one still unsatisfied,
Quicksilver-gold that breaks up in
One's very hands? Can you provide   1680
A game that I can never win,
Procure a girl whose roving eye
Invites the next man even as I lie
In her embrace? A meteoric fame
That fades as quickly as it came?
Show me the fruit that rots before it's plucked
And trees that change their foliage every day!

MEPHISTOPHELES. I shall perform as you instruct;
All these delights I can purvey.
But there are times in life, my friend,   1690
When one enjoys mere quiet satisfaction.

FAUST. If ever I lie down in sloth and base inaction,
     Then let that moment be my end!
     If by your false cajolery
     You lull me into self-sufficiency,
     If any pleasure you can give
     Deludes me, let me cease to live!
     I offer you this wager!

MEPHISTOPHELES.   Done!

FAUST.   And done again!
     If ever to the moment I shall say:
     Beautiful moment, do not pass away!   1700
     Then you may forge your chains to bind me,
     Then I will put my life behind me,
     Then let them hear my death-knell toll,
     Then from your labours you'll be free,
     The clock may stop, the clock-hands fall,
     And time come to an end for me!

MEPHISTOPHELES. We shall remember this; think well
     what you are doing.

FAUST. That is your right. This bet, which I may lose,
     Is no bravado. I must be pursuing
     My purpose: once I stand still, I shall be   1710
     A slave—yours or no matter whose.

MEPHISTOPHELES. At the doctoral feast* I shall display
     My willing servitude to you this very day.
     One small request—I am sure you'll understand;
     It's just in case—I'd like a line or two in your own hand.

FAUST. Poor pedant! Must it be in writing too?
     Is a man's plighted word a thing unknown to you?
     My spoken word must rule my life's whole course
     For ever: is this not enough?
     The world streams on with headlong force,   1720
     And a promise arrests me. What strange stuff
     Of dreams composes us! A pledge that binds
     Is a thing rooted in our minds,
     And we accept this. Happy is the man
     Of pure and constant heart, who can
     Regret no choice, no loss! But parchments signed and sealed

Are ghosts that haunt and daunt us; the word dies
Upon the very pen we wield,
And wax and leather tyrannize
Our lives. Well, devil, which is it to be: 1730
Bronze, marble, parchment, paper? Answer me:
What pen, what tool, what chisel shall I use?
The medium is yours to choose!

MEPHISTOPHELES. Come, come, sir, this excited flood
Of rhetoric's quite out of place.
The merest scrap of paper meets the case.
And—for your signature, a drop of blood.

FAUST. If that is all you want, I'll willingly go through
With such a farce to humour you.*

MEPHISTOPHELES. Blood is a juice with curious   1740
    properties.

FAUST. But you need have no fear that I will break*
This bond. To strive with all my energies—
Just that is what I undertake.
I have been too puffed up with pride:
I see now I belong beside
Merely the likes of you. With scorn
That mighty Spirit spurned me, Nature's door
Is closed, the thread of thought is torn,
Books sicken me, I'll learn no more.
Now let us slake hot passions in   1750
The depths of sweet and sensual sin!
Make me your magics—I'll not care to know
What lies behind their outward show.
Let us plunge into the rush of things,
Of time and all its happenings!
And then let pleasure and distress,
Disappointment and success,
Succeed each other as they will;
Man cannot act if he is standing still.

MEPHISTOPHELES. Nothing shall limit you; if you wish,   1760
    sir,
To sample every possible delight,
To snatch your pleasures in full flight,

Then let it be as you prefer.
Enjoy them boldly, grasp at what you want!

FAUST. I tell you, the mere pleasure's not the point!
To dizzying, painful joy I dedicate
Myself, to refreshing frustration, loving hate!
I've purged the lust for knowledge from my soul;
Now the full range of suffering it shall face,
And in my inner self I will embrace   [FRA 1770
The experience allotted to the whole
Race of mankind; my mind shall grasp the heights
And depths, my heart know all their sorrows and delights.
Thus I'll expand myself, and their self I shall be,
And perish in the end, like all humanity.

MEPHISTOPHELES. Oh, take my word for it, I who have
    chewed
For centuries on this stale food—
From birth to death a man may do his best,
But this old leavened lump he'll not digest!
We do assure you, such totality   1780
Is only for a god; perpetual light
Is God's alone, me and my kind
He has banished to darkness, and you'll find
You men must live with day and night.

FAUST. Yet I swear I'll achieve it!

MEPHISTOPHELES.   Bravely said!
But there's a problem, I'm afraid;
For time is short, and art is long.
Might I suggest you take along
With you some well-known poet? He will teach
You many things; his thoughts will reach   1790
Out far and wide, all sorts of virtues crown
Your noble head at his behest:
The courage of the lion,
The stag's velocity,
The Italian's fiery zest,
The north's tenacity!
He'll find out for you how to mingle guile
With magnanimity, and while
You're still a young warm-blooded man,

How to fall in love by a prearranged plan. 1800
The result, I'm sure, would be well worth meeting;
"Mr Microcosm!" shall be my respectful greeting.

FAUST. What am I then, if it's impossible
To win that crown of our humanity,
To be what all my senses ache to be?

MEPHISTOPHELES. You are just what you are. Do what
you will;
Wear wigs, full-bottomed, each with a million locks,
Stand up yards high on stilts or actor's socks—
You're what you are, you'll be the same man still.

FAUST. How uselessly I've laboured to collect 1810
The treasures of the human intellect,
And now I sit and wonder what I've done.
I feel no new strength surging in my soul
I'm not a hairsbreadth taller, I'm not one
Step nearer to the infinite goal.

MEPHISTOPHELES. My dear good sir, I fear your view
Of things is all too common in our day.
Revise it; and let's see what we can do
Before life's pleasures fleet away.
Confound it, man, one's hands and feet of course 1820
Belong to one, so do one's head and arse!
But all the things that give me pleasure,
Are they not mine too, for good measure?
Suppose I keep six stallions, don't you see
The strength of each of them's a part of me?
What a fine fellow I have grown,
Trotting with twenty-four feet of my own!
So come, drop all this cogitation, stir
Yourself, explore the world with me. I say
A philosophic ponderer 1830
Is like a poor beast led astray
By some malignant sprite, to graze on desert ground
When fine green grass is growing all around!

FAUST. How do we start?

MEPHISTOPHELES.   First we get out of here!
What sort of prison-hole is this? What mere
Shadow of life you live, when all you do

Just bores your pupils and bores you!
Let your fat colleagues take the strain!
Stop threshing empty straw! Why, even when
There's really something you could teach the poor lads,   1840
   then
It's something you're forbidden to explain.
Ah, I hear one of them outside your door!

FAUST. I can't see any students now.

MEPHISTOPHELES. He's waited a long time, poor chap,
   We'll have to comfort him somehow.
   Come, let me have your gown and cap.
   What a disguise! I'll look my best in it.

         [*He dresses up as* FAUST.]

Now leave all this to me and to my native wit.
I'll only need a quarter of an hour.
Meanwhile, make ready for our great Grand Tour!   1850

         [*Exit* FAUST.]

MEPHISTOPHELES [*in* FAUST'S *long gown*].
   Scorn reason, despise learning, man's supreme*
   Powers and faculties; let your vain dream
   Of magic arts be fortified with sweet
   Flatteries by the Spirit of Deceit,
   And you're mine, signature or none!—
   Fate has endowed him with the blind
   Impatience of an ever-striving mind;
   In headlong haste it drives him on,
   He skips the earth and leaves its joys behind.
   I'll drag him through life's wastes, through every kind   1860
   Of meaningless banality;
   He'll struggle like a bird stuck fast, I'll bind
   Him hand and foot; in his voracity
   He'll cry in vain for food and drink, he'll find
   Them dangling out of reach—ah, yes!
   Even without this devil's bond that he has signed
   He's doomed to perish nonetheless!

         [A STUDENT *enters*.]*   [UR

STUDENT. Sir, I'm a new arrival here
   And you're a famous man, I hear,

And so I've called to say hullo—   1870
Meaning no disrespect, you know!

MEPHISTOPHELES. You're too polite; I do my best,
I'm just a man like all the rest.
No doubt you've met my colleagues too?

STUDENT. I'd much prefer some advice from you!
I'll study everything with skill.
I've got some cash, lots of good will;
My mother told me: stay at home.
But I'm keen to learn, that's why I've come.

MEPHISTOPHELES. Well, well, you've arrived at the right   1880
college.

STUDENT. Quite frankly, though I thirst for knowledge,
I'm not quite sure if I shall stay!
These walls and halls scare me away.   [FRA
Everything seems to hem one in;
There's no green grass, no trees, and in
These lecture-rooms—oh goodness me,
I can't think straight or hear or see!

MEPHISTOPHELES. A matter of habituation,
That's all! Babes at their mother's breast
Will feed at first with hesitation,   1890
But soon show eagerness and zest.
Suck on at Wisdom's breasts, you'll find
She daily grows more sweet and kind.

STUDENT. Oh, I'll embrace her very gladly, sir!
But can you show me, please, the way to her?

MEPHISTOPHELES. Tell me first, without more ado,   [UR
Which Faculty appeals to you?

STUDENT. I want to be a learned man,
And find out everything I can—
All the whole universe contains,   1900
All about Nature, which Science explains.

MEPHISTOPHELES. Well, you're on the right road, that's
clear.
But you'll find a lot to distract you here!

STUDENT. Oh, I'll work hard, don't worry! Though   [FRA
    I'd like some fun too, that's to say
    Some free time now and then, you know,
    On a fine summer holiday!
MEPHISTOPHELES. Make good use of your time! It hurries
      past,
    But order and method make time last.
    So, friend, take my advice to heart: [UR 1910
    Hear lectures on Logic for a start.*
    Logic will train your mind all right;
    Like inquisitor's boots it will squeeze you tight,
    Your thoughts will learn to creep and crawl
    And never lose their way at all,
    Not get criss-crossed as now, or go
    Will-o'-the-wisping to and fro!
    We'll teach you that your process of thinking
    Instead of being like eating and drinking,
    Spontaneous, instantaneous, free,   1920
    Must proceed by one and two and three.
    Our thought-machine, as I assume,
    Is in fact like a master-weaver's loom:
    One thrust of his foot, and a thousand threads
    Invisibly shift, and hither and thither
    The shuttles dart—just once he treads
    And a thousand strands all twine together.
    In comes your philosopher and proves
    It must happen by distinct logical moves:
    The first is this, the second is that,   1930
    And the third and fourth then follow pat;
    If you leave out one or leave out two,
    Then neither three nor four can be true.
    The students applaud, they all say 'just so!'—
    But how to be weavers they still don't know.
    When scholars study a thing, they strive
    To kill it first, if it's alive;
    Then they have the parts and they've lost the whole,
    For the link that's missing was the living soul.
    *Encheiresis naturae,** says Chemistry now—   1940
    Mocking itself without knowing how.
STUDENT. I'm not quite sure if I understand.

MEPHISTOPHELES. You soon will; just carry on as
    planned.
  You'll learn reductive demonstrations
  And all the proper classifications.

STUDENT. I'm so confused by all you've said,
  It's like a millwheel going round in my head!

MEPHISTOPHELES. Your next priority should be
  Metaphysical philosophy!
  That will teach your shallow human brain   1950
  Profound thoughts which it can't contain,
  And for everything no one can understand
  High-sounding words will be ready to hand.
  But above all, this first term or two,
  Learn order and method in all you do.
  Five lectures will be your daily fare;
  When the bell rings, make certain you're there!
  And do your homework before you go,
  Learn all those paragraphs you must know,
  You can check then, without even a look,   1960
  That he's saying nothing that's not in the book;
  And yet take notes, never stop writing,
  Pretend it's the Holy Ghost dictating!

STUDENT. Oh, sir, you're absolutely right!   [FRA
  Notes are so useful, because then
  You can take your lecture back home again,
  And have it all down in black and white!

MEPHISTOPHELES. But come now, choose a Faculty!

STUDENT. I don't think Jurisprudence would be quite my
    line.

MEPHISTOPHELES. Well, well, I can't entirely disagree. 1970
  I know a bit about that discipline.
  Statutes and laws, inherited
  Like an old sickness, passed on by the dead
  Through endless generations, creeping down
  From land to land, from town to town!
  Sense becomes nonsense, good deeds dangerous;
  Our forebears are our burden. How
  About that natural law, new-born in each of us?
  Dear me, one never hears that mentioned now.*

STUDENT. I'm put off the subject by that one speech!   1980
   How lucky they are, the chaps you teach!
   Maybe Theology's what I should do.

MEPHISTOPHELES. I'd hate to be misleading you.
   In that particular science it is hard
   Not to stray from the path; be on your guard!
   Much poison lurks in it; you can't be sure
   Of knowing what will kill and what will cure.
   Here too, the wise beginner chooses
   One master, and swears by every word he uses.
   In short, hold fast to words!* They'll guide   1990
   You on the road to certainty,
   And Wisdom's gates will open wide.

STUDENT. But words must have some sense, it seems to me.

MEPHISTOPHELES. Yes, yes, but don't be bothered
    overmuch by that.
   It's just when sense is missing that a word comes pat
   And serves one's purpose most conveniently.
   Words make for splendid disputations
   And noble systematizations;
   Words are matters of faith; as you'll have heard,
   One can take no jot nor tittle from a word!*   2000

STUDENT. You must excuse me, asking all these questions,   [UR
   But I'm quite keen on Medicine too.
   I'd like a little word on that from you,
   I'm sure you have some good suggestions.
   Our three-year course is very short,
   With all those subjects to be taught!
   One needs a few tips just to start, you see,
   Before one can make progress on one's own.

MEPHISTOPHELES [aside]. I'm tired of this dry donnish
    tone;
   It's time for some more devilry.   2010
   [Aloud] The art of Medicine's easily defined.
   You study the whole world, both great and small,
   Only to find
   That God's creation can't be changed at all.
   Your far-flung scientific fantasies
   Are vain; we each learn only what we can.

But he who seizes opportunities,
He's the successful man!
Now, you're still fairly young and strong
And, I dare say, a bold lad too; 2020
Just let self-confidence carry you along,
And others will have faith in you.
Learn, above all, to handle women! Why,
In all their thousand woes, one sure
And certain cure
Will end their endless sob and sigh!
With a polite approach you'll put them at their ease,
And they'll be yours to treat just as you please.
A door-plate helps; she'll think: Now he
Has a superior degree! 2030
Then set your hands to work while bidding her good day,
And grope past years of other men's delay!
You'll press her tiny wrist just that much harder
To feel her pulse, and with sly ardour
Seize her about the slender waist,
To try if she's too tightly laced!

STUDENT. Well now, that's good advice! I see just what you
     mean!

MEPHISTOPHELES. My friend, all theory is grey, and
     green
The golden tree of life.

STUDENT.   Oh, bless my soul,
I think I must be dreaming! Might I call 2040
Another day, and trouble you again
And hear the rest of all your wisdom then?

MEPHISTOPHELES. What's in my power I'll gladly do.

STUDENT. There's just one thing I'd ask of you
Before I go, if you don't mind:
Your autograph—if you would be so kind.*

MEPHISTOPHELES. By all means.

     [He writes in the student's autograph book and returns it.]

STUDENT [reads]. Eritis sicut Deus, scientes bonum et
     malum.

               [He closes it reverently and takes his leave.]

MEPHISTOPHELES. Now heed my ancient serpent-aunt—
   her words were wise!—
  And be like God; you'll find it no light enterprise.   2050

              [Enter FAUST]*   [FRA

FAUST. Well, where do we go now?

MEPHISTOPHELES.   Wherever you like! We'll see
  The *beau monde* later, first the *bourgeoisie*.
  With what pleasure and profit you will pass,
  Without tuition-fees, from class to class!

FAUST. But what about my beard, my age?
  I'm no good on the social stage.
  The thing won't work; I've never known
  How to mix with people, living on my own.
  I feel inferior, I freeze;
  I always shall be ill at ease.   2060

MEPHISTOPHELES. My friend, all that will change a few
   days hence.
  You will learn *savoir-vivre* when you learn confidence.

FAUST. But how are we to leave here? Where
  Are your servants, where's your coach and pair?

MEPHISTOPHELES. One merely spreads one's cloak—
   you'll find
  It gives us aerial elevation.
  Though, please, this bold step for mankind
  Imposes luggage-limitation.
  I'll set the burners going, heat some air, and lo!
  We travel light, the earth lies far below.   2070
  Congratulations! See how soon it's done!
  Now your new way of living has begun!

8 · AUERBACH'S TAVERN IN LEIPZIG* [UR/FRA

[*A group of merry-makers.*]

FROSCH. Why don't you laugh? Where are your glasses?
  Just staring, just sitting on your arses!
  A set of bright sparks, I must say!
  By God, you're all damp squibs today.

BRANDER. That's your fault; why not show your famous
    wit?
  Some damn fool trick, some silly piece of shit.

FROSCH [*pouring a glass of wine over his head*]. Here's
    both at once!

BRANDER.   Twice filthy swine!

FROSCH. Well, it was your idea, not mine.   2080

SIEBEL. No quarrelling, or we'll chuck you out.
  Let's have a song, my hearties! Swig and shout!
  Come! Holla! Ho!

ALTMAYER.   Give me ear-plugs! This fellow,
  He's busting me for good with his great bellow!

SIEBEL. It's got to make the vault resound
  If it's to be the true *basso profondo* sound.

FROSCH. Right; out goes anyone who takes offence.
  Tra la la la la la!

ALTMAYER. Tra la la la la la!

FROSCH.   We're in good voice; commence!
      [*Sings.*] The Holy Roman Empire, we all love
        it so;*   2090
      But how it holds together, that's what we don't
        know.

BRANDER. A filthy song! Shame! A political song!
  A tedious song! My lads, thank God in daily prayer
  That running the Empire isn't your affair!
  I reckon it a blessing anyway
  That I'm not Emperor or Chancellor today.
  But someone here must be the boss:
  Let's choose a Pope, to lord it over us!*
  Come, you all know the rules as well as I,
  And what a chap must do to qualify!   2100

FROSCH [*sings*]. Fly away, nightingale, my pretty
         sweeting!
        Sing to my darling and bring her my greeting!

SIEBEL. No greeting! Damn all sweethearts!

FROSCH.   Let me be!
   Greetings and kisses she shall have from me.
       [*Sings.*] Oh let me in, the moon is high!
       Oh let me in, my love, 'tis I!
       By break of day I'll be away—

SIEBEL. All right then, sing, and sing her praises! One fine
   day
   I'll have the laugh on you, my friend.
   She double-crossed me, as she will you in the end.   2110
   May some randy hobgoblin be her Romeo,
   Canoodling with her at the crossroads! May
   Some old goat bleat goodnight to her on his way
   Home from the witches' sabbath! Go
   And serenade her, then! Real flesh and blood,
   Real decent chaps like us are much too good
   For such a slut! You make me sick.
   I'd serenade her windows with a brick!

BRANDER [*banging on the table*]. Gentlemen, pay
   attention, if you please!
   I'm a man of the world, as you'll allow.   2120
   We have love-sick folk among us, and for these
   Civility dictates that I must now
   Sing them a good-night song, as I know how.
   So listen to my fashionable strain,
   And all join heartily in the refrain!

               [*He sings.*]

       Down in the cellar there lived a rat,
       Where it was dark and smelly;
       It lived on butter and it got as fat
       As Doctor Luther's belly.
       The cook put down some poisoned cheese,   2130
       The rat began to choke and wheeze.
       You'd have thought it was in love, in love, in
         love!

CHORUS [*gleefully*]. You'd have thought it was in love,
         in love!

BRANDER. It raced around, it rushed outdoors,
       And drank from every drain, oh!

It scratched the walls and gnawed the floors,
But all its rage was vain, oh!
It leapt and hopped in mortal fear,
The poor beast knew its end was near;
You'd have thought it was in love, in love, in   2140
   love!

CHORUS. You'd have thought it was in love, in love!

BRANDER. Then to the kitchen by broad day
In terror it cavorted,
And there beside the fire it lay
And sadly twitched and snorted.
The cruel cook she laughed and said:
'I've cooked his goose, he'll soon be dead.
You'd have thought he was in love, in love,
   in love!'

CHORUS. You'd have thought he was in love, in love!

SIEBEL. What's the great joke then? Vulgar louts!   2150
A very noble art, to lay
Down rat-bane for those wretched brutes!

BRANDER. You're a rat-fancier, I dare say?

ALTMAYER. This pot-paunch with his balding pate!
Crossed love has made him meek and tame;
He sympathizes with the fate
Of the poor swollen rat—it feels and looks the same!

[*Enter* FAUST *and* MEPHISTOPHELES.]

MEPHISTOPHELES. The first thing now that I must do
Is find good company for you;
Life can so easily be fun! These folk   2160
Have made it one long feast and one long joke.
With little wit but with much pleasure
Round in this narrow ring they dance their measure,
Like kittens chasing their own tails.
So long as their headache's not too bad
And drinks on credit can be had,
This carefree idyll never fails!

BRANDER. Those two are travellers, you can see,
That's why they're acting so peculiarly.
They've only just arrived, I'd guess.   2170

FROSCH. You're right; one up to Leipzig! It's no less
  A town than Paris; living here's an education.

SIEBEL. Who are our visitors, d'you think?

FROSCH. Leave it to me! They'll have a glass to drink,
  And then they'll talk. I'll soon extract the truth;
  I'll tweak it out of them like a young kid's milk-tooth.
  They're from a noble family, I'd swear—
  They've got that arrogant ill-tempered air.

BRANDER. I think they're traders, come here for the fair.

ALTMAYER. Could be.

FROSCH.   Watch me, I'll find out who and   2180
  what and when.

MEPHISTOPHELES [to FAUST]. The common people never
  know
  The Devil, even when they've caught him.

FAUST.   Gentlemen,
  Good evening.

SIEBEL.   And we wish you both the same.

  [in an undertone, looking askance at MEPHISTOPHELES.]

  What's wrong with his foot? The fellow's lame.*

MEPHISTOPHELES. May we join you perhaps, and sit
  down here?
  To make up for the wine's inferior quality
  We shall be glad to have your company.

ALTMAYER. You seem to have a jaded palate, sir.

FROSCH. You were late leaving Rippach, I dare say;
  You dined there with Hans Arse, no doubt?*   2190

MEPHISTOPHELES. We didn't visit him today;
  But last time there was much to talk about.
  He spoke of each of you at length, and sends
  Most cordial greetings to his Leipzig friends.

                    [He bows to FROSCH.]

ALTMAYER [aside to FROSCH]. That's one for you!

SIEBEL.   A wily customer!

ALTMAYER.   I'll bet
  He knows a thing or two!

FROSCH.   Just wait, I'll get him yet.

MEPHISTOPHELES. Did we not hear, if I'm not wrong,
A group of practised voices joined in song?
It must be a rare treat to sing
With this fine vault re-echoing.   2200

FROSCH. No doubt you have a virtuoso's skill?

MEPHISTOPHELES. Alas, no; little aptitude, but much good
will.

ALTMAYER. Give us a song!

MEPHISTOPHELES.   If it amuses you,
I've quite a repertoire.

SIEBEL.   But sing one that's brand new!

MEPHISTOPHELES. We've just been travelling in Spain, a
fine
Country, the land of song and wine.
                    [Sings.] There was a king reigned over us,
                    He had a great big flea—

FROSCH. Hear that? A flea! Let's listen to the rest!
A flea's a cheerful sort of guest.   2210

MEPHISTOPHELES. There was a king reigned over us,
                    He had a great big flea;
                    He loved it as a father does,
                    And that was plain to see.
                    He called his tailor and said: 'There,
                    Now show what you can do!
                    This lord must have some clothes to wear,
                    He must have breeches too!'

BRANDER. But tell the tailor: Mark well what we've said!
Measure exactly, see to it   2220
Those breeches are a perfect fit;
One crease, and off will come your head!

MEPHISTOPHELES. So now the flea was richly dressed
                    In velvet and in silk,
                    With stars and crosses on his chest,
                    Like others of his ilk.
                    The king he made him minister,
                    And soon, as I've heard tell,

His cousins at the court they were
All ministers as well.   2230

The courtiers then did curse and groan,
Flea-bitten one and all;
The queen was bitten on her throne,
The servants in the hall.
Yet no one dared to kill those fleas,
Or dared to make a fuss.
But we can pick them off and squeeze
Them dead when they bite us!

CHORUS [*gleefully*]. But we can pick them off and squeeze
  Them dead when they bite us!   2240

FROSCH. Bravo! bravo! That was fine!

SIEBEL. Destruction to all fleas, I say!

BRANDER. Catch 'em and squash 'em, that's the way!

ALTMAYER. Three cheers for liberty! Three cheers for wine!

MEPHISTOPHELES. I'd gladly drink a toast to liberty
  If only you had wines of better quality.

SIEBEL. Now that's enough from you, Mr Pernickety!

MEPHISTOPHELES. The landlord wouldn't like it, I'm
    afraid,
  Or I'd invite these worthy guests to try
  A vintage from our own supply.*   2250

SIEBEL. Oh, I'll deal with the landlord; go ahead!

FROSCH. A glass of the best wine's a gift we'll thank you
    for,
  But fill our mouths full, if you please!
  If I'm to play the connoisseur,
  Large samples stimulate my expertise.

ALTMAYER [*aside*]. They're from the Rhineland, that's
    quite clear.

MEPHISTOPHELES. Fetch me a borer!

BRANDER.   What d'you want that for?
  D'you have your wine-casks just outside the door?

ALTMAYER. The landlord's got a tool-box over here.

MEPHISTOPHELES [*taking the borer*]. Now, which wine
    do you fancy?

FROSCH.   What!   2260
    Have you a whole variety?

MEPHISTOPHELES. You are free to choose, we have the lot.

ALTMAYER [*to* FROSCH]. Now you begin to lick your
    lips, hee hee!

FROSCH. Well! Hock will suit me, if the choice is mine.
    Home-grown products are best, God bless the Rhine!

MEPHISTOPHELES [*boring a hole in the edge of the table
    where* FROSCH *is sitting*]. Now find some wax and
    make some stoppers, quick!

ALTMAYER. Oh, this is some old conjuring-trick!

MEPHISTOPHELES [*to* BRANDER]. And you?

BRANDER.   I'll have champagne, if you don't mind;
    The very finest, the real bubbly kind!
        [MEPHISTOPHELES *bores; meanwhile one of the
        others has made the wax stoppers and pushes them into
        the holes.*]
    Foreigners have their uses, I suppose;   2270
    Home's best, but some good things just can't be had.
    A Frenchman stinks in every decent German's nose—
    But when one's drinking, well, their wine's not bad.

SIEBEL [*as* MEPHISTOPHELES *comes to his place.*]
    I must confess, dry wines are not for me;
    Give me a glass of something really sweet!

MEPHISTOPHELES [*boring*]. Tokay shall flow for you;
    just keep your seat.

ALTMAYER. Gentlemen, tell me honestly—
    You're surely just playing a joke on us!

MEPHISTOPHELES. Come, come! In such a noble company
    That would be most discourteous.   2280
    So tell me, without more ado,
    What wine can I now offer you?

ALTMAYER. Any you like, let's not waste time!
        [*The holes are all bored and stopped up.*]

MEPHISTOPHELES [*with strange gestures*].
                Grapes grow on the vine,
                Horns on the goat are mine,
                Wooden the vine-stem, grapes from wood,
                Wine from the table is just as good.
                Deep into Nature's mystery
                Our miracle delves; believe what you see!—
Now pull the stoppers out and swill.   2290

ALL [*as they draw the stoppers and the wine each of them
    asked for runs into his glass*]. Oh, precious nectar! Now
    we'll drink our fill!

MEPHISTOPHELES. But this wine, please, you must not
    spill!
               [*They drink glass after glass.*]

ALL [*singing*]. Oh now we're having a cannibal feast,
                Happy as five hundred swine!

MEPHISTOPHELES. This mob's on the free, watch them
    enjoying it!
FAUST. I think I'd like to leave now.
MEPHISTOPHELES.   Wait a bit,
    And their real bestiality will show!
    You've not seen half the fun, you know.
SIEBEL [*drinks carelessly, his wine spills on the ground and
    bursts into flame*]. Help! Hell's alight! Help! I'm on fire!

MEPHISTOPHELES [*commanding the flames*]. Sweet
    element, be still, be dark!   2300
    [*To the company.*] This time, just a slight purgatory-spark.

SIEBEL. What's the idea? Just you wait, my fine squire!
    We don't care for this sort of lark.

FROSCH. You'll pay for it if you try that again!

ALTMAYER. I think we'll take him outside and explain.

SIEBEL. How dare you, sir, how dare you come
    Here with this hocus-pocus stuff?

MEPHISTOPHELES. Cork your mouth, ancient wine-tub!
SIEBEL.   Skinny stick!
    Insult us, would you?

BRANDER.   That's enough!
Just wait, we'll kick him in the bum!   2310

ALTMAYER [*pulls a stopper from the table, fire leaps out at
    him*].
I'm burnt! I'm burnt!

SIEBEL.   It's magic! Draw
Your weapons! Wizards are outside the law!

[*They draw their knives and advance on* MEPHISTOPHELES.]

MEPHISTOPHELES [*with a solemn gesture*].
              False word and shape compel
              Mind and space by this spell!
              Be here, be there as well!

    [*They stop in astonishment and stare at each other.*]

ALTMAYER. Where am I? What a wonderland!

FROSCH. Vineyards! Can this be true?

SIEBEL.   And grapes right here to hand!

BRANDER. Look, under all these green leaves, see
These vines, these juicy grapes, bless me!

    [*He takes hold of* SIEBEL *by the nose. The rest do the
    same to each other and raise their knives.*]

MEPHISTOPHELES [*with another gesture*]. Illusion; let   2320
    their eyes go free! —
You'll not forget the Devil's little joke.

[*He vanishes with* FAUST, *the companions let go and recoil.*]

SIEBEL. What's the matter?

ALTMAYER.   What's this?

FROSCH.   Was that your nose I had?

BRANDER [*to* SIEBEL]. And I've got yours; now that's a
    funny thing.

ALTMAYER. I'm shaking! It was like some kind of stroke!
Get me a chair, I'm feeling bad!

FROSCH. But good God, what's been happening?

SIEBEL. Where is the fellow? If I find him
He'll not escape scot-free after our quarrel.

ALTMAYER. I saw him put the cellar door behind him—
   He rode out sitting on a barrel—   2330
   I've got lead weights in both my feet.
               [*Looking round at the table.*]
   God bless us! Is there any wine still there?

SIEBEL. It was a sham, all trickery and deceit.

FROSCH. But I was drinking wine, I'll swear!

BRANDER. And what about those grapes, and why—?

ALTMAYER. Now who says miracles are all my eye?

9 · A WITCH'S KITCHEN*   [FRA

[*A low hearth with a large cauldron hanging over the
fire. In the steam that rises from it various apparitions
are seen. A female baboon is sitting by the cauldron
skimming it, taking care not to let it run over. The male
baboon with their young sits nearby warming himself.
The walls and ceiling are decorated with strange witch-
paraphernalia.* FAUST *and* MEPHISTOPHELES *enter.*]

FAUST. I'm sick of all this crazy magic stuff!
   Is this your vaunted therapy,
   This mess of raving mad absurdity?
   Advice from an old witch! Am I to slough   2340
   Off thirty years, become as good as new,
   By swallowing her stinking brew?
   God help me now, if that's the best
   Hope you can offer! Has man's mind
   Devised no other method, can we find
   No nobler balm in Nature's treasure-chest?

MEPHISTOPHELES. You're talking sense again now, my
     dear sir!
   There is another means to your rejuvenation,
   But it's a very different operation;
   I doubt if it's what you'd prefer.   2350

FAUST. I wish to know it.

MEPHISTOPHELES.   Very well;
   You'll need no fee, no doctor and no spell.

Go out onto the land at once, begin
To dig and delve, be primitive
In body and mind, be bound within
Some altogether narrower sphere;
Eat food that's plain and simple, live
Like cattle with the cattle, humbly reap
The fields you have manured with your own dung;
Believe me, that will make you young   2360
And keep you young until your eightieth year!

FAUST. I'm not used to all that; it's no good now
Trying to learn the simple life. A spade
Is something I could never use.

MEPHISTOPHELES.   Then I'm afraid
The witch will have to show us how.

FAUST. Why do we need this hag? Can't you   [F.I.
Prepare the necessary brew?

MEPHISTOPHELES. The Devil's busy, sir! Why, I could
    build
A thousand bridges by the time that stuff's distilled!
I have the secret art, indeed,   2370
But not the patience I should need.
Quiet laborious years must run their course;
Time alone can ferment that subtle force.
And there's a deal of ceremony
To go with it—too weird for me.
The Devil taught the witch her tricks,
But she makes potions he can't mix.

                [*Seeing the animals.*]

Why, look! what charming kith and kin!*   [FRA
This is her manservant, that's her maid.

                [*To the animals.*]

It seems your mistress is not in?   2380

THE ANIMALS. Dining out!
            Up the chimney-spout!
            She's been delayed!

MEPHISTOPHELES. How long do her trips last, if I may
    be told?

THE ANIMALS. Till we leave the fire, till our paws get cold.

MEPHISTOPHELES [to FAUST]. Delightful creatures,
    don't you agree?

FAUST. I think they're dreary disgusting brutes.

MEPHISTOPHELES. Not at all; their conversation suits
    Me very well, as you can see.

So, what are you stirring there in that pot,   2390
You damnable apes? What mess have you got?

THE ANIMALS. It's charity soup, very light to digest.*

MEPHISTOPHELES. I'm sure your public will be impressed.

THE MALE BABOON [bounding up to MEPHISTOPHELES [FRA
    and coaxing him].

              O please, throw the dice!
              To be rich is so nice,
              It's so nice to be winning!
              Being poor isn't funny,
              And if I had money
              My head would stop spinning!

MEPHISTOPHELES. This monkey thinks a lucky thing   2400
    to do
Would be to play the lottery too!*

    [Meanwhile the young baboons have been playing with
    a large globe, which they roll forward.]

THE MALE BABOON. The world is this ball:
              See it rise and fall
              And roll round and round!
              It's glass, it will break,
              It's an empty fake—
              Hear the hollow sound!
              See it glow here and shine,
              See it glitter so fine!
              'I'm alive!' it sings.   2410
              O my son, beware of it,
              Keep clear of it:
              You must die, like all things!
              It's made of clay;
              Clay gets broken, they say.

MEPHISTOPHELES. What's the use of that sieve?*

THE MALE BABOON [*lifting it down*].
                If you were a thief
                I could tell straight away!

[*He scampers across to the female and makes her look through it.*]

                Look through the sieve!
                You can name the thief,   2420
                And you mustn't say.

MEPHISTOPHELES [*approaching the fire*].
                And what's this pot?

THE BABOONS. Poor ignorant sot!
                Doesn't know why the pot,
                Why the cauldron's there!

MEPHISTOPHELES. You insolent beast!

THE MALE BABOON. Take this whisk, at least,
                And sit down in the chair!

[*He makes* MEPHISTOPHELES *sit down.*]

FAUST [*who in the meantime has been standing in front of a mirror, alternately moving towards it and backing away from it*]*.

    Oh, heavenly image! What is this I see
    Appearing to me in this magic glass?   2430
    Love, carry me to where she dwells, alas,
    Oh, lend the swiftest of your wings to me!
    If I so much as move from this one spot,
    If I dare to approach her, then she seems
    To fade, I see her as in misty dreams!
    The loveliest image of a woman! Is this not
    Impossible, can woman be so fair?
    I see in that sweet body lying there
    The quintessence of paradise! How can one
    Believe such things exist beneath the sun?   2440

MEPHISTOPHELES. Well, if a god has worked hard for
    six days
    And on the seventh gives himself high praise,
    You'd think it would be reasonably well done!—

Look your fill at her now. I'll find
A little darling for you of that kind;
Then you can try your luck. If you succeed
In winning her, you'll be a happy man indeed!

[FAUST *keeps gazing into the mirror.*
MEPHISTOPHELES, *lolling in the chair and playing
with the whisk, goes on talking*].

Well, here I sit, a king enthroned in state;*
My sceptre's in my hand, my crown I still await.

THE ANIMALS [*who have been scampering about with each
other in a bizarre fashion and now bring a crown for
MEPHISTOPHELES, offering it to him with loud
screeches*].

    Oh sir, be so good   2450
    As to mend this old crown
    With sweat and with blood!

[*They handle the crown clumsily and break it into two
pieces, which they then scamper about with.*]

    Now it's done! It falls down!—
    We can talk, see and hear,
    We can rhyme loud and clear!

FAUST [*gazing at the mirror*].
Oh God! have I gone mad? I'm quite distraught!

MEPHISTOPHELES [*indicating the animals*].
I think I'm going a bit crazy too.

THE ANIMALS. And when our rhymes fit
    We're in luck: that's the thought,
    That's the meaning of it!   2460

FAUST [*as above*]. My heart's on fire, what shall I do?
Quick, let's leave now, let's get away!

MEPHISTOPHELES [*remaining seated, as above*].
Well, one must certainly admit
These apes are honest poets, in their way!

[*The cauldron, which the female baboon has been
neglecting, begins to boil over, and a great tongue of
flame blazes up into the chimney.* THE WITCH *comes
down through the flame, screaming hideously.*]

THE WITCH. Ow! ow! ow! ow!
  You damned brute, you damned filthy sow!
  Not minding the pot! You've burnt me now,
  You filthy brute!

        [*Seeing* FAUST *and* MEPHISTOPHELES.]

          What's this here? Who
          The hell are you?   2470
          Who let you in?
          What does this mean?
          May hell's hot pains
          Burn in your bones!

  [*She plunges the skimming-ladle into the cauldron and*
  splashes flames at FAUST, MEPHISTOPHELES *and*
  the animals. The animals whine.]

MEPHISTOPHELES [*reversing the whisk in his hand and*
  striking out with the handle at the glasses and pots].

          Split! split in two!
          That's spilt your stew!
          That's spoilt your cooking!
          I'm only joking,
          Hell-hag! You croon,
          I beat the tune!   2480

        [THE WITCH *recoils in rage and terror.*]

  Do you know me now? Skinny, cadaverous bitch,
  Do you know your lord and master? Why don't I
  Smash you to pieces, tell me why,
  You and your ape-familiars? Must I teach
  You some respect for my red doublet? What
  Is this cock's feather, eh? My face,
  Have I been hiding it? You learn your place,
  Old hag! Am I to name myself or not?

THE WITCH. Oh master, pardon my rude greeting!
  But where's your cloven hoof, your horse's leg?   2490
  And your two ravens? Sir, I beg
  To be excused!

MEPHISTOPHELES. Well, well, and so
  You are for once; it's true, I know,
  Some time has passed since our last meeting.

Besides, civilization, which now licks
Us all so smooth, has taught even the Devil tricks;
The northern fiend's becoming a lost cause—
Where are his horns these days, his tail, his claws?
As for my foot, which I can't do without,
People would think me odd to go about   2500
With that; and so, like some young gentlemen,
I've worn false calves since God knows when.

THE WITCH [*capering about*]. I'm crazy with excitement
    now I see
Our young Lord Satan's back again!

MEPHISTOPHELES. Woman, don't use that name to me!

THE WITCH. Why, sir, what harm's it ever done?

MEPHISTOPHELES. The name has been a myth too long.
    Not that man's any better off—the Evil One
    They're rid of, evil is still going strong.
    Please call me 'Baron', that will do.   2510
    I'm just a gentleman, like others of my kind.
    My blood's entirely noble, you will find;
    My coat of arms may be inspected too.

        [*He makes an indecent gesture.*]

THE WITCH [*shrieking with laughter*].
    Ha! ha! You haven't changed a bit!
    Still the same bad lad, by the looks of it!

MEPHISTOPHELES [*to* FAUST]. Mark well, my dear sir!
    This is how
One deals with witches.

THE WITCH.   Tell me now,
Gentlemen, what might be your pleasure?

MEPHISTOPHELES. A good glass of the you-know-what;
    But please, the oldest vintage you have got—   2520
    Years give it strength in double measure.

THE WITCH. Certainly! I've a bottle on this shelf,
    I sometimes take a swig from it myself;
    By now it's even quite stopped stinking.
    A glass for you can well be spared.
    [*Aside.*] But as you know, it's not for casual drinking—
    This man will die of it unless he's been prepared.

MEPHISTOPHELES. No, it will do him good—he's a good
    friend
  Of ours, and I can safely recommend
  Your kitchen to him. Draw your circle, say   2530
  Your spells, pour him a cup without delay!

> [THE WITCH, with strange gestures, draws a circle and
> places magic objects in it; as she does so the glasses and
> pots begin to ring and hum and make music. Finally she
> fetches a massive tome and puts the baboons in the circle,
> where they are made to act as a reading-desk for her and
> hold the torch. She beckons FAUST to approach her.]

FAUST [to MEPHISTOPHELES].
  Look, what use is all this to me?
  These crazy antics, all that stupid stuff,
  The woman's vulgar trickery—
  I know and hate them well enough!

MEPHISTOPHELES. Rubbish, man! Can't you see a joke?
  Don't be pedantic! You must understand,
  As a doctor she's got to hoke and poke
  If her medicine's to take effect as planned.

> [He makes FAUST step into the circle.]

THE WITCH [beginning to declaim from the book with great
    emphasis].*

              Now hear and see!   2540
              From one make ten,
              Take two, and then
              At once take three,
              And you are rich!
              Four doesn't score.
              But, says the witch,
              From five and six
              Make seven and eight;
              That puts it straight.
              And nine is one,   2550
              And ten is none.
              The witch's twice-times-table's done.

FAUST. She's obviously raving mad.

MEPHISTOPHELES. Oh, she has still much more to say!
   I know it well, the whole book reads that way.
   It's cost me more time than I had.
   A complete paradox, you see,*
   Fills fools and wise men with a sense of mystery.
   My friend, the art's both new and old:
   Let error, not the truth be told—   2560
   Make one of three and three of one;
   That's how it always has been done.
   Thus to their heart's content they dogmatize,
   Plague take the silly chattering crew!
   Men hear mere words, yet commonly surmise
   Words must have intellectual content too.
THE WITCH [continuing]. The lofty might
             Of wisdom's light,
             Hid from the vulgar throng:
             It costs no thought,   2570
             It's freely taught,
             We know it all along!
FAUST. What rubbish is the crone repeating?
   My head's half split by this entire
   Performance; it's like some massed choir
   Of fifty thousand idiots bleating.
MEPHISTOPHELES. Enough, enough, excellent sibyl!
   Bring
   Your cocktail, pour it, fill the cup
   Right to the brim, quick, fill it up!
   This drink won't harm my friend, he knows a thing   2580
   Or two already; many a strong potation
   He's swallowed during his initiation!

   [THE WITCH, with great ceremony, pours the potion
   into a cup; as FAUST raises it to his lips it flames up a
   little.]

Come, down with it! Don't dither so!
Soon it will warm the cockles of your heart.
You're practically the Devil's bedfellow,
And fire still makes you flinch and start!

   [THE WITCH opens the circle. FAUST steps out of it.]

Let's go! You must keep moving now.

THE WITCH. I hope my potion whets your appetite!

MEPHISTOPHELES [to THE WITCH]. And if I can do you
    a good turn somehow,
Just tell me on Walpurgis Night.   2590

THE WITCH. Here is a song, sir, you might like to sing;
    You'll find it has a special virtue in it.

MEPHISTOPHELES [to FAUST]. Do as I say, come, let's
    be off this minute;
You must let yourself sweat, this thing
Must soak right through your guts. Then you shall learn
How to appreciate your noble leisure,
And soon, to your consummate pleasure,
Cupid will stir in you, you'll feel him dance and burn.

FAUST. Let me look once more in the glass before we go—
    That woman's lovely shape entrances me.

MEPHISTOPHELES.   No, no!   2600
Before you in the flesh you soon will see
The very paragon of femininity.

    [Aside.] With that elixir coursing through him,
    Soon any woman will be Helen to him.*

10 · A STREET   [UR

[FAUST. MARGARETA passing by.]*

FAUST. My sweet young lady, if I may
    I will escort you on your way.

MARGARETA. I'm not a lady and I'm not sweet,
    I can get home on my own two feet.

        [She frees herself and walks on.]

FAUST. By God, but that's a lovely girl!
    More lovely than I've ever met.   2610
So virtuous, so decent, yet
A touch of sauciness as well!
Her lips so red, her cheeks so bright—
All my life I'll not forget that sight
It stirred my very heart to see

Her eyes cast down so modestly,
And how she put me in my place,
With so much charm and so much grace!

[*Enter* MEPHISTOPHELES.]

FAUST. Look, you must get that girl for me!

MEPHISTOPHELES. Which one?

FAUST.   She's just gone by.

MEPHISTOPHELES.   Ah, yes!   2620
She's just been making her confession.
Her priest gave her full absolution:
I sneaked up and was listening.
She's a poor innocent little thing,
With nothing whatever to confess.
I've no power over her, I fear.

FAUST. Why not? She's past her fourteenth year.

MEPHISTOPHELES. Come, this is Randy Andy talk!
You'd leave no flower on its stalk.
Pluck every favour, every prize   2630
That's pleased your self-conceited eyes—
But some things have to be eschewed.

FAUST. Now hear me, Dr. Rectitude!
Leave out the legal preachment stuff,
And let me tell you: either by
Tonight that sweet young thing shall lie
Between my arms, or you and I
Will have been together long enough.*

MEPHISTOPHELES. Be practical, my dear good sir!
I need two weeks of sniffing round   2640
To find out how to get at her.

FAUST. Two weeks! That child? Why, I'll be bound,
If I had even half a day
I'd not need the Devil to get my way.

MEPHISTOPHELES. Well, now you're almost talking
    French.
But with respect—take my advice:
Why bustle so to bed the wench?
Your pleasure with her will be twice

As keen after long preparation
And complicated titillation,   2650
To make her willing and soft to the touch;
In Italian tales you'll have read as much.

FAUST. I've appetite enough without
    All that.

MEPHISTOPHELES. But sir, be in no doubt—
    With this fair maid, I tell you plain,
    It's bound to be a long campaign;
    We'll not take her by storm. We must
    Use guile to satisfy your lust.

FAUST. Take me to where my darling lies!
    Get me some token, some sweet prize,   2660
    A garter, a kerchief from her breast—
    Something to set my heart at rest!

MEPHISTOPHELES. To demonstrate my willingness
    To serve your amorous distress,
    We'll lose not a moment in delay;
    I'll take you to her room this very day.

FAUST. And shall I see her? Have her?

MEPHISTOPHELES.   No!
    She'll be visiting a friend next door.
    But you'll be quite alone, and so
    In her private ambience you can glow   2670
    And gloat on pleasures still in store.

FAUST. Let's go now!

MEPHISTOPHELES. We must wait our chance.

FAUST. I'll take her a present; get one at once!   [Exit.]

MEPHISTOPHELES. Presents already? Very charming;
    he'll succeed.
I know some interesting places*
Where buried treasure's left its traces;
I'll reconnoitre . . . Yes, indeed!

11 · EVENING

[*A small well-kept room.*]

MARGARETA [*plaiting and binding up her hair*].
  I'd like to find out, I must say,
  Who that gentleman was today.
  A handsome man, I do admit,   2680
  And a nobleman by the looks of it.
  I could tell by something in his eyes.
  And he wouldn't have had the cheek otherwise.
    [*Exit.* MEPHISTOPHELES *and* FAUST *enter.*]

MEPHISTOPHELES. Come in, keep quiet! Come, don't
  delay!

FAUST [*after a pause*]. Leave me alone, please go away.

MEPHISTOPHELES [*taking a look round the room*].
  Very neat and tidy, I must say. [*Exit.*]

FAUST [*gazing up and about him*].
  Welcome, sweet twilight, shining dim all through
  This sanctuary! Now let love's sweet pain
  That lives on hope's refreshing dew
  Seize and consume my heart again!   2690
  How this whole place breathes deep content
  And order and tranquillity!
  What riches in this poverty,
  What happiness in this imprisonment!
    [*He sinks into the leather armchair by the bed.*]

Oh let me rest here: long ago, among
Their joys and sorrows, others sat on you,
Embraced and welcomed! Ah, how often too
Round this, their grandsire's throne, the children clung!
My love herself, at Christmas time, a young
Rosy-cheeked child, glad at some gift, knelt here   2700
Perhaps, and kissed his wrinkled hand so dear!
What order, what completeness I am made
To sense in these surroundings! It is yours,
Dear girl, your native spirit that ensures
Maternal daily care, the table neatly laid,

The crisp white sand strewn on the floors!
Oh godlike hand, by whose dear skill and love
This little hut matches the heavens above!
And here!

       [*He draws aside a curtain from the bed.*]

       What fierce joy seizes me! I could
Stand gazing here for ever. Nature, you   2710
Worked this sweet wonder, here the inborn angel grew
Through gentle dreams to womanhood.
Here the child lay, her tender heart
Full of warm life, here the pure love
Of God's creative forces wove
His likeness by their sacred art!

And I! What purpose brings me? What
Profound emotion stirs me! What did I
Come here to do? Why do I sigh?
Poor wretch! Am I now Faust or not?   2720

Is there some magic hovering round me here?
I was resolved, my lust brooked no delay—
And now in dreams of love I wilt and melt away!
Are we mere playthings of the atmosphere?

If she came in this instant, ah, my sweet,
How she would punish me! How small
The great Don Juan* would feel, how he would fall
In tears of languor at her feet!

MEPHISTOPHELES [*entering*]. Quick, she's down there,
    she'll be here any minute.

FAUST. Take me away! I'll never come again!   2730

MEPHISTOPHELES. Here's quite a heavy box with nice
    things in it;
I got it—somewhere else. Now then,
Into her cupboard with it, quick, before we're seen.
I tell you, when she finds that stuff
She'll go out of her mind; I've put enough
Jewellery in there to seduce a queen.
A child's a child, of course, and play's just play.

FAUST. I don't know if I should—

MEPHISTOPHELES.   Now what's the fuss about?
   You'd like to keep it for yourself, no doubt?
   Let me advise you then, Sir Lecher-Lust,   2740
   Stop wasting the fine time of day,
   And spare me further tasks! I trust
   You're not a miser too? I scratch my pate
   And bite my nails and calculate—

   [He puts the jewel-case in the cupboard and locks it up
   again.]

   Quick, we must go!—
   How I'm to please your sweetheart for you
   And make her want you and adore you;
   And now you hesitate
   As if this were your lecture-room
   Where in grey professorial gloom   2750
   Physics and metaphysics wait!
   We must go! [They leave.]

MARGARETA [coming in with a lamp].
   It's so hot and sultry in here somehow,

                  [She opens the window.]

   And yet it's quite cool outside just now.
   I've got a feeling something's wrong—
   I hope my mother won't be long.
   It's a sort of scare coming over me—
   What a silly baby I must be!

              [She begins singing as she undresses.]

      There once was a king of Thulè,*
      Of the far north land of old: 2760
      His dying lady he loved so truly
      She gave him a cup of gold.

      There was no thing so dear to the king,
      And every time he wept
      As he drained that cup at each banqueting,
      So truly his faith he kept.

      And at last, they say, on his dying day
      His kingdom was willed and told,

And his son and heir got all his share—
But the king kept the cup of gold.   2770

They feasted long with wine and song,
And there with his knights sat he,
In the ancestral hall, in his castle tall
On the cliffs high over the sea.

The old man still drank as his life's flame sank,
Then above the waves he stood,
And the sacred cup he raised it up,
Threw it down to the raging flood.

He watched it fall to the distant shore
And sink in the waters deep;   2780
And never a drop that king drank more,
For he'd closed his eyes to sleep.

[*She opens the cupboard to put her clothes in, and sees the jewel-case.*]

However did this pretty box get here?
I left the cupboard locked; how very queer!
Whatever can be in it? Perhaps my mother lent
Some money on it, and it's meant
As a security. Oh dear!
It's got a ribbon with a little key—
I think I'll open it, just to see!
What's this? Oh God in heaven, just look!   2790
I've never seen such things before!
These jewels would be what a princess wore
At the highest feast in the feast-day book!
I wonder how that necklace would suit me?
Whose can these wonderful things be?

[*She puts on some of the jewellery and looks at herself in the glass.*]

If even the earrings were only mine!
My, what a difference it makes!
We young girls have to learn, it takes
More than just beauty; that's all very fine,
But everyone just says 'she's pretty',   2800
And they seem to say it out of pity.

Gold's all they care
About, gold's wanted everywhere;
For us poor folk there's none to spare.

12 · A PROMENADE   [UR

[FAUST *walking up and down deep in thought. Enter*
MEPHISTOPHELES.]

MEPHISTOPHELES By the pangs of despised love! By the
   fires of hell!
I wish I knew something worse, to curse it as well!

FAUST. Whatever's the matter? You do look odd.
   What a sour face for a fine day!

MEPHISTOPHELES. May the devil take me, I would say,
   If I weren't the Devil myself, by God.   2810

FAUST. Are you right in the head? Excuse me if I smile;
   These rages aren't your usual style.

MEPHISTOPHELES. Just think: those jewels for Gretchen
   that I got,
A priest has been and swiped the lot!—
Her mother took one look, and hey!
She had the horrors straight away.
That woman's got a good nose all right,
Snuffling her prayer-book day and night,
With any commodity she can tell
Profane from sacred by the smell;   2820
And as for those jewels, she knew soon enough
There was something unholy about that stuff.
'My child', she exclaimed, 'ill-gotten wealth
Poisons one's spiritual health.
To God's blessed Mother it must be given,
And she will reward us with manna from heaven!'
How Meg's face fell, poor little minx!
It's a gift-horse after all, she thinks,
And whoever so kindly brought it—how can
There be anything godless about such a man?   2830
Ma sends for the priest, and he, by glory!

Has no sooner heard their little story
And studied the spoils with great delight,
Than he says: 'Dear ladies, you are quite right!
Who resists the tempter shall gain a crown.
The Church can digest all manner of meat,
It's never been known to over-eat
Although it has gulped whole empires down;
Holy Church's stomach alone can take
Ill-gotten goods without stomach-ache!'   2840

FAUST. It's common; many a king and Jew
Has a well-filled belly of that kind too.

MEPHISTOPHELES. So he sweeps every ring and chain
    and brooch,
As if they were peanuts, into his pouch;
Takes it no less for granted, indeed,
Than if it were all just chickenfeed—
Promises them celestial reward
And leaves them thanking the blessed Lord.

FAUST. And Gretchen?

MEPHISTOPHELES.   Sitting there all of a dither,
Doesn't know what to do or why or whether.   2850
Can't get the jewels out of her mind—
Or the gentleman who had been so kind.

FAUST. I can't bear my darling to be sad.
Get another lot for her! The ones she had
Weren't all that remarkable anyway.

MEPHISTOPHELES. Oh indeed, for my lord it's mere
    child's play!

FAUST. Do as I tell you!—And one thing more:
Get to know that friend of hers next door!
Do something, devil, stir your feet!
And get some more jewels for my sweet!   2860

MEPHISTOPHELES. With pleasure, sir, whatever you say.
                [Exit FAUST.]
He's just like all the lovesick fools I know;
To please their darlings they would blow
The sun and moon and stars out at one go. [Exit.]

13 · THE NEIGHBOUR'S HOUSE   [UR

MARTHA [alone]. My husband, may God pardon him!
    He didn't treat me right. For shame!
    Just went off into the world one day,
    Left me a grass widow, as they say.
    Yet I've never done him any wrong;
    I loved him truly all along. [She weeps.]   2870
    He may even be dead. Oh, my poor heart bleeds!
    —A death certificate's what one needs.*

            [Enter MARGARETA.]

MARGARETA. Martha!

MARTHA.   Gretchen dear! What a face!

MARGARETA. Martha, I feel quite faint! There's been
    This second box—I found it in
    My cupboard there—an ebony case
    Of the grandest jewels you ever saw;
    Much richer than the one before!

MARTHA. Now this time you mustn't tell your mother,
    Or the priest'll get it, just like the other.   2880

MARGARETA. Oh, look at this! Just look at this!

MARTHA [trying out some of the jewels on her].
    Aren't you a lucky little miss!

MARGARETA. But I can't wear them in the street, or go
    To church and be seen in them, you know.*

MARTHA. Just come whenever you can to me,
    And put on your jewels secretly—
    Walk about in front of the looking-glass here,
    And we'll enjoy them together, my dear.
    Then when there's a feast-day or some occasion,
    Let people see one little thing, then another,   2890
    A necklace at first, a pearl earring; your mother
    May not notice, or we'll make up some explanation.

MARGARETA. But all this jewellery—who can have   [FRA
    brought it?

I think there's something funny about it.

[*There is a knock at the door.*]

Oh God, perhaps that's my mother!

MARTHA [*looking through the peep-hole*]. No!
It's some gentleman I don't know—
Come in!

[*Enter* MEPHISTOPHELES.]

MEPHISTOPHELES. If I may make so bold!
Forgive me, ladies; I'm looking for
Frau Martha Schwertlein, who lives here, I'm told.

[*He steps back respectfully on seeing* MARGARETA.]

MARTHA. That's me; how can I oblige you, sir?   2900

MEPHISTOPHELES [*aside to her*]. Now that I know you,
    that will do;
You have a fine lady visiting you.
Excuse my taking the liberty;
I'll call again later when you're free.

MARTHA [*aloud*]. Do you hear that, child! What a rigmarole!
He takes you for a lady, bless your soul!

MARGARETA. Oh sir, you're much too kind to me;
I'm a poor young woman—this jewellery
I'm trying on, it isn't mine.

MEPHISTOPHELES. Why, it's not just the jewels that are   2910
    fine;
You have a manner, a look in your eyes.
Then I may stay? What a pleasant surprise.

MARTHA. Now, I'm sure your business is interesting—

MEPHISTOPHELES. I hope you'll pardon the news I bring;
I'm sorry to grieve you at our first meeting.
Your husband is dead, and sends his greeting.

MARTHA. What, dead? My true love! Alas the day!
My husband's dead! I shall pass away!

MARGARETA. Oh, don't despair, Frau Martha dear!

MEPHISTOPHELES. Well, it's a sad tale you shall hear.   2920

MARGARETA. I hope I shall never love; I know
  It would kill me with grief to lose someone so.

MEPHISTOPHELES. Joy and grief need each other, they
    can't be parted.

MARTHA. Good sir, pray tell me how he died.

MEPHISTOPHELES. In Padua, by St Anthony's side,
  There they interred your late departed,
  In a spot well suited, by God's grace,
  To be his last cool resting-place.

MARTHA. And have you brought nothing else for me?

MEPHISTOPHELES. Ah, yes; he requests you solemnly   2930
  To have three hundred masses sung for his repose.
  For the rest, my hands are empty, I fear.

MARTHA. What! no old medal, not a souvenir
  Or trinket any poor apprentice will lay by,
  Stuffed in his satchel, and would rather die
  In penury than sell or lose?

MEPHISTOPHELES. I much regret it, ma'am; but
    truthfully,
  Your husband wasn't one to waste his property.
  And he rued his faults, but his luck he cursed—
  The second more bitterly than the first.   2940

MARGARETA. Oh, why have people such ill luck! I'm sad
    for them.
  I promise to pray for him with many a requiem.

MEPHISTOPHELES. What a charming child you are! I'd
    say
  You deserve to be married straight away.

MARGARETA. Oh, I'm still too young, that wouldn't be right.

MEPHISTOPHELES. If a husband won't do, then a lover
    might.
  Why not? It's life's greatest blessing and pleasure
  To lie in the arms of so sweet a treasure.

MARGARETA. That's not the custom in this country, sir.

MEPHISTOPHELES. Custom or not, it does occur.   2950

MARTHA. Tell me the rest!

MEPHISTOPHELES.   I stood by his deathbed;
  It was pretty filthy, it must be said.
  But he died as a Christian, on half-rotten straw.
  His sins were absolved, though he felt he had many more.
  'I hate myself', he cried, 'for what I've done;
  Away from my trade, away from my wife to run.
  I'm tormented by that memory.
  If only she could forgive me in this life!—'

MARTHA [weeping]. Oh, he's long been forgiven by his
      loving wife!

MEPHISTOPHELES. '—But God knows, she was more to   2960
      blame than me.'

MARTHA. Why, that's a lie! What, lie at the point of death!

MEPHISTOPHELES. He was delirious at his last breath,
  If I am any judge of such events.
  'I had my time cut out', he said,
  'Providing her with children, then with bread—
  Which meant bread in the very widest sense.
  And then I got no peace to eat my share.'

MARTHA. Had he forgotten all my faithful loving care,
  Slaving for him all day and night?

MEPHISTOPHELES. Why no, he had remembered that   2970
      all right.
  He told me: 'When we sailed away from Malta,
  For my wife and brats I said a fervent prayer,
  And by heaven's will, our luck began to alter:
  We took a Turkish ship and boarded her—
  The mighty Sultan's treasure-ship! We fought
  Them bravely and deserved our prize.
  And as for me, this bold adventure brought
  Me in a dividend of some size.'

MARTHA. What's that? Where is it? Has he buried it?

MEPHISTOPHELES. Who knows now where the four
      winds carried it!   2980
  He fell in with a lovely lady-friend
  In Naples, visiting the place for fun;
  And fun he got—the kindnesses she'd done,
  They left their mark on him till his life's end.*

MARTHA. The scoundrel! Stealing his own children's bread!
  Not even want and poverty
  Could stop his vices and debauchery!

MEPHISTOPHELES. Well, there you are, you see; so now
    he's dead.
  If I were in your place, you know,
  I'd mourn him for a decent twelvemonth, then,   2990
  Having looked round a little, choose another beau.

MARTHA. Oh dear, after my first, it will be hard
  To find a second man like him again!
  He was a jolly fellow—everyone enjoyed him;
  He just was far too fond of wandering abroad,
  And foreign women, foreign wine,
  And it was that damned gambling that destroyed him.

MEPHISTOPHELES. Well, I daresay it was a fine
  Arrangement, if for his part he
  Allowed you equal liberty.   3000
  On such terms, I would hardly hesitate
  Myself to be your second mate.

MARTHA. Oh, sir, you like to have your little joke with me!

MEPHISTOPHELES [aside]. While there's still time I'd
    best get out of here;
  She'd hold the Devil to his word, that's clear.

[To GRETCHEN.]

And you, my child, are you still fancy-free?

MARGARETA. I don't quite understand.

MEPHISTOPHELES [aside]. Now there's sweet innocence!
  [Aloud.] Ladies, good day to you!

MARGARETA.   Good day!

MARTHA.   Sir, one more thing:
  I'd like to have some proper evidence—
  The details of my husband's death and burying.   3010
  I've always liked things orderly and neat;
  I want to read it in the weekly notice-sheet.

MEPHISTOPHELES. Indeed, ma'am; when two witnesses
  agree,

The truth's revealed infallibly.
I have a companion; he and I
Can go before the judge to testify.
I'll bring him here.

MARTHA.   Oh by all means do!

MEPHISTOPHELES. And this young miss will be here
    too?—
He's a fine lad; seen the world all right;
Very nice to ladies, very polite.   3020

MARGARETA. I shall blush with shame to meet him, I fear.

MEPHISTOPHELES. You need blush before no king, my
    dear.

MARTHA. I've a garden at the back; so, gentlemen,
Please come this evening, we'll expect you then.

14 · A STREET   [UR

[FAUST. MEPHISTOPHELES.]

FAUST. Well, what news now? Is it going ahead?

MEPHISTOPHELES. Ah, bravo! So you're well alight!
Gretchen will soon be in your bed.
We're to meet her at her neighbour's house tonight.
That Martha's a proper witch, good Lord,
I couldn't have picked you a better bawd.   3030

FAUST. Good.

MEPHISTOPHELES. But she asks a service of us too.

FAUST. That's fair enough; what do we have to do?

MEPHISTOPHELES. We swear a deposition, warranting
That her late husband's bones now are
Buried in hallowed ground in Padua.

FAUST. Brilliant; so first we have to travel there.

MEPHISTOPHELES. *Sancta simplicitas!* Why should we
    care?
Just testify; no need to make the visit.

FAUST. If that's your scheme, then I'll do no such thing.

MEPHISTOPHELES. Oh, holy Willie! That's your scruple,   3040
    is it?
So this is the first time in your career
That you'll have borne false witness? Have you not
Laid down authoritative definitions
Of God and of the world, of all that's there and here,
Man's mind and heart, his motives and conditions,
With brazen confidence, with all the pride you've got?
But pause to think—confess, as you draw breath:
Of all those matters you knew not a jot
More than of Martha Schwertlein's husband's death!

FAUST. You are, and always were, a sophist and a liar.   3050

MEPHISTOPHELES. And your standards of truth, I know,
    are so much higher.
In all good faith, tomorrow, we shall find
You turning little Gretchen's mind
With vows of love, and nonsense of that kind.

FAUST. It will come from my heart.

MEPHISTOPHELES.   A splendid vow!
Eternal love, faithfulness to the end,
Unique all-powerful passion—yes, my friend,
That will come from the heart too, will it now?

FAUST. Yes! Let me be! It shall!—This deep commotion
And turmoil in me, I would speak   3060
Its name, find words for this emotion—
Through the whole world my soul and senses seek
The loftiest words for it: this flame
That burns me, it must have a name!
And so I say: eternal, endless, endless—why,
You devil, do you call all that a lie?

MEPHISTOPHELES. I am right nonetheless.

FAUST.   Listen to me—
And understand, before I burst a lung:
Insist on being right, and merely have a tongue,
And right you'll be.   3070
But now let's go, I'm sick of all this chatter.
And you are right; I've no choice in the matter.

15 · A GARDEN   [UR

[MARGARETA *walking up and down with* FAUST,
MARTHA *with* MEPHISTOPHELES.]

MARGARETA. I'm quite ashamed, I feel you're being so kind
And condescending, just to spare
My feelings, sir! A traveller
Must be polite, and take what he can find.
I know quite well that my poor conversation
Can't entertain a man of education.

FAUST. One look, one word from you—that entertains
Me more than any this wise world contains.   3080
[*He kisses her hand.*]

MARGARETA. Sir, you put yourself out! How can you kiss
my hand?
It's so nasty and rough; I have to do
Such a lot of housework with it. If you knew
How fussy Mother is, you'd understand!
[*They pass on.*]

MARTHA. So, sir, you're always travelling, I believe?

MEPHISTOPHELES. Alas, constraints of duty and
vocation!
Sometimes a place is very hard to leave—
But it's just not one's destination.

MARTHA. I dare say, when one's young and strong,
It's good to roam the world and to be free;   3090
But there are bad times coming before long,
And creeping to one's grave alone—oh, you'd be wrong
To be a bachelor then, sir, believe me!

MEPHISTOPHELES. I view with horror that approaching
fate.

MARTHA. Then think again, while it's not yet too late!
[*They pass on.*]

MARGARETA. Yes, out of sight out of mind it will be!
And though you talk politely—after all,

You've many friends, and I'm sure they are all
More intellectual than me.

FAUST. My sweet, believe me, what's called intellect   3100
Is often shallowness and vanity.

MARGARETA.   How so?

FAUST. Oh, why can simple innocence not know
Itself, or humble lowliness respect
Its own great value, feel the awe that's due
To generous Nature's dearest, greatest boon—

MARGARETA. You'll sometimes think of me, and then forget
    me soon;
But I'll have time enough to think of you.

FAUST. So you're alone a lot?

MARGARETA. Oh yes, you see, our household's not
Big, but one has to see to it;   3110
And we've no maid. I cook and sweep and knit
And sew, all day I'm on my feet.
And my mother insists everything's got
To be so neat!
Not that she's really poor in any way,
In fact, we're better off than most folk, I should say.
We got some money when my father died,
A little house and garden just outside
The town. But mine's a quiet life now, that's true.
My brother's a soldier, he's not here.   3120
My little sister, she died too.
I had such trouble with her, the poor little dear,
And yet I'd gladly have it all again to do,
I loved her so.

FAUST.   A darling, just like you.

MARGARETA. I brought her up: she got so fond of me.
She was born after Father's death, you see,
And Mother was so desperately ill then
We thought she never would be well again,
And she got better slowly, very gradually.
She couldn't possibly, you know,   3130
Give the baby her breast; and so

I had to feed her, all alone,
With milk and water; she became my own,
And in my arms and on my breast
She smiled and wriggled and grew and grew.

FAUST. That must have been great happiness for you.

MARGARETA. But very hard as well, although I did my best.
At night she had her little cradle by
My bed; she'd hardly need to move, and I
Was wide awake.   3140
Then I would have to feed her, or else take
Her into bed with me, or if she went
On crying, I'd get up and jog her to and fro.
And then, the washing started at cock-crow;
Then I would shop and cook. That's how I spent
The whole of every blessed day.
So you see, sir, it's not all play!
But you eat well, and you sleep well that way.
                    [*They pass on.*]

MARTHA. We women do have an unlucky fate!   [F.I.
A confirmed bachelor's hard to educate.   3150

MEPHISTOPHELES. I'm sure it takes a lady of your kind,
Madam, to make one change one's mind.

MARTHA. But tell me truly now, sir: have you never   [UR
Lost your hard heart to any woman ever?

MEPHISTOPHELES. One's own fireside, we are so often
told,
And a good wife, are worth silver and gold.

MARTHA. I'm asking: have you never felt the inclination—?

MEPHISTOPHELES. I've always been treated with great
consideration.

MARTHA. I meant: have things not been serious at any time?

MEPHISTOPHELES. Trifling with ladies is a very serious   3160
crime.

MARTHA. Oh, you don't understand!

MEPHISTOPHELES.   That grieves me, I confess!
But I do understand—your great obligingness.
                    [*They pass on.*]

FAUST. You knew me again, sweetheart, immediately,
  Here in the garden? Is it really true?

MARGARETA. You saw me cast my eyes down, didn't you.

FAUST. And you've forgiven the liberty
  I took outside the church, the insulting way
  I spoke to you the other day?

MARGARETA. It was a shock—you see, it never had
  Happened before. No one ever says bad   3170
  Things of me, and I thought: did I somehow
  Seem lacking in modesty to him just now?
  He suddenly just thinks, quite without shame:
  'I'll pick this girl up'; maybe I'm to blame?—
  I must confess that something in my heart,
  I don't know what, began quite soon to take your part;
  In fact I got quite cross with myself, too,
  For not being quite cross enough with you.

FAUST. Oh my sweet!

MARGARETA.   Wait!
  [She picks a daisy and begins pulling off the petals one
  by one.]

FAUST.   What's this for? A bouquet?

MARGARETA. No!

FAUST.   What?

MARGARETA. You'll laugh at me; it's just a game we play. 3180
  [She murmurs as she picks off the petals.]

FAUST. What's this you're murmuring?

MARGARETA [half aloud].   He loves me—loves me not—

FAUST. You dear beloved little thing!

MARGARETA [continuing]. Loves me—not—loves
  me—not—
  [pulling off the last petal and exclaiming with joy].
  He loves me!

FAUST.   Yes, my love! The flower speaks,
  And let it be your oracle! He loves you:
  Do you know what that means? He loves you!

[*He clasps both her hands in his.*]

MARGARETA. I'm trembling all over!

FAUST. Don't be afraid! Oh, let my eyes,
My hands on your hands tell you what
No words can say: 3190
To give oneself entirely and to feel
Ecstasy that must last for ever!
For ever!—For its end would be despair.
No, never-ending! Never ending!

> [MARGARETA *presses his hands, frees herself and runs*
> *away. He stands lost in thought for a moment, then*
> *follows her.* MARTHA *enters with* MEPHISTOPHELES.]

MARTHA. It's getting dark.

MEPHISTOPHELES.   Yes, and we must be gone.

MARTHA. I would gladly invite you to stay on,
But this place has sharp eyes, and sharp tongues too.
It's as if they all had nothing else to do,
Day in, day out,
But try to sniff their neighbours' business out.   3200
It's wicked! But one can't escape their talk.
And our young pair?

MEPHISTOPHELES.   Gone fluttering up that garden walk;
Wild wayward butterflies!

MARTHA.   He seems to have found
His true love.

MEPHISTOPHELES. So has she. That's how the world goes
round!

16 · A SUMMERHOUSE*   [UR

> [MARGARETA *runs in, hides behind the door, puts a*
> *fingertip to her lips and peeps through a crack.*]

MARGARETA. He's coming!

FAUST [*entering*].   Little rogue! I've caught you now,
You tease! [*He kisses her.*]

MARGARETA [*throwing her arms round him and returning*
his kiss].

Darling, I love you so, I can't say how!

[MEPHISTOPHELES *knocks at the door.*]

FAUST [*stamping his foot*]. Who's there?

MEPHISTOPHELES.   A friend!

FAUST.   A beast!

MEPHISTOPHELES.   It's time to leave, I fear.

MARTHA [*entering*]. Yes, sir, it's getting late.

FAUST.   May I not escort you, then?

MARGARETA. My mother would—Goodbye!

FAUST.   Then I must go, my dear?
  Goodbye!

MARTHA.   *Adieu!*

MARGARETA.   Till we soon meet again!   3210

[FAUST *and* MEPHISTOPHELES *leave.*]

Oh goodness gracious, what a lot
Of clever thoughts in his head he's got!
I'm so ashamed, I just agree
With all he says, poor silly me.
I'm just a child and don't know a thing,
How can he find me so interesting?

17 A FOREST CAVERN*   [FRA

FAUST [*alone*]. Oh sublime Spirit!* You have given me,
  Given me all I asked for. From the fire
  You turned your face to me, and not in vain.
  You gave me Nature's splendour for my kingdom,   3220
  And strength to grasp it with my heart. No mere
  Cold curious inspection was the privilege
  You granted me, but to gaze deep, as into
  The heart of a dear friend. Before my eyes,
  Opened by you, all living creatures move
  In sequence: in the quiet woods, the air,
  The water, now I recognize my brothers.
  And when the storm-struck forest roars and jars,
  When giant pines crash down, whose crushing fall

Tears neighbouring branches, neighbouring tree-trunks   3230
    with them,
And drones like hollow thunder through the hills:
Then in this cavern's refuge, where you lead me,
You show me to myself, and my own heart's
Profound mysterious wonders are disclosed.
And when the pure moon lifts its soothing light
As I look skywards, then from rocky cliffs
And dewy thickets the ensilvered shapes
Of a lost world, hovering there before me,
Assuage the austere joy of my contemplation.

Oh now I feel this truth, that for mankind   3240
No boon is perfect. To such happiness,
Which brings me ever nearer to the gods,
You added a companion, who already
Is indispensable to me, although
With one cold mocking breath he can degrade me
In my own eyes, and turn your gifts to nothing.
He stirs my heart into a burning fire
Of passion for that lovely woman's image.*
Thus from my lust I stumble to fulfilment,
And in fulfilment for more lust I languish.   3250

[*Enter* MEPHISTOPHELES.]

MEPHISTOPHELES. Well, have you not tired yet of this
    life-style?
How strange that it still interests you!
No doubt it's good to try once in a while,
Till one moves on to something new!

FAUST. I wish you'd find some better occupation
Than to waste daylight bothering me.

MEPHISTOPHELES. Why now, I'll gladly let you be;
I take the hint; no need for explanation.
Such an ill-humoured, crazy customer
Would be no loss, my dear good sir!   3260
One slaves away all day and night
To please my lord, to guess what he'd prefer—
And there's no way to get it right.

FAUST. Oh yes, indeed, this tone's in character!
He plagues me and wants thanks for it as well.

MEPHISTOPHELES. What sort of life would you have
    had—just tell
  Me that, poor earthling!—without my
  Assistance? For some time I've cured
  Your scribble-scrabbling fancies; why,
  If I'd not been there, rest assured   3270
  You'd have already bid this world goodbye.
  And now in clefts and caves you sit
  Here like an ancient owl—what good is it?—
  Sucking some toad-like sustenance, all on your own,
  From this dank moss and dripping stone!
  A charming way to pass the year!
  You're the learned doctor still, I fear.

FAUST. Can you not understand how my life's strength
    increases
  As I walk here in these wild places?
  —Yes, if you could, you'd try to mar   3280
  My satisfaction, devil as you are!

MEPHISTOPHELES. What supernatural delight!
  Out on the mountains all the dewy night,
  Embracing earth and heaven with ecstasy,
  Swelling up into a divinity—
  Earth's guts yield to your thrusting aspiration,
  Your heart contains the six days of creation,
  So proud, so strong, such rapture, God knows what!
  A love that overflows and penetrates the lot:
  Mere mortal man no more! And then, my friend,   3290
  How does the lofty intuition end?—

            [*With a gesture.*]

I could mention how, but I'd better not.

FAUST. Shame on you!

MEPHISTOPHELES.   So! my commentaries offend
  Your modest ears, as well they may,
  And you cry shame! One must of course not say
  Out loud what modest minds are filled with anyway
  In short, good sir, by all means do
  Delude yourself if it amuses you;
  But you'll soon feel it's gone too far.

You're three parts dead again the way things are: 3300
Much more of it will wear you out,
You'll get the horrors, go clean mad no doubt.
Enough's enough!—Your sweetheart sits and waits;
She's trapped, she pines, she's grieving so!
Only on you she meditates;
You are her one great love, you know!
Your passion's first frenzy was a flood, as when
A stream overflows its banks as the snow melts in spring;
You poured it deep into her heart, poor thing—
And now your stream's run dry again.   3310
Might I suggest it would befit
Your majesty to leave this woodland throne,
Go to that poor young child and cheer her up a bit,
Reward her for her amorous moan?
The time hangs heavy on her hands;
She's watching the clouds; at her window she stands,
As they drift over the old town wall; she's all alone;
All day and half the night she sings:
If only I had a little bird's wings!
Sometimes she's blithe as a dove,   3320
Mainly she's sad, often she cries in streams,
Then she's quiet again, as it seems;
But always in love!

FAUST. You snake! you snake!

MEPHISTOPHELES [aside].   My venom begins to take!

FAUST. Let me alone, you monster! I forbid
Your tongue to speak that beautiful girl's name!
I desire her sweet body, I'm half mad
For it already; must you fan this flame?

MEPHISTOPHELES. What's it all for? She thinks you've   3330
    run away,
And there she's half right, I must say.

FAUST. She's always in my mind; no matter where
I am, I'm near to her, she's near to me;
Even the body of Christ rouses my jealousy
By having touched her lips when I'm not there.

MEPHISTOPHELES. Indeed, my friend! And what of the
      twin roes
   That feed among the lilies?* I begrudge you those!

FAUST. Clear off, disgusting pimp!

MEPHISTOPHELES.   Good! Your abuse
   Is so amusing. God himself, who made
   Us male and female, was the first to choose   3340
   That noble *métier*, joining man and maid.
   Come, let us end this scene of gloom!*   [UR
   Are you going, tell me, to your sweetheart's room,
   Or to your own last resting-place?

FAUST. What are the joys of heaven in her embrace?
   So close to her, her dear love warming me,
   Yet still I feel her misery!
   Who am I? The unhoused, the fugitive,
   The aimless, restless reprobate,
   Plunging like some wild waterfall from cliff to cliff 3350
   Down to the abyss, in greedy furious spate!
   And as I passed—she, childlike, innocent,
   A hut, a meadow on the mountain-slope,
   A home like that, such sweet content,
   Her little world, her little scope!
   And I, whom God had cursed,
   Rocks could not satisfy
   My rage to rive and burst
   And wreck as I rushed by!
   I had to ruin her, to undermine   3360
   Her peace; she was our victim, hell's and mine!
   Help me, you devil, to cut short this waiting,
   This fear! Let it be soon, if it must be!
   May her fate crush me, my own fate out-fating,
   And I be doomed with her, and she with me!

MEPHISTOPHELES. Well! now you're on the boil again,
      that's clear.
   Go to her, comfort her, you dunderhead!
   Because your silly brain can't see the way ahead,
   At once you imagine doomsday's near.
   One must keep fighting the good fight!   [FRA 3370
   You're well bedevilled now, you're one of us.

Devils must not despair, though sometimes they well
   might,
And that would be—devilish tedious.

18 · GRETCHEN'S ROOM*   [UR

[GRETCHEN *at her spinning-wheel, alone.**]

GRETCHEN.   My heart's so heavy,
            My heart's so sore,
            How can ever my heart
            Be at peace any more?

            How dead the whole world is,
            How dark the day,
            How bitter my life is   3380
            Now he's away!

            My poor head's troubled,
            Oh what shall I do?
            My poor mind's broken
            And torn in two.

            My heart's so heavy,
            My heart's so sore,
            How can ever my heart
            Be at peace any more?

            When I look from my window   3390
            It's him I must see;
            I walk out wondering
            Where can he be?

            Oh his step so proud
            And his head so high
            And the smile on his lips
            And the spell of his eye,

            And his voice, like a stream
            Of magic it is,
            And his hand pressing mine   3400
            And his kiss, his kiss!

My heart's so heavy,
My heart's so sore,
How can ever my heart
Be at peace any more?

My body's on fire
With wanting him so;
Oh when shall I hold him
And never let go

And kiss him at last 3410
As I long to do,
And swoon on his kisses
And die there too!

19 · MARTHA'S GARDEN   [UR

[MARGARETA. FAUST.]

MARGARETA. Promise me, Heinrich.*

FAUST.   Whatever I can!

MARGARETA. Then tell me what you think about religion.
I know you are a dear good man,
But it means little to you, I imagine.

FAUST. My darling, let's not talk of that. You know
I'd give my life for you, I love you so;
I wouldn't want to take anyone's faith away. 3420

MARGARETA. One must believe! That's not right what you
say!

FAUST. Ah, must one?

MARGARETA.   Oh, if only I could show you!
You don't respect the holy Sacraments, do you?

FAUST. I do.

MARGARETA. But you don't want them! You don't go
To Mass or to confession, that I know.
Do you believe in God?

FAUST.   My dear, how can
Anyone dare to say: I believe in Him?

Ask a priest how, ask a learned man,
And all their answers merely seem
To mock the questioner.

MARGARETA.   Then you don't believe?   3430

FAUST. My sweet beloved child, don't misconceive
My meaning! Who dare say God's name?
Who dares to claim
That he believes in God?
And whose heart is so dead
That he has ever boldly said:
No, I do not believe?
Embracing all things,
Holding all things in being,
Does He not hold and keep   3440
You, me, even Himself?
Is not the heavens' great vault up there on high,
And here below, does not the earth stand fast?
Do everlasting stars, gleaming with love,
Not rise above us through the sky?
Are we not here and gazing eye to eye?
Does all this not besiege
Your mind and heart,
And weave in unseen visibility
All round you its eternal mystery?   3450
Oh, fill your heart right up with all of this,
And when you're brimming over with the bliss
Of such a feeling, call it what you like!
Call it joy, or your heart, or love, or God!
I have no name for it. The feeling's all there is:*
The name's mere noise and smoke—what does it do
But cloud the heavenly radiance?

MARGARETA. Well, I suppose all that makes sense;
I think the priest says something like that too—
Just in the wording there's a difference.   3460

FAUST. It is what all men say,
All human hearts under the blessed day
Speak the same message, each
In its own speech:
May I not speak in mine?

MARGARETA. It sounds all very well, all very fine,
But there's still something wrong about it,
For you're not a Christian, I truly doubt it!

FAUST. Sweetheart!

MARGARETA.   It's always worried me
To see you keep such company.   3470

FAUST. What do you mean?

MARGARETA.   That man you have with you—
I hate him, upon my soul I do!
It pierces me to the heart like a knife.
I've seen nothing so dreadful in all my life
As that man's face and its ugly sneer.

FAUST. My poor child, why, there's nothing to fear!

MARGARETA. It's just that his presence offends me so.
I don't usually dislike people, you know!
And I'd gaze at you just as long as I can,
But it makes my blood freeze to see that man—   3480
And I think he's a scoundrel, anyway.
If I wrong him, God pardon what I say!

FAUST. Well, you know, some people just are rather odd.

MARGARETA. I wouldn't live with a man like that!
As soon as he steps through the door, you can tell
You're being looked so mockingly at
And half fiercely as well;
And he cares for nothing, not man nor God.
It's as if he'd a mark on his brow that said
That he never has loved, that his heart is dead.   3490
Each time you put your arms round me
I'm yours so completely, so warm, so free!
But I close up inside at the sight of him.

FAUST. Dear fancy, sweet foreboding whim!

MARGARETA. It upsets me so much, each time I see
Him coming, that I even doubt
If I still love you, when he's about.
Besides, when he's there, I never could pray,
And that's what's eating my heart away.
Dear Heinrich, tell me you feel the same way!   3500

FAUST. You've just taken against him, and that's all.

MARGARETA. I must go home now.

FAUST.   Oh, tell me whether
We can have some peaceful hour together,
Lie breast to breast and mingle soul with soul!

MARGARETA. Oh, if only I slept alone it would be all right,
I'd leave you my door unbolted tonight.
But my mother sleeps lightly, and if she
Were to wake up and catch us, oh goodness me,
I'd drop down dead on the very spot!

FAUST. My darling, there need be no such surprise.   3510
Look, take this little flask I've got:
You must put just three drops in her drink
And into a sweet, sound sleep she'll sink.

MARGARETA. What would I not do for your sake!
But she'll be all right again, she'll wake?

FAUST. Would I suggest it otherwise?

MARGARETA. I look at you, dear Heinrich, and somehow
My will is yours, it's not my own will now.
Already I've done so many things for you,
There's—almost nothing left to do.   3520

            [*Exit. Enter* MEPHISTOPHELES.]

MEPHISTOPHELES. Pert monkey! Has she gone?

FAUST.·   Still eavesdropping and spying?

MEPHISTOPHELES. I listened to it all most carefully.
The learned Doctor was catechized!
I hope he will find it edifying.
Girls always check up, if they're well-advised,
On one's simple old-world piety;
Their theory is, if he swallows all
That stuff, he'll be at our beck and call.

FAUST. To your vile mind, of course, it's merely quaint
That that dear loving soul, filled with her faith,   3530
The only road to heaven that she knows,
Should so torment herself, poor saint,
Thinking her lover's damned to everlasting death!

MEPHISTOPHELES. You supersensual sensual wooer,
   A pretty maid has led you by the nose.

FAUST. You misborn monster, spawn of fire and shit!

MEPHISTOPHELES. And physiognomy, how well she's
     mastered it!
   When I'm around she feels—just what, she's not quite
     sure;
   My face, forsooth! conceals some runic spell;
   She guesses I'm a genius certainly,*   3540
   Perhaps indeed the Devil as well.
   So, it's to be tonight—?

FAUST.   What's that to you?

MEPHISTOPHELES. I take a certain pleasure in it too!

20 · AT THE WELL   [UR

[GRETCHEN and LIESCHEN with water-jugs.]

LIESCHEN. You've heard about Barbara, haven't you?

GRETCHEN. No; I hardly see anyone.

LIESCHEN.   Well, it's true!
   She's done it at last; Sybil told me today.
   Made a fool of herself. That's always the way
   With those airs and graces.

GRETCHEN.   But what?

LIESCHEN.   It stinks!
   There's two to feed now when she eats and drinks!

GRETCHEN. Oh! . . .   3550

LIESCHEN. And serve her right at last, I say.
   Throwing herself at the lad for so long!
   Always on his arm, always walking along,
   Off to the villages, off to the dance;
   Oh, she had an eye to the main chance!
   Such a beauty, of course, she must lead the way!
   He courts her with pastries and wine every day;
   She's even so shameless, the little minx,

That she can accept presents from him, she thinks!
Cuddling and petting hour by hour— 3560
Well, now she's lost her little flower!

GRETCHEN. Poor thing!

LIESCHEN. Don't tell me you're sorry for her!
Why, all the rest of us, there we were,
Spinning,* our mothers not letting us out
In the evenings, while she's sitting about
In dark doorways with her fancy man,
Lingering in alleys as long as they can!
Well, now she'll have her church penance to do,
And sit in her smock on the sinner's pew!

GRETCHEN. But surely he'll marry her now!

LIESCHEN. Not he! 3570
A smart boy like that, there are fish in the sea
In plenty for him; he's not such a fool!
Anyway, he's left.

GRETCHEN. That's wrong of him!

LIESCHEN. Well,
If she gets him, she'll get the rest of it too.
The boys'll snatch the flowers from her head,
And we'll throw her none, just chopped straw instead!*
[Exit.]

GRETCHEN [as she walks home]. What angry things I used
to say
When some poor girl had gone astray!
I used to rack my brains to find
Words to condemn sins of that kind; 3580
Blacker than black they seemed to be,
And were still not black enough for me,
And I crossed myself and made such a to-do—
Now that sin of others is my sin too!
Oh God! but all that made me do it
Was good, such dear love drove me to it!

21 · BY A SHRINE INSIDE
THE TOWN WALL*

*[An icon of the Mater Dolorosa stands in the alcove
with vases of flowers in front of it.* GRETCHEN *puts
fresh flowers into the vases, then prays.]*

GRETCHEN. O Virgin Mother, thou
Who art full of sorrows, bow
Thy face in mercy to my anguish now!

O Lady standing by   3590
Thy Son to watch Him die,
Thy heart is pierced to hear His bitter cry.

Seeking the Father there
Thy sighs rise through the air
From his death-agony, from thy despair.

Who else can know
The pain that so
Burns in my bones like fire from hell?
How my wretched heart is bleeding,
What it's dreading, what it's needing,   3600
Lady, only you can tell!

Wherever I go, wherever,
It never stops, just never;
Oh how it hurts and aches!
When I'm alone, I'm crying,
I cry as if I'm dying,
I cry as my heart breaks.

The flower-pots by my window
I watered with tears like dew
When in the early morning   3610
I picked these flowers for you.

The early sun was gleaming,
I sat up in my bed
My eyes already streaming
As the new dawn turned red.

> Help! Save me from shame and death!—O thou
> Who art full of sorrows, thou
> Most holy Virgin, bow
> Thy face in mercy to my anguish now!

22 · NIGHT. THE STREET OUTSIDE GRETCHEN'S DOOR* [UR/F.I.

VALENTINE [*a soldier, Gretchen's brother*]. [UR

I used to drink with the other chaps; 3620
That's when one likes to boast. Perhaps
They'd start to sing their girl-friends' praises—
All lovely girls, like a ring of roses;
And round and round the full toasts went.
I'd sit there calm and confident,
With my elbows on the table-top;
Sit there and stroke my beard meanwhile,
Wait for their blethering to stop,
Then fill my glass, and with a smile
I'd say: All honour where honour's due! 3630
But in this whole land is there one girl who
Can compare with Meg, my sister so sweet,
One worthy to fasten the shoes to her feet?
Then clink! the toasts went round again,
And some of the fellows exclaimed: he's right!
She's the pride of her sex, she's the heart's delight!
And the boasters and praisers sat silent then.
And now—what now?—Shall I tear my hair,
Shall I run up the walls?—I could despair.
Every one of those blackguards now is free 3640
To sneer and wrinkle his nose at me;
I must sweat, like a debtor who can't pay,
At each chance remark that drops my way!
Oh, yes! I could knock out their brains! But why?
I still couldn't tell them they're telling a lie!

Who's there? Who's sneaking to her door? [F.I.
There are two of them, if I know the score.

If it's him, I'll take him while I can—
He'll not leave here a living man!

[Enter FAUST and MEPHISTOPHELES.]

FAUST. Look, through the window of the sacristy   [UR 3650
    The sanctuary-lamp gleams up and glows,
    Yet to each side, how dim, how weak it shows,
    As darkness clusters round it! So in me
    Night falls and thickens in my heart.

MEPHISTOPHELES. Well, I could act a tom-cat's part,
    Slinking the streets to find a way
    Up to the rooftops where I'll play!
    I feel a healthy appetite
    For some thieving, some lechery tonight.
    Walpurgis, Night of the Wild Witching,*   [F.I. 3660
    Is coming soon; already I'm twitching
    With expectation. Just you wait!
    One doesn't sleep through that fine date.

FAUST. Is that your buried gold that's rising now,*
    Back there? It blooms, it shines at us somehow!

MEPHISTOPHELES. Quite so; you soon will have the pleasure
    Of lifting out the pot of treasure.
    I took a squint into it too;
    Fine silver coins I've raised for you.

FAUST. Was there no jewellery you could find?   3670
    My mistress loves those golden toys.

MEPHISTOPHELES. I did see something of the kind;
    A necklace. Pearls that are her eyes.*

FAUST. That's good; it makes me sad to go
    Without a gift to her, you know.

MEPHISTOPHELES. Come now, you should get used to ladies;
    Sometimes one enjoys their favours gratis.
    But look! The stars are in the sky,
    And being a gifted artist, I
    Will now sing her a moral song,   3680
    To confuse her sense of right and wrong.

[He sings, accompanying himself on a zither.]

Who stands before
Her sweetheart's door
Once more, once more,
With early morning starting?
Poor Kate, beware!
You'll enter there
A maid so fair—
No maid you'll be departing!

Men must have fun,   3690
But when it's done
They'll up and run—
They're thieves, why should they linger?
Poor darlings all,
Beware your fall:
Do nothing at all
Till you've got the ring on your finger!

VALENTINE. Who are you serenading here?
  Damned rat-catcher!* The devil take
  Your zither first; God's blood! I'll make   3700
  Him take the singer next, d'you hear?

MEPHISTOPHELES. The instrument's a write-off, I'm
  afraid.

VALENTINE. Now draw, and there'll be corpses made!

MEPHISTOPHELES. Doctor, don't back away! Now, quick!
  Keep close to me, move as I do.
  Come on, out with your tickle-stick!
  Now lunge! I'll parry him for you.

VALENTINE. Well, parry this one!

MEPHISTOPHELES.   Certainly!

VALENTINE. And that!

MEPHISTOPHELES.   Why not?

VALENTINE.   The devil it must be!
  What fencing's this? I think my hand's gone lame.   3710

MEPHISTOPHELES [to FAUST]. Strike now!

VALENTINE [falling]. Oh God!

MEPHISTOPHELES.   Now the poor lout is tame!

But now let's go! We must get out of here:
They'll start a hue and cry, and all that chatter.
The police I can deal with, but I fear
The High Assize is quite another matter.*

[*Exit with* FAUST.]

MARTHA [*at her window*]. Come out! Come out!

GRETCHEN [*at her window*].   Please, fetch a light!

MARTHA. They're cursing and shouting! There's a fight!

THE CROWD [*gathering*]. There's someone dead, there's one!

MARTHA [*coming out of her house*]. Where did the
    murderers run?

GRETCHEN [*coming out of her house*]. Who's lying here?

THE CROWD.   Your mother's son.   3720

GRETCHEN. Oh God in heaven! What have they done!

VALENTINE. I'm dying; it's a thing soon said,
    And even sooner the thing's real.
    You women-folk, why weep and wail?
    Just hear me speak before I'm dead.

[*They all gather round him.*]

Meg, listen: you're still a poor young chit,
    You've not yet got the hang of it,
    You're bungling things, d'you see?
    Just let me tell you in confidence:
    Since you're a whore now, have some sense   3730
    And do it properly!

GRETCHEN. My brother! God! What do you mean?

VALENTINE. Leave God out of this little scene!
    What's done is done, I'm sorry to say,
    And things must go their usual way.
    You started in secret with one man;
    Soon others will come where he began,
    And when a dozen have joined the queue
    The whole town will be having you!

Let me tell you about disgrace: 3740
    It enters the world as a secret shame,

Born in the dark without a name,
With the hood of night about its face.
It's something that you'll long to kill.
But as it grows, it makes its way
Even into the light of day;
It's bigger, but it's ugly still!
The filthier its face has grown,
The more it must be seen and shown.

There'll come a time, and this I know,   3750
All decent folk will abhor you so,
You slut! that like a plague-infected
Corpse you'll be shunned, you'll be rejected,
They'll look at you and your heart will quail,
Their eyes will all tell the same tale!
You'll have no gold chains or jewellery then,
Never stand in church by the altar again,
Never have any pretty lace to wear
At the dance, for you'll not be dancing there!
Into some dark corner may you creep   3760
Among beggars and cripples to hide and weep;
And let God forgive you as he may—
But on earth be cursed till your dying day!

MARTHA. Commend your soul to God's mercy too!
   Will you die with blasphemy on you?

VALENTINE. Vile hag, vile bawd! If I could take
   You by the skinny throat and shake
   The life out of you, that alone,
   For all my sins it would atone.

GRETCHEN. Oh, brother—how can I bear it—how—   3770

VALENTINE. I tell you, tears won't mend things now.
   When you and your honour came to part,
   That's when you stabbed me to the heart.
   I'll meet my Maker presently—
   As the soldier I'm still proud to be.

                    [He dies.]

23 · A CATHEDRAL*

[*A Mass for the Dead. Organ and choral singing.*
GRETCHEN *in a large congregation. An* EVIL
SPIRIT *behind* GRETCHEN.]

THE EVIL SPIRIT. How different things were for you,
    Gretchen,
  When you were still all innocence,
  Approaching that altar,
  Lisping prayers from your little
  Worn prayer-book;   3780
  Your heart had nothing in it
  But God and child's play!
  Gretchen!
  What are you thinking?
  What misdeed burdens
  Your heart now? Are you praying
  For your mother's soul, who by your doing
  Overslept into long, long purgatorial pains?
  Whose blood stains your doorstep?
  —And under your heart is there not   3790
  Something stirring, welling up already,
  A foreboding presence,
  Feared by you and by itself?

GRETCHEN. Oh God! Oh God!
  If I could get rid of these thoughts
  That move across me and through me,
  Against my will!

THE CHOIR. *Dies irae, dies illa**
        Solvet saeclum in favilla.
            [*Organ.*]

THE EVIL SPIRIT. God's wrath seizes you!   3800
  The Last Trumpet scatters its sound!
  The graves shudder open!
  And your heart
  That was at rest in its ashes
  Is resurrected in fear,

Fanned again to the flames
Of its torment!

GRETCHEN. Let me get away from here!
It's as if the organ
Were choking me   3810
And the singing melting
The heart deep down in me!

THE CHOIR. *Judex ergo cum sedebit,*
            Quidquid latet adparebit,
            Nil inultum remanebit.

GRETCHEN. I can't breathe!
The great pillars
Are stifling me,
The vaulted roof
Crushes me!—Give me air!   3820

THE EVIL SPIRIT. Hide yourself! Sin and shame
Cannot be hidden.
Air? Light?
Woe on you!

THE CHOIR. *Quid sum miser tunc dicturus?*
            Quem patronum rogaturus,
            Cum vix justus sit securus?

THE EVIL SPIRIT. Souls in bliss
Have turned their faces from you.
They shrink from touching you,   3830
For they are pure!
Woe!

THE CHOIR.
            Quid sum miser tunc dicturus?

GRETCHEN. Neighbour! Your smelling-salts!
                [She faints.]

24 · WALPURGIS NIGHT*   [F.I.

[*The Harz Mountains, near Schierke and Elend.* FAUST
and MEPHISTOPHELES.]

MEPHISTOPHELES. Wouldn't you like a broomstick?
    I confess
  I wish I had a randy goat to ride!
  We'll never reach the summit at this pace.

FAUST. I've still got my two legs, a stout stick at my side,
  And they're quite good enough for me.
  Our route's not long—why make it less?   3840
  These valleys are a labyrinth; let's see
  Them first, then climb the rocky heights!
  Look how that stream pours down perpetually:
  The walk's worth while to see such sights.
  The birch-trees are all touched by spring
  Already, even the pines revive;
  Do our limbs too not come alive?

MEPHISTOPHELES. Well, frankly, I can't feel a thing.
  My limbs are in a wintry mood;
  I'd prefer frost and snow along this road.   3850
  How gloomily the humpbacked moon is rising,
  With what a feeble red belated glow!
  With every step one takes, it's not surprising
  One bumps into some tree or rock. I know:
  I'll call a will-o'-the-wisp! Excuse me. Why,
  There's one, blazing like merry hell. What ho,
  My little friend! Approach us, please!
  Stop wasting all that energy,
  And light our way uphill.

WILL-O'-THE-WISP.   I'll try,
  Out of respect for you, my lord, to force   3860
  My wayward nature; but we like to tease,
  And normally pursue a zigzag course!

MEPHISTOPHELES. I see; you like to imitate mankind.
  Well, just go straight if you don't mind,
  Or I'll blow out your flicker with one puff!

WILL-O'-THE-WISP. You're master here, I see that well
    enough!
  I'll do my best to do just as you say.
  But the whole mountain's magic-mad tonight, good sir,
  And you must not be too particular
  If a will-o'-the-wisp's to show the way!   3870

  [FAUST, MEPHISTOPHELES, WILL-O'-THE-WISP,
              singing in turn.]*

          World of magic, land of dreams!
          We have entered you, it seems.
          Wisp, lead well and show your paces;
          We must get there, we must hurry
          In these wild, wide-open places!

          Trees and trees in quick succession:
          See them pass us, see them scurry!
          Feel the beetling cliffs' oppression,
          Hear those rocks as the winds roar,
          How their long snouts snort and snore!*   3880

          Through the rocks and through the grasses
          Streams and streamlets swift descending,
          Murmuring water, murmuring voices:
          Are they singing love's unending
          Sweet complaint from days gone by?
          How we hope, and how we sigh!
          And an echo, like the story
          Of old times, still makes reply.

          Night-owl, screech-owl: can you hear them?
          Pie and peewit territory: 3890
          All awake as we pass near them.
          Bloated long-legged salamanders
          Haunt the thicket; all around us
          Twisting roots that would ensnare us,
          Slither snakelike from the sand,
          Writhing from the rocks to scare us;
          Trunk-knots, tree-growths, how they thrive,
          Thick and fleshy, long and live,
          Each a reaching polyp-hand,

Tangled tentacles to bind us!   3900
Mice in many-coloured hosts
Scuttle over moss and moor,
And a million fireflies lure
Us to follow, glittering ghosts
Swarming densely to confound us.

Are we coming? are we going?
Are we standing? There's no knowing!
All is whirling, all is flowing!
Rocks and trees with weird grimaces
Shift their shapes and change their places;   3910
Wild fires wander, teeming, growing.

MEPHISTOPHELES. Hold fast to me! This middle summit
Will suit us; there's a fine view from it.
Look! This is my lord Mammon's night:*
His mountain gold shines rich and bright.

FAUST. How strangely through the hollows glimmering
Like a false dawn the dull light glows!
Into crevasses glinting, shimmering,
Into each deep abyss it goes.
Clouds drift, a vapour rises, yet   3920
Through veils of mist that radiance gleams:
It trickles like a rivulet,
Or in a full flood bursts and streams.
There down the wider vale meandering
It winds in channels by the score,
Till into close confinement wandering
It flows in single course once more.
But here, nearby, like scattered sand
Of gold, what sparks fly upwards! and
The mountain face—look, its entire   3930
Breadth, depth and height are catching fire!

MEPHISTOPHELES. Mammon lights up our palace for
these feasts;
A splendid show, you must admit.
You're lucky to have been at it.
Ah! Here come some of our wild guests.

FAUST. How the gale rages through the air!
How furiously it lashes at my head!

MEPHISTOPHELES. It will lash you right off the precipice;
    take care!
    Grab those old ribs of rock, or you'll be dead.
    A mist thickens the night.   3940
    Hear the storm in the woods! The owls
    Are startled into flight.
    Hear now, in those ever-green halls,
    The columns crack, the boughs moan
    As they split! On every side
    The mighty tree-trunks groan!
    Their roots creak, gaping wide!
    In fearful chaos they all
    Crash together as they fall,
    And through the half-choked clefts of this   3950
    Their ruin, the winds howl and hiss.
    Do you hear voices in the sky?
    Far away? And nearby?
    Yes! There it rages, up and along
    The whole mountain, a torrent of witching song!

WITCHES [in chorus]. Where have the Brocken witches
            been?
        Stubble is yellow, young corn is green.
        Now we meet again, and up we ride!
        Lord Capercailzie will preside.*
        So come away, let's make a start!   3960
        A goat can stink, a witch can fart!

A VOICE. Look, here comes Mother Baubo now!*
    She's all by herself, she rides a sow!

CHORUS. Well, let's pay honour where honour's due.
        Lead on, Dame Baubo, and we'll ride too!
        A proper dame and a proper swine,
        And the whole witch-rabble follows in line!

A VOICE. Which way did you come?

A VOICE.   By the Ilsenstein!
    Looked into the owl's nest as I passed;
    She got a surprise!

A VOICE.   Oh to hell with you!   3970
    Stop riding so fast!

A VOICE. I'm scratched to the bone!
  Just look what she's done!

WITCHES [in chorus]. The way is wide, the way is long;
                The devil take this crazy throng!
                The broomstick scratches, the pitchfork pokes,
                The mother bursts, the baby chokes.*

WARLOCKS [half chorus]. We're lagging behind at the
                women's tails,
                We're crawling after them like snails;
                For on the way to Satan's bed   3980
                A woman starts a mile ahead.

WARLOCKS [the other half]. Why worry?
                We still win these races!
                A woman's mile's a thousand paces:
                But let her hurry as she can—
                One jump's enough if you're a man!

A VOICE [above]. Come up from the tarn! You must follow
  us now!

A VOICE [from below]. We want to come, but we don't
  know how.
  The water washes us bright and clear,
  But we're barren for ever, we're still stuck here.

BOTH CHORUSES. The wind is silent, the stars hide,   3990
                The dull moon covers its face as we ride.
                A thousand sparks of hell-fire fly
                As the witching chorus rushes by!

A VOICE [from below]. Wait for me! Wait, or I'll be left
  Behind!

A VOICE [from above]. Who calls from the rocky cleft?

VOICE [below]. Take me with you! Take me with you! Stop!
  For three hundred years already I've climbed,
  And still I can never get to the top.
  I want to be there with my own kind.

BOTH CHORUSES. Fly on a broom--handle, fly on a stick; 4000
                A pitchfork or goat will do the trick!
                If you can't get off the ground today
                You're lost for ever anyway.

HALF-WITCH [*below*]. I can't keep up, I can't keep abreast,
  I'm always so far behind the rest.
    When I'm at home I don't feel right,
    Yet I don't belong on Walpurgis Night.

CHORUS OF WITCHES. Witch-unction lifts our spirits
                    high;*
          Any old trough will travel the sky,
          Any old rag will do for a sail.   4010
          You must fly tonight, or you'll always fail!

BOTH CHORUSES. And as we hover round and round
          The top,* let's skim along the ground;
          Let the blasted heath be occupied
          By the witch-clanjamphry far and wide!

          [*They settle on the ground.*]

MEPHISTOPHELES. They push, they shove, they rush,
  they rattle,
  They tug and swirl, they hiss and prattle,
  They blaze and sputter and burn and stink!
  It's a real witch-world, don't you think?
  Keep close, or we'll be swept apart somehow.   4020
  Where are you?

FAUST [*in the distance*].   Here!

MEPHISTOPHELES.   What, all that far away?
  I must assert my landlord's rights. Make way!
  Squire Voland's here.* Make way, sweet rabble! Now,
  Doctor, catch hold of me! and with some haste,
  With one leap, we'll escape from this *canaille*;
  It's all too crazy, even for my taste.
  Look, there's a light, there's quite a special glow;
  Those bushes over there have caught my eye.
  Let's slip in there now, come, let's go!

FAUST. What a spirit of paradox you are! Well then,   4030
  Lead on! An excellent idea, to climb
  The Brocken on Walpurgis Night, and spend the time
  Hiding out in some isolated den!

MEPHISTOPHELES. Look how that jolly camp-fire gleams!
  A pleasant social gathering, it seems.

One's not alone in select company.

FAUST. But the summit's where I'd rather be!
There's swirling smoke there, fire from hell.
The mob streams up to Satan's throne;
I'd learn things there I've never known.   4040

MEPHISTOPHELES. And meet new mysteries as well.
Let the great mad world go its way;
It's cosy here, so why not stay?
The great world, as you know, by subdivision
Turns into small worlds; it's an old tradition.
Why, look! young naked witchlings, fresh and sweet!
Older hags too, more wisely dressed.
Don't let me down; let's do our best!
It's not much trouble, and it's such a treat.
Listen, there's music of some kind!   4050
Damned whining noise. But still, one mustn't mind.
Come; come with me—it's plain what we must do:
We'll go in, I'll present you. I'll renew
Your debt of gratitude to me! And so,
My friend, how do you like it? It's not small;
One can't see where the place ends. Look at all
Those fires burning in a row!
One can dance here, talk, drink, make love or cook a meal;
Just tell me where you'll get a better deal!

FAUST. And what role will you play to make our entry   4060
here?
The Devil, or perhaps a sorcerer?

MEPHISTOPHELES. I like to go incognito on most occasions;
But on a gala night one wears one's decorations.
The Garter, alas, I've never merited,
But here my cloven hoof will stand me in good stead.
Look at that big fat snail crawling our way!
She's got sensitive feelers on her snout,
She lost no time smelling me out.
Disguise is useless here, try as one may.
We'll go from fire to fire; come, let's start!   4070
You are the wooer, and I speak your part.

[To a group sitting round dying embers.]

What are you doing here, you ancient gentlemen,
Right at the end, sitting apart so surly
And not among the youthful hurly-burly?
You'll be alone enough when you're at home again.

A GENERAL. Who'd trust a nation now? No matter what
One's done for them, great deeds or not—
Whether it's women or the people's praise,
Only the young win either nowadays.

A MINISTER. The good old times, where did they go?   4080
This modern world's hopelessly incorrect.
That was the golden age, you know,
When you and I were treated with respect.

A PARVENU. And we didn't do badly then, we made
Our little pile, though moralists might frown.
But now we're trying to consolidate,
And suddenly it's all turned upside down.

AN AUTHOR. Where are there readers now, for prose or
    verse,
For any work of moderate good sense?
As for young people, bless their impudence   4090
And sheer conceit, one's never known it worse.

MEPHISTOPHELES [suddenly looking very old].
The nation's ripe for the last trump, I fear,
Since this is my last climb up here.
My cask is drained down to the dregs,
Which means the world must be on its last legs.

A PEDLAR-WITCH*. Gentlemen, pause a moment, if you
    please!
Don't miss this opportunity!
I offer goods in great variety:
Where did you last see things like these?
Yet, though my stall's unique, you'll find   4100
Not one thing among all this lot
That in some way, some time, has not
Injured the world or harmed mankind.
No dagger here that's not shed blood, no cup
That has not poured its deadly juice
Into some wholesome life to burn it up;

No jewel that could not seduce
A lovely girl, no sword that by some traitor's blow,
Dealt from behind, has not struck down his foe!

MEPHISTOPHELES. Cousin, the times have overtaken   4110
     you.
What's done is done, what's said is said!
Try peddling novelties instead!
Nothing will sell unless it's new.

FAUST. I almost could forget myself today.
This is some fairground, I must say!

MEPHISTOPHELES. The whole mob streams and strives
     uphill;
One thinks one's pushing, and one's pushed against
     one's will.

FAUST. What woman's that?

MEPHISTOPHELES.   Look at her carefully;
Her name is Lilith.*

FAUST.   Who?

MEPHISTOPHELES.   Adam's first wife. Beware!
There is strong magic in her hair;   4120
She needs no other ornament. That net
Can catch young men, and doesn't let
Her victims go again so easily.

FAUST. There's two of them, one old, one young; and I'll be
     bound
They've both been covering the ground.

MEPHISTOPHELES. Today it's practically non-stop.
Come, let's join in, look! they've begun another hop.

FAUST [dancing with the young witch].
A pleasant dream once came to me:
I saw a lovely apple-tree,
And two fine apples hanging there;   4130
I climbed to pick that golden pair.

THE FAIR ONE. You men were always apple-mad;
Adam in Eden was just as bad.
I've apples in my garden too—
How pleased I am to pleasure you!

MEPHISTOPHELES [*with the old witch*].
    A naughty dream once came to me:
    I saw a cleft and cloven tree.
    It was a monstrous hole, for shame!*
    But I like big holes just the same.

THE OLD WITCH. Greetings, Sir Cloven-Hoof, my dear!   4140
    Such gallant knights are welcome here.
    Don't mind the outsize hole; indeed,
    An outsize plug is what we need!*

MR ARSEY-PHANTARSEY.* Damned spirit-rabble! Stop
    this insolence!
    Hasn't it been quite clearly proved to you
    You don't exist as proper people do?
    You have no standing, yet you even dance!

THE FAIR ONE [*dancing*]. What is he doing at our ball?

FAUST [*dancing*]. Oh, he's the skeleton at all
    These feasts. Others just dance, but he evaluates.   4150
    Each step we take, he thinks it must,
    If it's to count, be learnedly discussed.
    Any step forward is what most he hates;
    Shuffle round in a circle, if you will,
    As he does in his own old mill,
    And no doubt he'll approve—especially
    If you ask his opinion courteously.

MR ARSEY-PHANTARSEY. This is outrageous! Why are
    you still here?
    The world has been enlightened! You must disappear!
    —Damned lawless sprites, they dance on, nothing   4160
    daunted.
    We state the rules, and still that house in Tegel's haunted!*
    All my life long I've tried to sweep away
    This superstitious junk. It's an outrage, I say!

THE FAIR ONE. Then clear off, and stop being such a bore!

MR ARSEY-PHANTARSEY. I tell you spirits flat, I'll stand
    no more
    Of this! It's spiritual bullying.
    My spirit's scope can't cope with such a thing!

[*The dance continues.*]

Today, I see, I'm having no success.
Still, it's travel-material nonetheless;*
I'll write it up. And one day, 'pon my soul,   4170
I'll get devils and poets under my control.

MEPHISTOPHELES. He'll sit down in a swamp now;
    that's the way
He gets relief. Fat leeches make a meal
Of his backside, and so his spirits heal,
His visions and his brains all melt away!

[To FAUST, *who has stopped dancing.*]

Why have you let that pretty creature go,
Who danced and sang so charmingly?

FAUST. Ugh, as she sang, didn't you see?
A red mouse jumped out of her mouth!

MEPHISTOPHELES.   Quite so!
Remarkable! Be glad at least   4180
It was no grey and common little beast.
This is an hour of dalliance, you know!

FAUST. Then I saw—

MEPHISTOPHELES. What?

FAUST.   Mephisto, look! Right over there:
A young girl stands, so pale, so fair,
All by herself! How slowly she moves now,
As if her feet were fastened somehow!
And as I look, it seems to me
It's poor dear Gretchen that I see!

MEPHISTOPHELES. Let it alone! That is no wholesome
    vision,
But a dead thing, a magic apparition;   4190
I warn you to avoid it. Come,
And keep your distance, or its stare will seize
Your living blood, almost to stone you'll freeze.
You have heard of the Gorgon, I presume.

FAUST. It's true, it's true! Those eyes are open wide,
Closed by no loving hand! I know

Gretchen's sweet body which I have enjoyed,
Her breast that lay by mine not long ago!

MEPHISTOPHELES. Gullible fool! That's the enchanter's art:
    She takes the shape of every man's sweetheart!   4200

FAUST. Alas, what anguish, what delight!
    I cannot tear my eyes from this one sight!
    How strange it is: her lovely neck's arrayed
    With one encircling scarlet thread,
    No wider than the edge of a knife-blade!*

MEPHISTOPHELES. Yes, yes, I see it too. She can transport her head
    Under her arm if you prefer;
    Perseus, as you know, beheaded her.
    You are obsessed by these illusions still.
    Come, let's just climb this little hill.   4210
    It's like Vienna's new suburban park;
    What fun! And if they've not deluded me,
    It's actually a theatre. What a lark!
    What's going on?

MR AT-YOUR-SERVICE. The show starts again presently!
    It's a new piece, the last of seven.
    That's how our plays are always given.
    A dilettante wrote all these;
    The cast are dilettantes too.
    My dilettante-duty, if you please,
    Is now to raise the curtain; so, good sirs,   4220
    Excuse me!

MEPHISTOPHELES. Well met here, the pack of you!
    The Blocksberg's the right place for amateurs.

25 · A WALPURGIS NIGHT'S DREAM* [F.I.
or
THE GOLDEN WEDDING OF OBERON
AND TITANIA

[*An Intermezzo.*]

THE STAGE CARPENTER.

> This stage won't need old Mieding's skill:*
> We've got no work to do here.
> Dull soggy valleys, one old hill,
> And that's the total view here!

A HERALD.

> A marriage in its fiftieth year
> Is golden by duration.
> And they've stopped quarreling too, I hear:
> That's gold for jubilation.   4230

OBERON.

> Spirits, I'm here—and where are you?
> Show yourselves now, you devils!
> Your king and queen are wed anew,
> So let's begin our revels!

PUCK.

> Puck's here, my lord! I dance, I spin,
> I'm light of foot! You'll find me
> Among a hundred others in
> The giddy throng behind me.

ARIEL.

> Ariel's song is sweet and pure:
> Some ugly frumps revere it,   4240
> But it can also please and lure
> When lovely ladies hear it.

OBERON.

> Couples, if in the married state
> You look for calm contentment,
> Do as we've done and separate!
> Distance will lend enchantment.

TITANIA.

> When wife and husband can't agree,
> Immediately advise them:
> 'Madam, go south! and sir, go north!'
> That will de-polarize them.   4250

FULL ORCHESTRA [fortissimo].

> Fly-Snout and Gnat-Nose, here we are,
> With kith and kin on duty:
> Frog-in-the-Leaves and Grasshopper—
> The instrumental tutti!

A SOLO.

> Look, here comes Mr Bagpipe-Squeeze,*
> Alias Sir Soap-Bubble!
> He has to whinge and whine and wheeze,
> His blunt nose gives him trouble.

A SPIRIT STILL UNDER CULTIVATION.

> Toad-belly, spider's feet, a pair
> Of wings! A puny baby!   4260
> Hardly an animal so far;
> But a tiny poem, maybe.

A YOUNG COUPLE.

> We walk, short-stepped but high of heart,
> Through honeydew and flowers.
> Yes, you can trot with agile art,
> But flight is not yet ours.

A CURIOUS TRAVELLER.

> Is this not some stage trick again?
> Unless my eyes deceive me
> I see the godlike Oberon plain;
> Though no one will believe me.   4270

AN ORTHODOX BELIEVER.

> I see no claws, I see no tail!
> Yet there's no doubt about them:
> These goblins, like the gods of Greece,
> Are devils even without them.

A NORTHERN ARTIST.

> At present, all I can perceive
> Is sketchy, to be sure;

                   But I'll be ready soon to leave
                   On my Italian Tour.

A PURIST.

                   How did I get here? What a stew
                   Of lechery! The whole place full   4280
                   Of half-dressed witches; only two
                   Are powdered, how disgraceful!

A YOUNG WITCH.

                   Powder is like a petticoat
                   For ladies old and greying:
                   I'm naked on my billy-goat,
                   And know what I'm displaying!

A MATRON.

                   We'll not waste words on you; we know
                   Our manners and our duties.
                   You're young and fresh, but even so,
                   May you soon rot, my beauties!   4290

THE CONDUCTOR.

                   Fly-Snout and Gnat-Nose! This striptease
                   Performance is distracting.
                   Frog and Grasshopper, if you please!
                   Keep time while I'm conducting!

A WEATHERVANE [turning one way].

                   What better company does one need!
                   This place is simply swarming
                   With nubile maidens, and indeed
                   With nice young men; how charming!

THE WEATHERVANE [turning the other way].

                   I wish the earth would spring a crack
                   And swallow up the lot of them!   4300
                   I'd disappear to hell and back
                   Myself, just to get shot of them!

THE XENIA.*

                   Gadflies and bugs is what we are,
                   We're nasty little nippers;
                   We honour Satan, our papa,
                   With these respectful capers.

AUGUST VON HENNINGS.

> Just hear them buzz, just see them swarm,
> Like simple children playing!
> You'd almost think they meant no harm—
> That's what they'll soon be saying.   4310

THE MUSE-MASTER.

> I'm happy to be on the loose
> Among this Blocksberg rabble:
> Witches are easy to seduce—
> The Muse is much more trouble.

THE SOMETIME GENIUS OF THE AGE.

> One must be well-connected! Come,
> I'll launch you! Many asses
> Have climbed the Blocksberg's hump, there's room
> On Germany's Parnassus.

THE CURIOUS TRAVELLER.

> 'Tell me, who's that so tall and stiff?
> How pompously he paces!'   4320
> He's hunting Jesuits! Sniff by sniff
> He's smelling out their traces.

A CRANE.*

> 'When fishing for men's souls, one tries
> Both clear and troubled waters.'
> He'd undertake to missionize
> The Devil's own headquarters.

A WORLDLING.

> For pious folk, all means will serve
> When faith's to be expounded;
> Even on the Blocksberg, I observe,
> Conventicles are founded.   4330

A DANCER.

> 'Is that some further chorus? Why
> This sound of distant drumming?'
> It's just the bitterns' mating-cry,
> Their dreary bogland booming.

THE DANCING-MASTER.

> The bent ones leap, the dull ones hop—
> How can they call this dancing?

If they could see themselves, they'd stop
Their skipping and their prancing.

THE FIDDLER.

This lot all hate each other's guts
And long for mutual slaughter;   4340
Orpheus's lyre tamed wild brutes,
Bagpipes keep these in order.

A DOGMATIST.

Let doubters rail and critics bawl,
I'll stand by my conviction.
If there's no Devil after all,
These devils here are fiction!

AN IDEALIST.

The power of my Fantasy*
Today seems much augmented.
I must say, if all this is me,
I'm temporarily demented.   4350

A REALIST.

Is Substance now no longer sound,
Is something wrong with Matter?
I once stood four-square on the ground:
Today I'm all a-totter.

A SUPERNATURALIST.

I am delighted to be here
And pleased to meet these creatures;
For devils prove to me that there
Are higher spirit-natures.

A SCEPTIC.

They search for buried truth; maybe
The flames will lead them wrong here.*   4360
Devil and *doubt* both start with D,
So I think I belong here.

THE CONDUCTOR.

Grasshopper! Frog! I'll not endure
This clumsy ululation.
Fly-Snout and Gnat-Nose! Think of your
Professional reputation!

THE CLEVER ONES.

> We're the new *Sans-souci* élite,*
> A merry lot of clowners!
> We made no headway on our feet,
> So now we're upside-downers.   4370

THE INEPT ONES.

> Once we were shod, and got our share,
> By dancing court-attendance;
> God help us now! Our feet are bare
> In these days of independence.

WILL-O'-THE-WISPS.

> We're from the bogs and swamps, and here
> We come to join these revels.
> We may be humbly born, but we're
> Now smart and dashing devils!

A SHOOTING STAR.

> O dear, I've fallen from on high,
> A brief and brilliant meteor!   4380
> And now flat in the grass I lie:
> Who'll help me to my feet here?

THE HEAVY BRIGADE.

> Make way, make way! As we dance round*
> The grass is all downtrodden.
> We're spirits too, but spirits can
> Be very heavy-shodden.

PUCK.

> You clodhopping calf-elephants,
> How ponderously you trample!
> Puck shall be clumsiest in this dance:
> Just follow my example!   4390

ARIEL.

> Nature gave wings to some, in some
> The spirit elevates you.
> Follow me, I am light, so come!*
> The rose-red hill awaits you!

THE ORCHESTRA [*pianissimo*].

> The drifting mist, the veil of cloud,
> Are touched by dawning day now:

Leaves rustle, and the reeds are stirred—
And all is blown away now.*

26 · A GLOOMY DAY. OPEN COUNTRY.*   [UR

[FAUST and MEPHISTOPHELES.]

FAUST. In misery! In despair! Pitiably wandering about
the country for so long, and now a prisoner! Locked up
in prison as a criminal and suffering such torment, the
sweet hapless creature! So this is what it has come to!
This!—Vile treacherous demon, and you told me nothing!—Yes, stand there, stand there and roll your devilish
eyes in fury! Stand and affront me by your unendurable
presence! A prisoner! In utter ruin, delivered over to evil
spirits and the judgement of cold heartless mankind! And
meanwhile you lull me with vulgar diversions,* hide her <10>
growing plight from me and leave her helpless to her
fate!

MEPHISTOPHELES. She is not the first.

FAUST. You dog! You repulsive monster! Oh infinite
Spirit,* change him back, change this reptile back into
the form of a dog,* the shape he used so often when it
amused him to trot along ahead of me at night, suddenly
rolling at the feet of innocent wayfarers and leaping on
their backs as they fell! Change him back into his
favourite shape, let him crawl before me in the sand on <20>
his belly, let me trample this reprobate under my feet!—
Not the first!—Oh grief, grief that no human soul can
grasp, to think that more than one creature has sunk to
such depths of wretchedness, that the sins of all the
others were not expiated even by the first, as it writhed
in its death-agony before the eyes of the eternally merciful God! I am stricken to my life's very marrow by the
misery of this one girl—and you calmly sneer at the fate
of thousands!

MEPHISTOPHELES. Well, here we are again at the end <30>
of our wit's tether, the point where your poor human
brains always snap! Why do you make common cause

with us, if you can't stand the pace? Why try to fly if
you've no head for heights? Did we force ourselves on
you, or you on us?

FAUST. Stop baring your greedy fangs at me, it makes me
  sick!—Oh you great splendid Spirit, who deigned to
  appear to me, who know my heart and my soul, why did
  you chain me to this vile companion, who gorges his
  appetite on ruin and drinks refreshment from destruc- <40>
  tion?

MEPHISTOPHELES. Have you done talking?

FAUST. Save her! Or woe betide you! May the most hideous
  curse lie upon you for thousands of years!

MEPHISTOPHELES. I cannot loose the Avenger's bonds
  or open his bolts!—Save her!—Who was it who ruined
  her? I, or you?

  [FAUST glares about him in speechless rage.]

Are you snatching for the thunder? A good thing it was
not given to you wretched mortals, to blast your
adversary when he makes an innocent reply! That's the <50>
way of tyrants, venting their spleen when they're in an
embarrassing pass.

FAUST. Take me to her! I'll have her set free!

MEPHISTOPHELES. And what of the risk you'll run?
  I tell you, on that town there lies blood-guilt by your
  hand. Over the grave of the man you killed there hover
  avenging spirits, waiting for the murderer to return.

FAUST. Must I hear that from you too? May the murder
  and death of a world come upon you, you monster! Take
  me to her, I tell you, and free her!   <60>

MEPHISTOPHELES. I will take you, and I will tell you
  what I can do. Have I all the power in heaven and earth?
  I will bemuse the gaoler's senses, you can take his keys
  and bring her out with your own human hand! I'll keep
  watch, the magic horses will be ready, and I'll carry you
  both to safety. That I can do.

FAUST. Let's go at once!

27 · NIGHT. IN OPEN COUNTRY.   [UR

[FAUST and MEPHISTOPHELES storming past on
black horses.]

FAUST. What's that moving around on the gallows-mound?*

MEPHISTOPHELES. I don't know what they're doing and   4400
stewing.

FAUST. Up and down they hover, they stoop, they swoop.

MEPHISTOPHELES. A guild of witches!

FAUST. They're scattering something, it's a ritual deed.

MEPHISTOPHELES. Ride on! Ride on!

28 · A PRISON   [UR/F.I.

FAUST [with a bundle of keys and a lamp, by a small iron
door].
That shudder comes again — how long a time
Since last I felt this grief for all man's woe!
She lies behind this cold, damp wall, I know;
And her loving heart's illusion was her crime.
Do I pause as I enter this place?
Am I afraid to see her face?   4410
Quick! She must die if I keep hesitating so.

[He grasps the lock. Margareta's voice sings from inside.]
Who killed me dead?
My mother, the whore!
Who ate my flesh?
My father, for sure!
Little sister gathered
The bones he scattered;
In a cool, cool place they lie.
And then I became a birdie so fine,
And away I fly—away I fly.*   4420

FAUST [unlocking the door].
She doesn't know her lover's listening at the door,
Hearing the clank of chains, straw rustling on the floor.

[*He enters the cell.*]

MARGARETA [*hiding her face on her straw mattress*].
Oh! Oh! They're coming! Bitter death!

FAUST [*softly*]. Quiet! Quiet! I've come to set you free.

MARGARETA [*crawling towards his feet*].
If you are human, then have pity on me!

FAUST. You'll waken the gaolers, speak under your breath!

[*He takes up her chains to unlock them.*]

MARGARETA [*on her knees*]. Oh, hangman, who gave you
    this power
Over me? Who said
You could fetch me at this midnight hour?
Have pity! Tomorrow morning I'll be dead,   4430
Isn't that soon enough for you?

[*She stands up.*]

I'm still so young, still so young too!
And already I must die!
I was pretty too, and that's the reason why.
My lover was with me, now he's far away.
They tore my garland off, and threw the flowers away.
Why are you clutching at me like this?
Oh spare me! What have I done amiss?
Let me live! Must I beg you, must I implore
You in vain? I've never even seen you before!   4440

FAUST. How can I bear this any more!

MARGARETA. I'm in your power now, I'm ready to go.
Just let me feed my baby first.
I was cuddling it all last night, you know.
They took it from me; that was just
To hurt me. I killed it, is what they say.
Now things will never be the same.
They're wicked people: they sing songs against me!
There's an old tale that ends that way —
Who told them it meant me?   4450

FAUST [*throwing himself at her feet*].
It's your lover, I'm here at your feet, I came
To free you from this dreadful place!

MARGARETA [*kneeling down beside him*].
  Oh, let's kneel, and call on the saints for grace!
  Look, under that stair,
  Under the door,
  Hell's boiling there!
  You can hear the voice
  Of his angry roar!

FAUST [*aloud*]. Gretchen! Gretchen!   4460

MARGARETA [*hearing her name*]. That was my lover's
    voice!

        [*She jumps to her feet. Her chains fall off.*]

  Where is he? I heard him call to me.
  No one shall stop me, I am free!
  To his arms I'll fly,
  On his breast I'll lie!
  He stood and called 'Gretchen'! I recognized him!
  Through the wailing and gnashing of Hell so grim,
  Through the Devil's rage, through his scorn and sneer,
  I knew it was his voice, so loving and dear!

FAUST. I am here!

MARGARETA.   It is you! Oh, tell me once again!   4470
  [*Embracing him.*] It's him! It's him! Where's all my
    suffering, then?
  Where are my chains, my prison and my fear?
  It's you! You've come to rescue me from here
  And I am saved!—
  I think it's here again, that street
  Where I first saw you; and by and by
  We're waiting again, Martha and I,
  In that lovely garden where we used to meet.

FAUST [*trying to leave with her*]. Come! Come with me!

MARGARETA.   Oh stay!
  I love being anywhere when you're not away!   4480

              [*Caressing him.*]

FAUST. No, don't delay!
  Or we shall have to pay
  Most bitterly for this!

MARGARETA. What, you've forgotten so soon how to kiss?
  We're together again, my sweetest friend,
  And our kissing's come to an end?
  In your arms, why do I tremble so?
  A whole heaven used to close in on me,
  You spoke and you looked so lovingly;
  I was stifled with kisses, you'd never let go.   4490
  Oh kiss me now!
  Or I'll show you how!

[*She embraces him.*]

Oh! Your lips are dumb,
They've nothing to say!
Why has your love gone cold?
Who can have come
Between us to take it away?

[*She turns away from him.*]

FAUST. Come! Follow me! Darling, you must be bold!
  I'll hug you later on ten-thousandfold,
  Just follow me now! It's all I ask of you!   4500

MARGARETA [*turning to him*]. But is it you, can it be
  really true?

FAUST. It's me! Come!

MARGARETA.   You undid my chains, they fell apart,
  And you will take me back to your heart.
  How is it you don't find me a vile thing?
  Do you really know, my dear, who you are rescuing?

FAUST. Come! Come! The deep night's giving way to dawn!

MARGARETA. My mother's dead; I poisoned her, you see.
  I drowned my child when it was born.
  Hadn't it been God's gift to you and me?
  To you as well—It is you! Can I trust   4510
  This not to be a dream?
  Your hand! Your dear hand!—Ugh, but it's wet! You must
  Wipe off the blood! To me there seem
  To be bloodstains on it. Oh my God,

What did you do!
Put away your sword,
I beg of you!

FAUST. Forget what happened, let it be!
You are killing me.

MARGARETA. Oh no, you must survive!   4520
I'll tell you about the graves now, I'll describe
Them to you. You must arrange all this,
Tomorrow as ever is.
You must choose the places. Mother must have the best,
And my brother right next to her with his,
And me a little further off—
But not too far! Just far enough.
And my little baby at my right breast.
There'll be no one else to lie with me!—
When I clung to your side so tenderly,   4530
Oh, that was so blessed, a joy so sweet!
But I can't seem to do it now as I could;
When I come, I seem to be dragging my feet,
And you seem to be pushing me back somehow.
Yet it's still you, you're still gentle and good!

FAUST. If you feel that it's me, come with me now!

MARGARETA. Out there?

FAUST. Into freedom!

MARGARETA.   If my grave's out there,
If death is waiting, come with me! No,
From here to my everlasting tomb   4540
And not one step further I'll go!—
You're leaving? Oh Heinrich, if only I could come!

FAUST. You can! Just want to! I've opened the door!

MARGARETA. I can't leave; for me there's no hope any more.
What's the use of escaping? They'll be watching for me.
t's so wretched to have to beg one's way
Through life, and with a bad conscience too,
And to wander abroad; and if I do,
In the end they'll catch me anyway!

FAUST. I'll stay with you always!   4550

MARGARETA. Quick, oh, quick!
  Save your poor baby!
  Just follow the path
  Up the stream, uphill,
  Over the bridge,
  The wood's just beyond;
  In there, on the left, by the fence—
  He's in the pond!
  Oh, catch hold of him!
  He's struggling still,   4560
  He's trying to swim!
  Save him! Save him!

FAUST. Oh, stop, stop! Think what it is you say!
  Just one step, and we're on our way.

MARGARETA. Oh, quick, let's get to the other side
  Of the hill! My mother sits on a stone
  Up there—oh it's cold, I'm so terrified!—
  My mother's sitting up there on a stone,
  She's wagging her head, she's all alone,
  Not beckoning, not nodding her poor heavy head;   4570
  She slept so long that she'll never wake.
  She slept so that we could be happy in bed!
  Oh, those were good times, and no mistake.

FAUST. If persuasion's no use, if that's how it must be,
  I'll have to carry you off with me.

MARGARETA. Don't touch me! Put me down! No, no!
  I'll not be compelled! Don't clutch me so!
  I was always willing, as well you know.

FAUST. The day's dawning! Oh sweetheart! Sweetheart!

MARGARETA. The day! Yes, it's day! The last day dawning! 4580
  I thought it would be my wedding morning.
  Now you've been with Gretchen, don't tell anyone.
  Oh, my garland's spoilt!
  What's done is done!
  We'll meet later on;
  But I shan't be dancing.
  I can't hear them, but the crowd's advancing.
  There are so many there,

The streets and the square
Are all full; the bell tolls; they break the white rod.*   4590
Oh how they bind me and seize me, oh God!
Now I'm on the execution-chair,
And at every neck in this whole great throng
The blade strikes when that sword is swung.
The world lies silent as the grave.

FAUST. Oh why was I born, at such a cost!

MEPHISTOPHELES [appearing outside the door].
Come! One more moment and you're lost!
What's all this dallying, parleying and dithering!
My night-steeds are quivering,*
The sun's nearly risen.   4600

MARGARETA. What's that? It came out of the floor of my
          prison!
It's him! It's him! Send him away!
He can't come! This place is sacred today!
He wants me!

FAUST.   You're to live!

MARGARETA.   Oh my God, I await
Your righteous judgment!

MEPHISTOPHELES [to FAUST].
          Come! Come! Or I'll leave
You both to your fate!

MARGARETA. Oh Father, save me, do not reject me,
I am yours! Oh holy angels, receive
Me under your wings, surround me, protect me! —
Heinrich! You frighten me.   4610

MEPHISTOPHELES. She is condemned!

A VOICE [from above]   She is redeemed!

MEPHISTOPHELES [to FAUST].
Come to me!
     [He vanishes with FAUST.]

[MARGARETA'S] VOICE [from the cell, dying away].
          Heinrich! Heinrich!

EXPLANATORY NOTES

1 Introduction p. xliv (*Chorus Mysticus*), . . . *lay beyond us*: taking *unzulänglich* (in accordance with Goethe's probable intention) in its older sense of 'unreachable, inaccessible' (now *unzugänglich*) rather than in its modern sense of 'inadequate'.

2 Ibid., *visible*: taking account of the semantic association between *Ereignis* (now = 'event', but formerly often *Eräugnis*, i.e. 'manifestation') and *Auge* (eye).

3 1–32, *Dedication*: this and the other two 'prefaces' to *Faust* as a whole (*Prelude on the Stage* and *Prologue in Heaven*) were probably (the *Dedication* certainly) all written in the summer of 1797 at the time of Goethe's second resumption of work on what is now 'Part One' (cf. Introd., pp. xxvi ff.). In the four stanzas of *Dedication* the 48-year-old poet apostrophizes the fictions of his imagination of the *Urfaust* period, the friends of his youth, and the world of his youth generally. (The theme of nostalgia for lost youth recurs in the *Prelude*, 184–97.) In the 1808 edition the words *mein Leid ertönt* in line 21 ('my woes are heard') was noted as a misprint for *mein Lied ertönt* ('my song is heard'), but this correction was not made in the later editions published during Goethe's lifetime, either because he overlooked it or because he accepted *Leid* as giving a good enough alternative sense. The reading *Lied* which I have used therefore remains controversial.

4 33–242, *Prelude on the Stage*: cf. previous note, and Introd., pp. xxvii f. Although the scene contains nothing that seems specifically relevant to *Faust*, the Clown ('*Lustige Person*') may be thought of as representing the comic element in the play, including Part Two, which has often been insufficiently appreciated even by German readers. In productions, the Clown (if the scene was included at all) has usually been played by the same actor as Mephistopheles, and this seems to be in keeping with Goethe's intention; similarly, the Poet and the Director may be thought to parallel Faust and 'the Lord' respectively.

5 243–353, *Prologue in Heaven*: cf. Introd., pp. xxviii–xxxv. The general conception is based on Job 1: 6–12. The traditional name 'Mephistopheles' for Faustus's devil, going back to the earliest chapbooks, is of uncertain derivation, and Goethe also leaves his position in the demonological hierarchy unclear.

6 334 f.: the Serpent of the Garden of Eden story (Genesis 3), thought of as the archetypal tempter and thus related to the Devil.

7 339, *ironic scold*: *Schalk* in modern German has come to mean merely 'mischievous rogue', but Goethe is here probably using it in an idiosyncratic sense (developed under the influence of a Swiss usage known to him and of certain literary and personal encounters) which implies someone possessed by *esprit de contradiction* and given to mocking, negativistic attitudes. Goethe drew attention to this special sense of *Schalk* in a minor literary work written a year or two after the *Prologue*, called *The Good Women*, a short story or conversation-piece in which the concept *Schalk* is lightheartedly analysed with application to one of the female characters. In the case of Mephistopheles the word emphasizes his negative and sardonic view of things and his usual expression of this in cold and witty intellectual irony. For the translation 'the ironic scold' an acceptable though less exact alternative would be 'the Ironist'.

8 342 (German text 343): *als Teufel schaffen* could mean 'create (be creative) as the Devil (i.e. in his devilish fashion)' or 'be busily active (in devilish fashion)'; both senses are probably intended.

9 354–605: the *Urfaust* begins with this sequence, and thus rather more than half of the scene *Nacht* consists of material originally written between 1772 and 1775. Goethe followed the puppet-play tradition (derived from Marlowe) of introducing Faust with his monologue about the futility of learning.

10 354 ff., 360: in the traditional medieval division of the academic faculties, 'Philosophy' embraced the Arts subjects, in which Faust has taken the degree of Master: he is also Doctor in the three higher faculties, of Law, Medicine, and Theology (cf. the similar classification in the Student scene, 1896–2036).

11 362: this suggests that Faust is perhaps in his thirties; in the Scene *A Witch's Kitchen*, witten about fifteen years later, Goethe seems to think of him as about 50 (2340 f.).

12 420, *Nostradamus*: Michel de Notredame, a sixteenth-century French astrologer. His work, which includes no known books on magic, was not directly known to Goethe, who here fictionally associates him with Faust.

13 429 (stage direction): Goethe derived the idea of the 'Sign of the Macrocosm' from his early alchemical and astrological reading, which included such works as the *Opus mago-cabbalisticum et theosophicum* of Georg von Welling (1652–1727) and the *Paradoxical Discourses or Uncommon Opinions on the Macrocosm and Microcosm* by Franziskus Merkurius van Helmont (1618–99). In the traditional language of such studies, the 'great order'

(macrocosm) of Nature was distinguished from the human 'little order' (microcosm), and the two were held to be magically related in complex ways which could be represented in signs and diagrams. Cf. also Note 14.

14 459 (stage direction): no precise antedecent or source is known for the 'Earth Spirit' which Faust here invokes, and it seems to be essentially an original invention by the young Goethe. Its status and its relationship to Faust and Mephistopheles are only ambiguously indicated in the text, and this question has been endlessly discussed. In the Spirit's self-definition in 501–9, which is perhaps the key passage, it appears as the creative and destructive force of terrestrial Nature, weaving 'the living garment of God' (strictly, 'of the Deity', *der Gottheit*); and in another *Urfaust* scene (Sc. 26) Faust remembers it as a 'great, splendid' spirit. On the other hand, it appears from that same scene (cf. Note 124) to be associated with Mephistopheles and to be in some way his master. It is a 'spirit of the earth', not of heaven. In biblical tradition the Devil is a god or ruler of 'this world', and in the Faust chapbook which Goethe had read he is twice referred to as 'the earthly god' (*der irdische Gott*). It is also notable that in the original *Urfaust* version of the stage direction after 459 the Spirit was described as appearing to Faust not only 'in a red flame' but also 'in a repugnant form' (*in widerlicher Gestalt*), a phrase which Goethe later deleted. This 'earthy' spirit thus seems to have diabolic as well as divine or God-serving attributes. It has been suggested that whereas the 'Sign of the Macrocosm' (cf. Note 13 and lines 430–53) symbolizes a kind of lofty mystical contemplation, the Earth Spirit represents physical activity and involvement with the processes of earthly life, so that Faust in turning from the former to the latter (454–61) is making a momentous decision which will put him in the power of Mephistopheles. This has been seen as a modernized, attentuated echo of the motif in the old Faustus tradition whereby, as in Marlowe's play, Faustus ignores the counsels of a good angel and accepts those of an evil spirit. Moreover, the Earth Spirit's closing words in the present scene (512 f.) are scarcely intelligible except as a scornful relegation of Faust to the more suitable companionship of the baser spirit Mephistopheles. For further discussion of the Earth Spirit problem see Introd., pp. xxiv f. and xxxi f.

15 519: Faust's 'famulus' or academic servant was called Christoph Wagner in the first Faust-book of 1587. Anachronistically, Goethe uses the figure of Wagner to represent aspects of eighteenth-century culture which he wishes to ridicule (com-

placent faith in man's rational faculties and in academic learning, the assumption that moral edification is the essential purpose of art and rhetorical skill its essential means, the optimistic doctrine of automatic progress, etc.). Faust's speeches express the critique of these values by the young Goethe and his generation.

16 606 ff.: this is the beginning of the later-added 'infill material' (cf. Introd., pp. xxxv f.) with which Goethe closed the gap in the *Urfaust* version between the departure of Wagner and the entry of the Student (1868). Nearly all of it was written between 1798 and 1801 (lines 598–601 were also inserted at this stage as a bridge-passage connecting the scene Night with the ensuing Easter Day sequence (737–1177)). Faust's second soliloquy is partly a restatement of some of the themes already introduced in the opening *Urfaust* material (354–417); these are developed in a more 'classical' verse style and intermingled with further general reflections. It is notable that Goethe does not (as might have seemed natural or logical) choose Faust's decision to commit suicide (686–736) as the point at which to introduce Mephistopheles; instead, the latter's appearance is deferred until after a sequence of scenes (737–1237) which establish Faust in a more affirmative mood and in which Christian symbolism is prominently used.

17 737–807: the angelic and other choruses heard by Faust are presumably a supernatural intervention, like the spirit voices in Sc. 7, and not real singing from a nearby church. Goethe is thought to have begun writing this part of Sc. 4 on 9 April 1798, which was Easter Monday, shortly after hearing Karl Heinrich Draun's oratorio, *The Death of Jesus* (1775).

18 770–8: Goethe here adds a new dimension to Faust by ascribing to him a youthful period of fervent religious belief, referred to again in 1023–9, and reminiscent of Goethe's own Pietistic phase in his early twenties.

19 941–8: to establish some continuity between this later-written scene of the Easter walk and the Wagner scene of the *Urfaust* material, Goethe reintroduces the figure of Wagner as the narrow-minded bookish pedant, the contrasting foil to the visionary Faust (cf. 522 ff., 602–5, and 1147–63).

20 997–1055: in the folk tradition Faust was a peasant's son, reputed to have acquired out-of-the-way scientific knowledge and to be able to cure people with herbs and potions. In Goethe's version his father was a doctor and alchemist, like that of Paracelsus to whom an allusion is perhaps intended. Faust describes (1038–47)

his father's alchemical experiments, using the esoteric jargon of the art: chemical substances of different colours would be 'married' in a retort and forced by heat and evaporation from this 'bridal chamber' into another, in which an iridescent deposit would appear (the 'Young Queen', thought to possess healing powers). In Book VIII of his autobiography, *Poetry and Truth*, the elderly Goethe described with a certain irony the similar experiments he himself had carried out at the age of 20 in his parents' house in Frankfurt.

21 1110–25: the inner polarity of which Faust here speaks appears to resolve itself into a conflict between dependence on sensuous earthly experience on the one hand and intellectual aspiration on the other (the latter impulse also being ascribed to Wagner). There is no very clear continuity between the conflict expressed in these terms and Faust's state of mind in the *Urfaust* material, where he seemed to be utterly repudiating what Wagner stood for. Nor does Faust's ensuing wish (1118–21) to be borne aloft, not to his intellectual ancestors (as in 1117) but to 'new many-coloured life', seem to correspond exactly to either of the 'two needs' referred to in the preceding lines; it may, however, represent a synthesis between the two.

22 1126–41: Wagner's highly poetic speech about the wind-demons seems scarcely in keeping with his elsewhere established role of rationalist and pedant.

23 1148: according to the legend Faust possessed a familiar demon in the form of a large, black, hairy dog with fiery eyes called Prestigiar, which changed colour when stroked. This chapbook motif is alluded to in the sinister *Urfaust* prose scene, *A Gloomy Day*, but in the present passage (and more especially in the ensuing conjuration scene, 1178–322) it is treated as an essentially comic theme, in keeping with the classical Goethe's more detached attitude to folkloristic material of this kind (cf. Introd., p. xxiii).

24 1176: it seems to have been common, in Goethe's time and later, for students in Germany to keep dogs. (This is alluded to, for example, in Adalbert Stifter's story, *The Recluse*, published in 1844.)

25 1178–2072: this important sequence, presenting Faust's encounter and negotiation with Mephistopheles, consists officially of two substantial and complex scenes which it has become the established convention (following Goethe's own final version of the text) to designate as '*Faust's Study (I)*'' and '*Faust's Study (II)*'

(although in fact they are respectively the second and third scenes to take place in Faust's study). The division between them at 1529 is a dramatically unexplained hiatus, due simply to the abandonment of Goethe's original intention to insert a further scene at this point. The additional scene, for which only a fragmentary sketch survives, was to have featured a public academic disputation between Faust and Mephistopheles. On the evidence of a letter to Schiller which appears to allude to it, *Faust's Study (I)* (1178–529) was written in April 1800; compared with its sequel (1530–2072), which combines material (including the Student scene) written at all three of the composition-stages of Part One, it has a more integrated and logical character.

26 1184 f., 1215–23: these statements may seem inconsistent with Faust's profession of disbelief in 765. The Christian symbolism which Goethe felt artistically constrained to introduce both in this scene and in the newly written latter part of *Night* (606–807) is, however, strongly associated with the affirmation of earthly life and with the theme of activity.

27 1224–1237: Faust's retranslation of ἐν ἀρχῇ ἦν ὁ λόγος (John 1:1) as 'in the beginning was the Deed' is not in itself alien to the Christian conception of the divine Logos as the active creative principle, but in Goethe's emphasis it both continues the *Urfaust* polemic against empty words (385, 552f., etc.) and stands out as a key statement of the theme of ceaseless activity which is central to the 1797–1801 material (cf. Introd., pp. xxxiv f.). In *Night* (705) Faust has even envisaged death as the entry to a new sphere of 'pure activity', a conception in keeping with Goethe's own later statement, reported by Eckermann (4 February 1829), that his conviction of man's survival after death 'is derived from the idea of activity'. As Faust restates his central positive principle, the dog (Mephistopheles as the antagonist of creation) howls in protest; the motif recalls the Devil's attempts to interrupt Luther as he worked on his translation of the Bible.

28 1258, *King Solomon's Key*: the *Clavicula Salomonis*, a popular handbook of spells for the conjuration of elemental spirits, first extant in the sixteenth century and still in use in the eighteenth.

29 1272: the 'Spell of the Four' conjured spirits of the four elements, fire, water, air, and earth; 'incubus' (1290), in one of its meanings, was another name for the earth-goblin whose underground activities extended to cellars and houses. Faust's use of these commands will cause the dog, if it is an elemental, to reveal itself in its true shape; if it is a devil it can be conjured with the crucifix (1298–1309) or a symbol of the Trinity (1319).

EXPLANATORY NOTES 155

30 1333 f.: Faust alludes to biblical names for the Devil such as Beelzebub (lord of flies), Apollyon (destroyer), diabolus (slanderer, liar).

31 1395 f.: the five-pointed star or pentagram has been associated since antiquity with various symbolisms. It was used by the Pythagoreans and the Gnostics as well as in the cabbalistic and alchemical systems of medieval Jewish and Christian thought, and still plays a part in Satanistic rituals. As a deformed or five-clawed 'witch-foot' it was an apotropaic magical sign in Germanic folklore. Goethe found it reproduced and discussed in a book on magic and witchcraft published in 1666 under the title *Anthropodemus Plutonicus* by Johannes Schultze ('Johannes Prätorius'), a seventeenth-century popular writer on such subjects. Geometrically and graphically the pentagram is a figure of some interest, definable as a regular pentagon whose five sides are also the bases of outward-pointing identical isosceles triangles, or as an interlocking system of five identical capital 'A's whose crossbars are the sides of the pentagon, or as five straight lines each of which begins and ends at two of five equidistant points on the circumference of a circle enclosing the figure. The pentagram thus consists of five intersecting and joining straight lines of equal length; and when the sign was, for example, drawn with consecrated chalk on a threshold as a charm against witches, it was considered important to trace these lines continuously without raising the chalk from the ground, and to take care that there was no break at any of the five angles.

32 *Faust's Study (II)*: on the problems arising from this scene (particularly from 1583–634 and 1675–706) cf. Note 25 and Introd., pp. xxxvi–xxxix.

33 1656–9: this straightforward bargain involving Faust's damnation in 'the next world' seems to be an artistically necessary concession by Goethe to the old Faust tradition. As in the *Prologue* (318–21; cf. Introd., p. xxx) its importance is immediately played down by Faust's dismissive reply (166–70).

34 1712: the reference to a 'doctoral feast' is an unexpunged trace of Goethe's original intention to write a further scene (cf. Note 25) between *Faust's Study (I)* and *Faust's Study (II)*; after abandoning this idea he characteristically left the reference standing, as well as the hiatus between the two scenes.

35 1738 f.: it is to be presumed that during or immediately after these words Faust actually does write on a piece of paper and sign his name with blood. Goethe, again characteristically, dis-

dains to insert any stage direction to this effect; like the motif of the afterlife (cf. Note 33), that of the written bond, dismissively ridiculed by Faust here and in his preceding speech, seems intended as a concession to tradition. Nor are we given any indication of what Faust writes; presumably it is an undertaking that if he loses his 'wager' (1698) the 'pact' will come into effect, that is to say he will be bound by the condition proposed by Mephistopheles in 1656-9. The 'paper signed in blood' is mentioned only twice more in the whole of the remainder of *Faust*, namely in two rather less than serious passages of Part Two (lines 6576-9 and 11,613; cf. Introd., p. xliii). In general Goethe's reduction of the contract with the Devil to a bet reduces its seriousness (cf. Introd., pp. xxxvii). The quite different assumptions of the old Faust chap-books required a less urbane treatment of the theme, as may be judged from the following extract:

. . . In audacity and transgression, Doctor Faustus executed a written instrument and document to the evil spirit. This was a blasphemous and horrible thing, which was found in his lodging after he had lost his life. I will include it as a warning to all pious Christians, lest they yield to the Devil and be cheated of body and soul . . . When these two wicked parties contracted with one another, Doctor Faustus took a penknife, pricked open a vein in his left hand (and it is the veritable truth that upon this hand were seen graven and bloody the words: *o homo fuge—id est*: o mortal fly from him and do what is right), drained his blood into a crucible, set it on some hot coals and wrote as here followeth: 'I, Johann Faustus, Dr., do publicly declare with mine own hand in covenant and by power of these presents: Whereas, mine own spiritual faculties having been exhaustively explored (including the gifts dispensed from above and graciously imparted to me), I still cannot comprehend; and whereas, it being my wish to probe further into the matter, I do propose to speculate upon the *Elementa*; and whereas mankind doth not teach such things; Now therefore have I summoned the spirit who calleth himself Mephostophiles [*sic*], a servant of the Hellish Prince in Orient, charged with informing and instructing me, and agreeing against a promissory instrument hereby transferred unto him to be subservient and obedient to me in all things; I do promise him in return that when I be fully sated of that which I desire of him, twenty-four years also being past, ended and expired, he may at such a time and in whatever manner or wise pleaseth him order, ordain, reign, rule and possess all that may be mine: body, property, flesh, blood, etc., herewith duly bound over in eternity and surrendered by covenant in mine own hand by authority and power of these presents, as well as of my mind, brain, intent, blood and will. I do now defy all living beings, all the Heavenly Host and all mankind, and this must be. In confirmation and contract whereof I have drawn out mine own blood for certification in lieu of a seal. —Doctor Faustus, the Adept in the *Elementa* and in Church Doctrine.'

(Translation from *The History of Dr Faustus*, ed. H. G. Haile; see Bibliography.)

36 1741–69: these lines, the last twenty-nine of the 'infill material' written in the third composition-phase, connect the foregoing negotiation with that part of the present scene (1770–867) which Goethe had written already and published ten years earlier (cf. Introd., pp. xxi f.). As a linking passage designed to minimize the appearance of a join, it picks up some threads from the earlier versions, alluding to the Earth Spirit (1746 f.), to Faust's longing for communion with nature (1747 f.), his disillusionment with learning (1748 f.), and his desire to experience all the joys and sufferings of mankind (1754–8); his next speech (1765–75, which contains the actual join, 1769 f.) also clearly echoes lines 464–7 of the original Earth Spirit conjuration.

37 1851–67: Mephistopheles' Iago-like soliloquy (the only major soliloquy by Mephistopheles in Part One) is probably the most important passage in the *Fragment* version of 1790, and sets out the relatively traditional devil's-bargain scenario with which Goethe was still operating at that stage; for further discussion of this point cf. Introd., pp. xxxviii f. In lines 1855 and 1866 incidentally ('. . . signature or none', '. . . bond that he has signed') the German original does not expressly mention the blood-signed document (cf. Note 35).

38 1868–2050: the episodic satirical scene between Mephistopheles and the Student is essentially *Urfaust* material from the early 1770s, paralleling in important respects the scene between Faust and Wagner (cf. Note 15) which was also written at|that time. It is notable that Mephistopheles (used|with|scant or ironic regard for his diabolic role) is here just as much a spokesman for the young Goethe as Faust in the Wagner scene. In both cases the naïve interlocutor hears a polemic on 'Storm and Stress' lines against narrow academic pedantry, the bandying of empty words, 'grey theory' that draws no nourishment from the 'golden¯tree of life' (2038 f.). The Student scene incorporates the young Goethe's recollections of university life at Leipzig in the late 1760s, particularly of the teaching methods which he had found so antiquated and uninspiring. The original version also alluded, in a long and pleasingly ribald passage, to the living-conditions suffered by Leipzig students in those days; this was excised when the scene underwent revision at the *Fragment* stage, but the passages on Law and Theology (1968–2000) were now added to

complete this ironic review of the traditional four faculties (cf.
Note 10).

39 1911–41: in Book VI of his autobiography Goethe later recalled
the Leipzig foundation-course in logic: '. . . I found it strange to
be told that those mental operations which I had performed with
the greatest of ease since childhood must be pulled apart, isolated
and virtually destroyed if I was to understand how to carry them
out correctly.'

40 1940, *encheirisis naturae*: 'an intervention by the hand of Nature'
—a pompous pseudo-explanatory concept (used by one of
Goethe's teachers at Strasbourg) which made nonsense of the
scientist's claim to have discovered the essential truth.

41 1972–9: this Rousseauistic polemic in favour of 'natural law',
delivered a little incongruously through Mephistopheles, again
represents the view of the young Goethe, himself a practising
lawyer at that time, although the passage about Law was in fact
added at the *Fragment* stage (cf. Note 38).

42 1990–2000: in the passage satirizing theology, added for the 1790
version (cf. Note 38), Goethe continues the anti-verbalist polemic
of the *Urfaust* (cf. 385, 552–7, 3453–7) which remained one of
his characteristic themes; it recurs in Sc. 9 (2554–66) which he
also wrote at the *Fragment* stage (cf. Notes 60 and 79).

43 2000: Matthew 5:18 ('jot'=the letter iota). It is possible (cf. Notes
42 and 60) that Goethe is also alluding satirically to the Christ-
ological controversy at the Council of Nicaea (AD 325), in which
the difference of one iota between ὁμοούσιος (of the same
nature [as the Father]) and ὁμοιούσιος (of similar nature) had
vast doctrinal consequences.

44 2046 ff.: it was then customary for students to carry autograph
books in which to collect the signatures of academics. Mephistopheles writes the words of the Serpent in Eden (Genesis 3:5,
'you shall be as God, knowing good and evil').

45 2051–72: a linking passage added for the 1790 *Fragment*. In 2069
Goethe alludes to a technological breakthrough of that age, the
first hot-air balloon flights by the Montgolfier brothers in 1783;
similar balloon experiments were now also being conducted by
the Weimar court apothecary Buchholz.

46 2073–336: the tavern scene, like the scene with the Student (see
Note 38), is *Urfaust* material, recalling Goethe's university days
at Leipzig. Auerbach's wine-cellar near the market-place was a
well-known meeting-place for students, with sixteenth-century

murals depicting scenes from the Faust legend. Goethe originally wrote it almost entirely in prose, but versified and otherwise revised and improved it at the *Fragment* stage. The names and conversation of the revellers suggest student terminology and humour, though it is not clear that they are all students.

47 2090 f.: the 'Holy Roman Empire of the German Nation', for centuries a ramshackle and largely nominal instution and now in terminal decline, was a commonplace target of satire in the young Goethe's day.

48 2098 ff.: an allusion to the student custom of electing as 'king' or 'pope' the performer of the most impressive drinking feat.

49 2184: Mephistopheles' 'cloven hoof' is also alluded to in 2490, 4065, and 4140.

50 2189 f.: in Rippach, a village near Leipzig, the landlord's name in the young Goethe's time was Hans Ars, which lent itself to student ribaldry as *Hans Arsch* (Simple Simon, poor sucker, stupid prick; cf. Note 65).

51 2250–91: the magical trick of extracting wine from a table (performed in the original version of the scene by Faust himself) is Faust-book material, as is the motif (featured in one of the Auerbach murals) of Faust riding astride a wine-cask (2330).

52 2337–604: Goethe is thought to have written much of the *Witch's Kitchen* scene in the garden of the Villa Borghese in Rome in the spring of 1788. This rather incongruous setting is perhaps reflected in the scene's curious mixture of ironic and grotesque elements with the kind of folkloristic material he had used in the *Urfaust* (cf. Introd., p. xxiii).

53 2378–428: Goethe may have derived the baboons and their antics (the ape playing with the globe for instance) from certain grotesque motifs in sixteenth- and seventeen-century Flemish painting, examples of which he could have seen in Dresden.

54 2392, *charity soup*: the word *Bettelsuppe* was later used by Goethe in a letter to Schiller (26 July 1797) referring to a literary work of very inferior quality as 'real soup-kitchen stuff, suited to the taste of the German public'.

55 2401, *the lottery*: this is thought to allude to the passion for gambling current in Italy at the time of Goethe's visit.

56 2416–21: the sieve, as a device for sorting good things from bad, was in popular superstition also able to discriminate honest men from scoundrels.

57 2429–40: for Faust's vision of perfect feminine beauty in the magic glass Goethe is thought to have had in mind a naked Venus such as Titian's in Florence or Giorgione's in Dresden.

58 2448–53 (and cf. 2427 f.): as token sceptres, or symbols of refinement and therefore of status, fly-whisks or bushy-topped fans have been used by potentates in certain cultures (in Africa in the present century for instance), and it seems possible that Goethe found some earlier European or non-European example of this in one of the authors or artists who were his sources for this scene. The associated passage about the broken crown may be an allusion to the precarious state of the French monarchy in the years immediately before the Revolution. Goethe had been interested in the notorious scandal at the French court about a diamond necklace (1785) and later published a minor dramatic work (*Der Groß-Cophta*, 1791) about the adventurer Cagliostro and his involvement in this affair.

59 2540–52: it has been suggested that this nonsense-rhyme ironically disguises an allusion to the doctrine of numerical 'magic squares' which Goethe encountered in his alchemistic reading. One such square is the ternary acrostic illustrated below, in which each of the six horizontal and vertical lines of figures adds up to 15:

10	2	3	(15)
0	7	8	(15)
5	6	4	(15)

(15) (15) (15)

The witch's words can be read in such a way as to fit this pattern. Thus, 1 is replaced by 10, to which 2 and 3 are added making us 'rich' with 15 (lines 2541–4); 4–5–6 becomes 0–7–8 (2545–8), and 'that puts it straight' (literally 'that completes it') in the sense that the figure can now easily be completed by entering in the third row the three numbers not yet used—with the exception of 9 which may be taken to stand for the square as a whole. Lines 2550 f. could then mean that 9 is one of the 'magic' square numbers but 10 is not.

60 2557–62: Goethe had no patience with the apophatic paradoxes of theology, and here takes occasion to satirize the dogma of the Trinity by comparing it to the witch's numerical

abracadabra, or perhaps to the 'three in one' magic square (cf. Note 59). The polemically anti-Christian tendency in Goethe's thinking was particularly evident at the time of the Italian journey (cf. Introd., p. xxi) when this scene was written. It is also of interest that Mephistopheles' two phallic gestures (stage directions after 2513 and 3291) both occur in scenes added at this time.

61 2603 f.: on the possible significance of the allusion to 'Helen' at this point see Introduction, p. xxiii. Mephistopheles' remark in any case serves as a transition to the Gretchen sequence which Goethe, having already written it about fifteen years earlier, now attaches to the present *Fragment* material.

62 2605: the Gretchen scenes, which begin here, are taken from the *Urfaust* with very little alteration, and may be regarded as the early core of the tragic action of *Faust* Part I (cf. Introd., pp. xvii–xx). For his stage and dialogue directions Goethe uses the full form of the heroine's name (in German 'Margarete') chiefly in the scenes before she is seduced (Sc. 10, 11, 13–16, 19) but also in the final scene just before her death (Sc. 28). In the remaining scenes (nearly all after the seduction but including 18) he uses the diminutive form 'Gretchen'; this form is also nearly always used when she is addressed or referred to within the dialogue itself, though variants of the diminutive ('Margretlein', 'Gretelchen') occur once or twice (e.g. Sc. 12, 13).

63 2635–8. these lines appear to indicate an early, *Urfaust* conception, not elsewhere developed, of the relationship between Faust and Mephistopheles, in which the latter is a servant whom Faust still has the power to dismiss.

64 2675 ff.: in popular belief, the Devil has knowledge of buried treasure and the power to raise it (cf. 2821 f. and 3664–75).

65 2727, *the great Don Juan*: the German is *der große Hans*, meaning merely something like 'the fine big fellow, the great boaster' with no specific reference to the legendary *machó* hero whose name is the Spanish form of Hans. (Nor, of course, has it anything to do with the name 'Johannes' which became attached to the traditional Faustus.) The phrase is comparable to the common use in popular German of the name 'Hans' with an ironic or disparaging adjective or noun attached to it, as in 2628 where Mephistopheles tells Faust that he is now talking *wie Hans Liederlich* (literally 'like Jack the lecher, Jack libertine') and in the implied 'Hans Arsch' of 2190 (cf. Note 50).

66 2759, *Thule*: pronounced as two syllables. The Romans gave the

name *'ultima Thule'* (of uncertain derivation) to a semi-
legendary island at the northernmost limit of their known world.
The ballad is, however, quintessentially Germanic in character.
Goethe is thought to have written it in 1774, at the same period
as the *Urfaust* scenes and perhaps independently of them (but
cf. Introd., p. xviii).

67 2872, *death certificate* (cf. 3012 'weekly notice-sheet', i.e. weekly
advertiser): such things existed in the eighteenth-century though
not in the sixteenth. This is one minor example of the anachron-
isms in *Faust*, which Goethe did not of course intend as a realistic
reconstruction of the historical Faust's period, and into which
eighteenth-century themes and details are freely mixed (cf.
Note 15).

68 2883 f.: the sumptuary laws of Goethe's day forbade or strictly
limited the wearing of jewellery by girls of modest social station
(by a Frankfurt police regulation of 1731, for instance, a manual
worker's daughter was allowed only one gold chain and one gold
ring, of a total value not exceeding 50 florins, and a maidservant
no ornament at all). Gretchen is also not entitled to be addressed
as *Fräulein* ('young lady', as in 2605 or 2906) but only as *Jungfer*
or *Jungfrau* (young woman).

69 2981–4: syphilis, thought to have been brought back from Haiti
in 1493 by Columbus's first expedition, broke out seriously in
Naples when the city was besieged by the French in 1495. It
became widely known as *le mal de Naples*, the Neapolitan disease,
and was a dreaded scourge of sixteenth-century Europe.

70 3205–16 (A *Summerhouse*): it is not certain that the action of
Sc. 16 immediately follows that of Sc. 15, though productions
generally treat these as one continuous scene. It may be argued
that the stage direction after 3194 leads naturally to that before
3205, and that there is similar continuity between 3195 and
3207 f.; on the other hand, the relevance of 3213 f. to the dialogue
in Sc. 15 is less obvious.

71 3217–373 (A *Forest Cavern*): cf. Introd., pp. xxiv f. and the
composition-synopsis (pp. lvi f.). This scene, with the exception
of one important passage (cf. Note 75), belongs entirely to the
Fragment stage and was probably at least partly written when
Goethe was in Italy. In the *Fragment* it follows Sc. 19 and 20,
which means that it was originally conceived and composed as a
scene occurring *after* the seduction of Gretchen. In the 1808 text
it is inserted into the Gretchen sequence immediately after Sc. 16
and thus at a point *before* her fall (cf. Introd., p. xxv). Goethe's

reasons for this rearrangement have been much discussed but not clarified. As usual he made no consequential emendations to his earlier-written material, so that, for example, lines 3249 f., 3307–10, 3336 f., and 3345–65 read rather oddly in their new context.

72 3217: the 'sublime Spirit' whom Faust addresses can only be the Earth Spirit, in view of the reference to his appearance in fire (3218 f.) which echoes the *Urfaust* scene 460–517, and of the retention (3241–6) of the *Urfaust* idea (cf. Introd. pp. xxiv f. and Note 124) that the Earth Spirit gave or attached Mephistopheles to Faust. Goethe thus seems, in the 1790 *Fragment*, to be still using his original demonological scenario, which the not yet written *Prologue in Heaven* was to modify significantly ten years later (cf. Introd., pp. xxxi f.). In this *Fragment* scene the Earth Spirit is clearly also intended, appropriately enough, as a reinforcing link between the opening *Urfaust* soliloquy in which Faust communed with Nature (386–459, etc.), and the present soliloquy (3217–39) which is a classicized version of the same theme.

73 3248: the phrase 'that lovely woman's image' (literally 'that beautiful image', *jenes schöne Bild*) evidently refers to Faust's vision in the magic mirror of the contemporaneously written *Witch's Kitchen* scene, at least as much as to Gretchen (whose actual name is never mentioned in A *Forest Cavern*). This synthesis of the particular and the general dignifies and 'classicizes' Faust's passion, in accordance with the general tendency of the *Fragment* material (cf. Introd., pp. xxiii f.).

74 3336 f.: an allusion to Song of Solomon 4: 5: 'Thy two breasts are like two fawns that are twins of a roe, which feed among the lilies.'

75 3342–69: these lines were written at the *Urfaust* stage and originally belonged to a different dramatic context, at a much later point in the Gretchen story. At the *Fragment* stage, having decided not to publish yet that concluding part of the *Urfaust* material, Goethe nevertheless retrieved this one passage containing Faust's outburst of remorse, and inserted it here into the new *Forest Cavern* scene. About ten years later, for purposes of the final version, he repositioned A *Forest Cavern* (and thus for the second time repositioned the remorse speech) by bringing it forward to a point well before Gretchen's seduction (cf. Note 71). Dramatically the speech makes less good sense here, but intrinsically it remains, in its general import, perhaps the most crucial document of the young Goethe's original tragic conception of the figure of Faust (cf. Introd., p. xxv).

76 3374: the rest of the Gretchen sequence (Sc. 18–23, and 26–8) is like Sc. 10–16 nearly all *Urfaust* material, only very slightly revised except for the important expansion of Sc. 22 (Valentine's death, cf. Note 84), and the versification of the Prison scene (Sc. 28, cf. Note 122). These two revisions were carried out during the third composition-phase, to which the interpolated Walpurgis Night material (Sc. 24 and 25) also belongs.

77 3374–413, Sc. 18: this famous lyrical piece, unlike *The King of Thule* in Sc. 11, is strictly speaking not a song sung by Gretchen but a personal spoken soliloquy in a dramatic context. It has, of course, lent itself to many musical settings, of which Schubert's is the best known, and in any case the distinction between drama and opera in *Faust* cannot be drawn absolutely (cf. Note 94).

78 3414: the historical Faust's first name was Georg and that of his legendary counterpart was Johann (cf. Introd., pp. xiii f.) It is pointless to speculate on whether Goethe preferred to think of him as 'Heinrich Faust' or whether Faust merely uses the name 'Heinrich' to Gretchen as a *nom d'amour*. There is no evidence that she knows his real name or identity at all, a fact which makes the ending (4610 ff.) all the more poignant.

79 3455 (3456 in the German text), 'The feeling's all there is' (*Gefühl ist alles*): the lapidary German words are frequently quoted as the young Goethe's central 'Storm and Stress' slogan, and taken to mean that nothing in life is so important as emotion generally or sexual emotion in particular. In the context of Faust's speech, however (which is one of Goethe's most important and characteristic utterances on the subject of religious belief), it is clear, despite the omission of the definite article before *Gefühl*, that 'feeling' stands in antithesis to 'name' in the following line, and that the sense of the statement is thus less wide and primarily theological: 'God', and indeed all life, is a mystery that cannot be put into words or given a 'name' at all (cf. 3432). The young Goethe continues here the anti-verbalist polemic delivered by Faust in his opening soliloquy (354–85) and scene with Wagner (534–69), as well as ironically by Mephistopheles in his scene with the student (1948–53, etc.). In Faust's present speech to Gretchen the eroticism that colours his language is, of course, also undeniable.

80 3540: 'genius' was the cult-concept first made fashionable by the 'Storm and Stress' movement of the 1770s, the detractors of which also ironically referred to it as the 'genius period' (*Geniezeit*).

81 3563 f.: the hard labour of spinning is the realistic background

to Gretchen's 'song' in Sc. 18; cf. also the account of her domestic tasks which she gives to Faust, Sc. 15, 3109–48.

82 3575 f.: literally, 'the boys will tear off her bridal wreath (*Kränzel*), and we'll scatter chopped straw (*Häckerling*) outside her door'. These were two punitive social ceremonies inflicted on 'fallen' women. The snatching off of the wreath or garland (as the symbol of virginity, cf. 3561 'her little flower') is referred to again in Gretchen's last scene (4436, 4583). The dread of such penalties, particularly of the public 'church penance' (3568 f.), often drove girls to infanticide as an attempt to conceal their guilt. In the Duchy of Weimar public penance was abolished in 1786, with Goethe's concurrence as a member of the Council of State, though he supported the retention of the death penalty for infanticide. It may be noted that church penance for fornication or adultery was also the custom in eighteenth-century Scotland, and is alluded to by Robert Burns in his ballad about an unmarried mother *The Rantin' Dog the Daddie o't* (written in about 1785), where he calls the penance-stool 'the creepy-chair'. Goethe greatly admired Burns (though he would not necessarily have known this poem).

83 3587–619: the shrine is in the narrow space (called in German *der Zwinger*) between the town wall and the houses nearest to it. The icon recalls the thirteenth-century hymn attributed to Giacopone da Todi (*Stabat Mater dolorosa*) which describes the sorrow of the Virgin as she witnesses the Crucifixion.

84 3620–775, *Night. The street outside Gretchen's door*: it is clear from certain allusions in the *Urfaust* text (corresponding to 4512–17, 4525 and lines <55 ff.> of the prose scene, Sc. 26) that the killing of Gretchen's brother by Faust was part of the young Goethe's original plan. At that stage, however, he only wrote two disconnected fragments of the dramatic scene in which this takes place—they were indeed perhaps not even originally conceived as parts of the same scene. These were Valentine's soliloquy (3620–45), and a passage of dialogue between Faust and Mephistopheles, part of which contained Faust's remorse speech and was later transferred to *A Forest Cavern* (cf. Note 75 and the composition-synopsis; the dialogue 3650–9 originally continued as 3342–69). It was not until 1806 that Goethe completed the Valentine scene, adding lines 3646–9 and 3660–775 in which he nevertheless very successfully recaptured the style and spirit of the *Urfaust*.

85 3660–3: these lines too were inserted at the final stage to establish

a link between this scene and the Walpurgis Night sequence which Goethe had now added (cf. Note 93).

86 3664–73: this rather mysterious passage is a further allusion (cf. Note 64) to the power of the Devil over precious metals and jewellery. The treasure was supposed to 'bloom' with an eery light as it rose.

87 3672 f.: the German merely says 'I did see something like a kind of pearl necklace'. Pearls were thought to symbolize tears (and therefore to be unlucky for a lover to give or a bride to wear); the motif of a necklace for Gretchen also reappears with sinister effect in 4203 ff. I have added to Mephistopheles' words a Shakespearian allusion which is not out of keeping with the scene (cf. Notes 88 and 89).

88 3682–97: Mephistopheles' ironic serenade is freely adapted from one of Ophelia's songs in *Hamlet*, in her 'mad' scene (IV.v) which was already paralleled in the *Urfaust* Prison scene (cf. Note 127):

> Tomorrow is Saint Valentine's day,
>   All in the morning betime,
> And I a maid at your window.
>   To be your Valentine:
> Then up he rose, and donned his clothes,
>   And dupp'd the chamber door;
> Let in the maid, that out a maid
>   Never departed more.
>
> By Gis and by Saint Charity,
>   Alack, and fie for shame!
> Young men will do't, if they come to't;
>   By Cock they are to blame.
> Quoth she, before you tumbled me,
>   You promised me to wed:
> So would I ha' done, by yonder sun,
>   An thou hadst not come to my bed.

In his version Goethe uses the name *Katrinchen* (Kate) which commonly occurs in German folksongs of similar purport.

89 3699: Shakespeare's Mercutio challenges Juliet's cousin Tybalt with the words 'Tybalt, you rat-catcher, will you walk?' *Romeo and Juliet* was the only Shakespeare play Goethe himself translated, and this seems to be a conscious echo, another being probably Faust's enforced flight from the town after killing Valentine, which is comparable to Romeo's banishment after killing Tybalt. There is also a certain affinity between Juliet's nurse and Gretchen's *confidante* Martha, and perhaps between Mercutio generally and Mephistopheles.

90 3714 f.: Mephistopheles distinguishes between minor offences and those crimes which went before courts that could pass the death-sentence and were thus regarded as having divine authority.

91 3776–834, The Cathedral: in the Urfaust this scene preceded the original fragmentary version of that of the death of Valentine (cf. Note 84). The Urfaust stage direction specifically stated that the requiem being sung was for Gretchen's mother (and that 'all her relations' were present). The implication of 3787 f. is that her mother has died from the effects of the sleeping-potion (cf. 3510–15, 4507, 4570 ff.) which has presumably been administered on a number of occasions. The Fragment ended with the cathedral scene, Goethe having at that time decided to withhold all the subsequent Urfaust material. In the final version, having completed the Valentine scene, he placed the cathedral scene after it instead of before it, so that the order of Gretchen's concluding appearances (evidently intended at the Urfaust stage to be, more naturally, By a Shrine—The Cathedral—Valentine scene—The Prison) now becomes (21) By a Shrine—(22) Valentine scene—(23) The Cathedral—(28) The Prison. From the point of view of dramatic realism this new sequence is rather less plausible than the original one, since the completed Sc. 22 makes it clear that Gretchen's situation has become a public scandal, and leaves her implicated in her brother's death as a witness at least, whereas the now following cathedral scene gives the impression that her pregnancy (3790–3) is still a relatively private matter. In the repositioned Sc. 23 Goethe now inserts an allusion to Valentine's death (3789) into the words of the 'evil spirit' who externalizes Gretchen's remorseful thoughts, but deletes the reference to her mother and family from the stage-direction.

92 3798 f., 3813 ff., 3825 ff.: the words about the Last Judgement sung by the choir are verses from the Dies irae sequence in the Mass for the Dead ('Day of dread, that day of ire, when the world explodes in fire . . . When the Judge ascends his throne, every secret shall be known, all for sin must then atone . . . Then, poor wretch, what shall I say? Who then shall be my strength and stay, when even just men fear that day?'). The evil spirit echoes other phrases from the sequence.

93 3835–4222 Walpurgis Night: St Walpurgis or Walburga, abbess of Heidenheim in Franconia, was born in England and died in 779; her name appears to be derived from 'Wolborg', a 'good fortress' (against evil, by her purity) and she was invoked in aid against witchcraft. Her day, 1 May, is also an ancient pagan spring festival, and she is thus associated by antithesis with the

witches' sabbath which was traditionally supposed to take place on the Brocken during the previous night. The Brocken or Blocksberg, known to the Romans as Mons Bructerus, is the main summit of the Harz Mountains and at 3,745 ft. the highest mountain in central Germany. Schierke and Elend are two villages a few miles from it. Goethe had climbed the Brocken in December 1777, and revisited the Harz district in 1783 and 1784. The mention of Walpurgis Night in the *Witch's Kitchen* scene (2590) may mean that he already intended at the *Fragment* stage to use this material for *Faust* (cf. also 2113 f. in *Auerbach's Tavern*, revised at this time, and Note 123). In the traditional Faustus literature there is never any mention of the Walpurgis legend, and it seems that before Goethe the only combination of the Faust and Blocksberg themes was in a comic epic called *Walpurgis Night* (1756) by Johann Friedrich Löwen, a very minor writer from the Harz district; the serious association of the two legends is thus essentially a Goethean contribution. His actual writing of the Walpurgis Night scenes belongs to the third composition phase, chiefly between 1799 and 1801. Sources that influenced him included the *Anthropodemus Plutonicus* by 'Prätorius' (Schultze, cf. Note 31), the same author's *Blockesberges Verrichtung* (The Blocksberg Ceremony) of 1669, and a large engraving by Michael Herr (1591–1661) which depicts the grotesque revels of witches and demons. It is of interest in this connection that the last witch-burning in Germany had not taken place until 1782.

94 3871–911: Goethe here explicitly adopts an operatic treatment (cf. Note 77) as in the latter part of Act III of Part Two.

95 3879 f.: among various strangely shaped rocks in the Brocken area (with names such as Devil's Pulpit, Witch's Altar, etc.) two are known as the 'Snorers' owing to a peculiar local sound-effect in high wind.

96 3914–33: 'Mammon', as the diabolic personification of gold and material wealth generally, appears in the New Testament, the medieval mystery plays, Milton's *Paradise Lost*, etc. The Harz Mountains have for centuries been an important mining area for silver and other metals, though the yield of gold has been very small and there is no mine on the Brocken itself. Goethe had some expertise in geology and mineralogy, and it is on his own knowledge and local observations that Faust's fantastic vision of glowing gold in the valleys and cliffs is partly based. His source Prätorius also mentions veins of metal in the 'Blocksberg' area. On the 'diabolic' nature of buried treasure cf. Notes 64 and 86.

97 3959, *Lord Capercailzie*: the original is *Herr Urian*, a name for
the Devil formed from *Ur-jan*, i.e. '*Ur-Hans*', a kind of primal
male figure (cf. Old Nick, Auld Hornie, etc., and Note 65). It also
became popularly identified with *Urhahn* or *Auerhahn* (capercailzie, wood grouse; *Hahn*=cock). In one episode of Thomas
Mann's novel *Doctor Faustus* (1947) the Devil appears as 'Mr
Capercailzie'.

98 3962, *Baubo*: a figure from classical mythology (the lewd nurse
of the earth-goddess Demeter).

99 3977: according to Goethe's sources, witches who had been
made pregnant by demons would sometimes get rid of their
offspring by miscarriage as they rode to the sabbath.

100 4008, *witch-unction*: the witches smeared a magic 'salve' on
themselves and their supposed means of transport; the reference
may be to hallucinogenic drugs rubbed into the skin to induce
sexual excitement and fantasies of flying. Prätorius reports that
salves derived from the corpses of newly born children who had
been murdered before baptism would bring about a trance-like
state in which the soul left the body and flew to the Blocksberg.

101 4013: the Brocken summit is rounded, with very scanty vegeta-
tion.

102 4023, *Voland*: an old name for the Devil which Goethe found in
Prätorius. The medieval forms *fāland*, *vālant*, etc. are associated
with earlier Germanic words meaning fear or horror.

103 4096–113: the pedlar-witch may have been suggested to Goethe
by one of his pictorial sources. For the list of her wares there are
possible approximate parallels in Shakespeare's *Macbeth* (the
ingredients of the witches' cauldron) and in Burns's poem *Tam
o' Shanter* (1790). In the latter, the hero witnesses a sabbath in
which 'auld Nick' in the form of a black shaggy dog (cf. Note 23)
sits playing the pipes, and an altar is covered with sinister objects
recalling bloody deeds. It has also been suggested that the objects
peddled by Goethe's witch have an associative connection with
the Gretchen tragedy (poison, jewels, a sword). We should note,
however, that Goethe treats the motif even more ironically than
Burns (esp. in 4110–13).

104 4119: 'Lilith', as a kind of mythical primal witch, was to be
found in Prätorius and in the Blocksberg literature generally.
From the fact that the Book of Genesis offers two versions of the
creation of Woman, Rabbinical tradition had concluded that
Adam must have been married twice, and his first wife acquired
the name Lilith, meaning a kind of demon. The word occurs in
the Bible only once, in a passage (Isaiah 34:14) from which it has

been variously translated (screech owl, night hag, lamia, kobold).

105 4138 f., 4142 f.: the German words corresponding to these indecent particulars have generally been replaced by dashes in the printed editions since 1808.

106 4144–75, Mr Arsey-Phantarsey: Goethe's word is Proktophantasmist, from πρωκτός (anus) and φάντασμα (apparition); the last syllable is also homophonous with the German word for dung (Mist). The victim of this rancorous satire was Friedrich Nicolai (1733–1811), a critic and minor writer from Berlin who in his day had been a worthy representative of the German literary Enlightenment. In 1775 Nicolai had written a parody of Goethe's recently published novel, The Sorrows of Werther, and the young Goethe had replied with a verse epigram even more scatological than the Walpurgis Night passage. For Goethe and his friends Nicolai typified the worst kind of narrow-minded 'enlightened' philistinism, and he remained a target of satire. At about the time when the Walpurgis Night scenes were being written, this arch-rationalist and dedicated campaigner against superstition was plagued for weeks on end by inexplicable ghostly apparitions; he attributed these to high blood-pressure, and was cured of them by the application of leeches to his backside (4172–5). Having little sense of the ridiculous, he then gave a lecture on his experience to the Berlin Academy, which was published in 1799. This bizarre incident was mercilessly exploited by the young Romantic writers as well as by Nicolai's old enemy Goethe, who had vowed in 1775 to punish him by making him appear in Faust. The resulting 'Proktophantasmist' passage is an amusing if tasteless in-joke for some of the poet's contemporaries, but like other satirical material in the Walpurgis Night sequence (4072–95, 4210–398) and in A Witch's Kitchen (esp. 2390–428, 2448–64) it seems wholly irrelevant to the Faust story.

107 4161: in 1797 hauntings had been reported in the head forester's house in Tegel, just north of Berlin; they had been investigated by a commission which concluded that they were a practical joke.

108 4169: Nicolai was also a tireless travel-writer, whose Account of a Journey through Germany and Switzerland in the year 1781 had appeared in twelve volumes between 1783 and 1796.

109 4203–8: apparitions presaging imminent or future executions are a folklore motif. A book which Goethe is known to have read (The Infernal Proteus by Erasmus Francisci von Finx, 1690) contains the anecdote of a maidservant who has killed her illegitimate child and who sees in the moonlight the ghost of a woman carrying her severed head in her hands.

110 4209 22: these last fourteen lines are a later-written transition to Sc. 25 (cf. Note 111).

111 4223–398, A *Walpurgis Night's Dream*: this 'intermezzo', so called because it was originally to have been followed by another Blocksberg scene (cf. Note 121 and Introd, pp xxxix f), consists entirely of a series of satirical epigrams about half of which had been written in 1797, two or three years before the *Walpurgis Night* itself, and had at first not been intended as part of *Faust* at all. In his periodical *The Almanach of the Muses* for that year, Schiller had published a collection of about 400 epigrams in the classical distich style, written in collaboration by himself and Goethe; they were caustically satirical, directed against all and sundry on the contemporary German literary scene, and appeared under the ironic title (borrowed from Martial) of *Xenia*, i.e. 'parting gifts' for guests. Later in the same year Goethe offered Schiller a further series (this time in rhymed quatrains) suggesting that they should appear in the 1798 *Almanach* as a sequel to the *Xenia*. Schiller, however, did not wish to continue this campaign which had stirred up much animosity, and Goethe agreed that the idea should be dropped, adding surprisingly that the new epigrams, the number of which he had now doubled, 'might well be best accommodated in *Faust*'. Goethe's references to *Faust* in his letters to Schiller at this time of resuming work on it are often ironical (cf. Introd., p. xxvii), and most commentators take what seems to be the common-sense view that the forty-four *Dream* epigrams remained essentially irrelevant to the play and were simply dumped into it, rather as Goethe also inserted miscellaneous collections of aphoristic material into his novels *Wilhelm Meister* and *The Elective Affinities*. None of the epigrams alludes to Faust or Mephistopheles or indicates that either of them is present; some (evidently among those written later) maintain a tenuous connection with the Walpurgis Night theme by mentioning devils or witches, or by the recurrent suggestion that some kind of unruly dance is in progress, accompanied by an 'orchestra' of animal noises. Most of them seem to be veiled allusions to minor and forgotten contemporaries of Goethe, though the conclusive identification of these is usually no longer possible and is of little interest in any case. The title of the intermezzo is of course whimsically derived from that of *A Midsummer Night's Dream*, and Goethe passingly includes figures from this play (Oberon, Titania, Puck) and from *The Tempest* (Ariel), but these Shakespearian associations are quite undeveloped and their significance remains unclear. Nor is there

the slightest explanatory value (as some commentators suppose) in the fact that Goethe may have wished to allude to the verse romance *Oberon* (1780) by his older contemporary Wieland, or to the operetta *Oberon, King of the Elves* by another minor contemporary, Paul Wranitzky, which he had himself produced at the Weimar court theatre in 1796. In practice the *Walpurgis Night's Dream* contains no substantive allusion to either of these works, or to Shakespeare's play, beyond the mere use of the names at the beginning and end of the sequence.

112 4223 f.: Johann Martin Mieding, whose death in 1782 Goethe commemorated in a poem, had worked as a stage carpenter at the Weimar court theatre.

113 4255 f.: the description evokes some grotesque creature, possibly a frog; a similar motif seems to occur in 4259 f. The satire in both these quatrains is perhaps literary, as in 4263–6.

114 4303–18: for the polemical 'Xenia' cf. Note 111. One of their victims was August von Hennings (1746–1826), a totally unimportant *littérateur* who edited a periodical at first called *The Genius of the Age* and later (after 1800) *The Genius of the Nineteenth Century*. He also published in 1798 and 1799 a six-volume anthology called *Der Musaget*, i.e. the leader or master of the Muses, in which some of Goethe's work was referred to disparagingly.

115 4323–6: according to Goethe himself in a conversation with Eckermann in 1829, the 'crane' is the Swiss religious writer and preacher Johann Kaspar Lavater (1741–1801). As a young man Goethe had been friendly with him for a time, but later found his narrowly doctrinaire Pietism distasteful. Lavater is further alluded to in the following epigram and possibly also in the preceding one.

116 4347–54: the two philosophical positions here parodied are that of post-Kantian, especially Fichtean, subjective idealism which regards the external world as a product of the mind, and that of realism or empiricism which insists on its objective reality.

117 4360: the 'flames' seem to be the spectral flickerings that are supposed to lead the initiate to buried treasure (cf. Note 86).

118 4367–82: these quatrains probably refer to various émigré types of the years following the French Revolution.

119 4383–6: the allusion is probably not to the revolutionary masses in a literal sense, but once again to what Goethe elsewhere calls

'literary *sans-culottes*'; the ensuing comments by Puck and Ariel (4387–94) also seem to suggest this.

120 4393 f.: Ariel's summons to the 'hill of roses' (*Rosenhügel*) remains obscure, and no light is cast on it by pointing out that there are rose-bushes round Oberon's palace in Canto 12 of Wieland's epic (cf. Note 111). Ariel's words may possibly be a reference to the dawning day, as are perhaps those of the next quatrain which closes the 'dream'.

121 (after 4398): Goethe originally (cf. Introd., p. xxxix) intended a further scene at this point, in which the *Walpurgis Night* sequence would end climactically with a satanistic ritual at the top of the mountain. His surviving manuscript draft for it includes the following disjointed notes:

After the Intermezzo. Solitude A wild place Trumpets sounded Lightning and thunder from above Pillars of fire, smog, fog. A rock jutting out. It is Satan. A great crowd round him. [. . .] Satan's speech etc. Presentations. Investitures.

There are some verse sketches, mainly satirical material of a trivial and indecent kind (notably a passage in praise of Satan's enormous anal cavity) but also further prose jottings in a more serious vein:

Midnight. The spectacle vanishes. Volcano. Chaotic dispersal. [. . .] On red-hot ground. The apparition naked Her hands behind her back   Not covering her face or her private parts   Singing   Her head falls off The blood spurts up and puts out the fire Night A rushing sound Witch-children chattering   From which Faust learns that Faust Meph

The 'apparition' seems to be the 'pale young girl' taking the form of Gretchen (4190; the word *Idol* is used in both passages), and the last words of the note seem to lead directly into the scene *A Gloomy Day* (Sc. 26) in which Faust has learnt of Gretchen's plight.

122 (Sc. 26, 27, 28): these last three *Urfaust* scenes were all omitted from the 1790 *Fragment*, which ended with Gretchen fainting in the cathedral. They were originally in prose, and at the *Fragment* stage Goethe evidently felt that he could neither versify them nor publish them unversified (cf. Introd., pp. xxiv, xl f.). When he finally turned his attention to them again in 1798, he versified and considerably extended the Prison scene itself, but decided to leave the other two as they were, with only slight emendations, and adding the title *A Gloomy Day. Open country* to Sc. 26. The short Sc. 27 (*Night. In open country*) may have originally been thought of as prose, but in the German it has a strong rhythmic character

and the first and fifth lines do in fact rhyme; the editions have accordingly always treated it as if it were free verse and resumed the line-numbering at 4399. A *Gloomy Day* is thus of special interest as the only prose scene in *Faust*, as well as for other reasons (cf. Notes 124 and 125).

123 <10>, *vulgar diversions*: this phrase, occurring as it does in the *Urfaust* text, may indicate that even at that stage the young Goethe was planning to incorporate in *Faust* a *Walpurgis Night* scene or something equivalent to it. There is already a fleeting allusion to the Blocksberg in the *Urfaust* version of *Auerbach's Tavern* (made clearer in the revised *Fragment* text, 2113 f.), though this may not be significant.

124 <14>f. *Oh infinite Spirit* and <37> *Oh you great splendid Spirit*, etc.: it is clear that Faust is addressing the Earth Spirit, who 'deigned to appear to him' (481 f.) and who, in the archaic *Urfaust* conception which these passages vestigially represent, was evidently thought of (at least by Faust) as having control over Mephistopheles and as being responsible for the latter's relationship to Faust (<38>f.; cf. 3243 f.). On the question of the status of the Earth Spirit cf. Introd., pp. xvi f., xxiv f., xxxi f., and Notes 14 and 72. It may be noted that Faust's present description of the Spirit (<38>) as a being who 'knows my heart and my soul' seems hardly consistent with its scornful attitude to him in 512 f. and in the scene of its appearance generally (cf. also 1747), and some commentators have even speculated that there was another (lost) *Urfaust* scene in which it reappeared and treated Faust more benignly.

125 <15–20>, *the form of a dog . . . his favourite shape*: this, too, seems to be a surviving archaic conception, peculiar to the *Urfaust*, of Faust's dealings with Mephistopheles. In it, the latter not only assumed the shape of a dog as in the old Faust-book (cf. Note 23) but also frequently accompanied Faust in this form. The breed of dog is not specified, but it was evidently large enough to terrify 'innocent wayfarers'. This curious scenario is compatible with the chapbook material but in no way compatible with Goethe's final version, where Mephistopheles adopts canine form only once, to insinuate himself into Faust's company at their first meeting, in the comical shape of a poodle (1147–323). As usual Goethe did not delete the earlier dog passage when revising the prose scene, and it therefore remains as another detail which we can explain historically but not dramatically.

126 4399, *gallows-mound*: in German *Rabenstein*, literally 'ravens' rock'. When criminals were hanged or broken on the wheel,

the rough stone-built mound on which (for better public viewing) they were executed was generally outside any town, because their bodies would be left there unburied and would attract ravens and crows. Such places were of course uncanny. Faust and Mephistopheles ride past one on their way to the town in which Gretchen is awaiting her relatively merciful execution by beheading in the market-square (4588–94), after which she evidently expects to be buried (4521–6). The witches at the gallows-mound are reminiscent of those in *Macbeth*; the scene is also thought to have been influenced by Gottfried August Bürger's famous Storm and Stress ballad *Lenore* (1774), in which a lover returning from the grave to fetch his mistress carries her off through the night, and on their way they ride past a place of execution with spirits hovering round it.

127 4412–20: in the Shakespearian parallel scene, the crazed Ophelia in *Hamlet* sings 'snatches of old songs' which like much else in her wild talk have a folkloristic character. The source for Gretchen's song at this point is the old tale of the Juniper Tree, of which many versions are known in Europe. In it a little boy is killed by his mother or stepmother and unknowingly eaten by his father; his sister buries his bones under the tree, whereupon he turns into a bird and sings:

> My mother she killed me,
> My father he ate me,
> My sister Mary-Annie
> All my bones she found,
> My bones in a silk cloth she bound,
> And laid them under the juniper tree:
> Kee-witt! kee-witt! what a fine bird am I!

At the time of writing the *Urfaust* in the early 1770s Goethe must have known some version of this story, or at least of the song (probably he had heard the tale from his mother as a child). In 1809, a year after the appearance of *Faust* Part One but quite independently of it, a Low German version of *The Juniper Tree* (*Von dem Machandelboom*) was sent to the brothers Jacob and Wilhelm Grimm as a contribution to their forthcoming collection of folk-tales, and in 1812 they published it in their first volume. In Gretchen's version the song is poignantly distorted to fit her own case, the boy calling his mother 'the whore' who killed him. In 4449 f. she again refers to an old *Märchen* or folk-tale (not necessarily the same one) which she feels has some reference to herself. On the relevance of folk-culture to the Gretchen drama generally cf. Introd., p. xviii.

128   4590: the ceremonies at a public execution such as Goethe had in
      mind here included the tolling of a bell (the 'poor sinner's bell',
      Armesünderglöcklein) as the prisoner was conveyed through the
      streets to the scaffold, and the breaking of a white rod above his
      head in token of final condemnation. The prisoner was tied to a
      chair and beheaded with a special executioner's sword.

129   4599 f.: Mephistopheles' magic horses will vanish at daybreak.